Developing Professional Practice in the Early Years

Developing Professional Practice in the Early Years

Shirley Allen, Mary Whalley,
Maureen Lee and Angela Scollan

Open University Press

Open University Press
Mcgraw-Hill Education
8th Floor, 338 Euston Road
London
England
NW1 3BH

First published 2020

Senior Commissioning Editor: Hannah Kenner
Editorial Assistant: Karen Harris
Content Product Manager: Ali Davis

A catalogue record of this book is available from the British Library

ISBN-13: 9780335264766
ISBN-10: 033526476X
eISBN: 9780335264773

Library of Congress Cataloging-in-Publication Data
CIP data applied for

Typeset by Transforma Pvt. Ltd., Chennai, India

Fictitious names of companies, products, people, characters and/or data that may be used herein (in case studies or in examples) are not intended to represent any real individual, company, product or event.

Printed in Great Britain by Bell and Bain Ltd, Glasgow

MIX
Paper from
responsible sources
FSC
www.fsc.org   FSC® C007785

Praise for this book

"This publication supports the development of practitioners working in early years. A foundation of knowledge is provided through chapters relating to children's learning and development with a clear focus on leading practice through professional reflection. Inclusion of key areas that drive high quality provision include: promoting relationships, enabling environments and the importance of collaborative practice. Case study materials ensure practitioners can identify the application of theory in practice. The structure and clear layout make the material easily accessible."

Janine Ryan, Head of Department of Education,
Health and Community Practice,
Doncaster College and University Centre, UK

"Developing Practice in the Early Years is essential navigation to help early childhood professionals steer safe passage through their challenging yet rewarding work with young children and families in England. Packed full of useful information and key theoretical perspectives which are brought to life with extracts from practice and opportunities for reflection, this well-structured book offers invaluable guidance for experienced practitioners and early childhood students alike. The authors have created a treasure trove for professional development that will prove an important addition to any early childhood practitioner's bookshelf."

Jane Murray PhD, Associate Professor, Centre for Education and
Research, University of Northampton, UK

Contents

About the authors

Shirley Allen is a Senior Lecturer in Early Childhood Studies at Middlesex University and a Senior Fellow of the Higher Education Academy. She was a primary teacher for several years before moving to the University of Hertfordshire in 2005 to work on Early Years and Primary initial teacher training programmes. She moved to Middlesex University in 2007 to lead the Early Years Professional Status programme and has worked on CPD programmes for early childhood professionals and initial teacher training routes at Middlesex. Shirley is programme leader for the Learning and Teaching undergraduate degree and has written on the subjects of learning theories and early years pedagogy and practice.

Maureen Lee has moved into independent consultancy. Her consistent focus now and in previous roles (as a teacher, local authority adviser and Director of Best Practice Network) has been on enabling developing professionals to recognise both their strengths and areas that need further development to improve outcomes for children. Maureen has taken a lead in establishing rigorous and supportive graduate leadership programmes for early years practitioners across England – initially focused on Early Years Professional Status and more recently on Early Years Teacher Status. Maureen has served on national expert panels and working groups focused on setting the vision and frameworks for the development of a highly skilled and qualified children's workforce. Maureen writes regular articles for early years journals, always focused on showcasing excellent practice in settings and is delighted to volunteer at a school in Essex.

Angela Scollan is a Senior Lecturer in Early Childhood Studies and Education Studies at Middlesex University. Previously, she has worked as a Manager and Foundation Degree Coordinator in a further education college and as a freelance Early Years Ofsted Inspector. In 2010, Angela opened her own training company, 'Emerald Early Years and Education', offering bespoke training and CPD to promote high-quality, sustainable and reflective early years leadership and provision. Since the early 1990s, Angela has worked directly with and for children, positioning her practice within a trans-disciplinary approach and as a rights-based advocate. Her teaching philosophy, research and writing focus on the child first. Angela has recently completed research on the Erasmus+ project, 'SHARMED', observing how facilitation and the use of digital resources encourage shared memories and dialogue in 48 primary and secondary schools in Italy, Germany and England.

Mary Whalley is an independent consultant and local school governor but started work as a nursery/infant school teacher before moving into a training role, first in further education and then in higher education. She has also worked as a registered Ofsted Inspector. Mary was involved in the development and delivery of one of the first Sector-endorsed Foundation Degrees in Early Years at Leeds Metropolitan (now Beckett) University and then the subsequent full honours degree in young children's learning and development. Through her work as a tutor and assessor with the Early Years Professional graduate leader programme, Mary developed a particular research interest in leadership in early childhood and has contributed to early childhood literature on leadership of practice. Her doctoral study focused on graduate pedagogical leadership with children from birth to 30 months.

We recommend this book strongly to you and trust that it enables you, the early childhood professional, to learn, grow and develop as you continue on your unique professional learning journey.

List of figures and tables

Figures

Tables

Introduction

This book aims to address a range of aspects that early childhood professionals should understand and develop about practice with children in their earliest years. It is premised on a belief that our youngest children both need and have a right to high-quality provision from informed and committed practitioners. The arena of early childhood policy and practice is constantly changing and we have drawn on a number of significant research reports, legislation and regulatory guidance to highlight some of these changes. The need for professionals to access appropriate knowledge and information has never been greater, as we rise to the challenge and opportunities of new situations and issues.

Who is the book for?

This book is for both people on initial study programmes and those already in practice, including the many that are engaged in further study. This list is not exhaustive but includes: students on foundation degrees and childhood studies degrees; those undertaking initial teacher training for work with young children; qualified teachers working in the Early Years Foundation Stage (EYFS) or Key Stage 1; early years professionals; early years teachers; and those in positions of leadership and management in early childhood settings. All should find this book a valuable tool to support both their and their colleagues' professional learning and development. There are also strong practical elements to the book to support the application of learning to high-quality practice with young children.

Given the variety of practice or training roles readers of the book may have, we have chosen to use the generic term *early childhood professional* to embrace all – and more. In using this term, we acknowledge the diversity of roles within early childhood settings and a history of confusion over a range of practitioner titles that have been in use at different times (MacNaughton 2003). With the emphasis of the book on developing *professional* practice, using the term 'early childhood professional' will enable the reader to focus on the complexity of 'being professional' in contemporary early childhood practice.

Some readers will already be working in early childhood settings, while others will be having placement experiences as part of their study programmes and, thus, have the opportunity to experience and learn from work with young children prior to qualification. We have aimed to include everyone in the tasks and case studies. We use the word *setting* to mean any registered out-of-home provision for young children, aged from birth to seven. This includes home-based practice (childminders), voluntary pre-schools, private nurseries, full day-care settings, maintained settings such as children's centres and school provision (EYFS and Key Stage 1).

The book is largely written within the context of early childhood provision and practice in England, with specific reference to the underpinning principles and practice promoted within the EYFS framework (DfE 2017). This was a framework introduced in England in 2008 for practice with children from birth to five and, although there have since been revisions, it is the 2017 framework to which we refer. Across the chapters of the book, you will find many references to research and practice from a wider global perspective; thus, we believe this book has relevance to early childhood professionals across the world. Indeed, we acknowledge the significant contribution to contemporary practice in early childhood education and care (ECEC) from many countries and understand that globalisation continues to affect the lives of young children in both majority and minority worlds (Edwards 2019).

How to use the features of the book

Developing professional practice involves the building of theoretical knowledge. Each chapter of the book will help you to engage with some of the challenging concepts and ideas that underpin current policy and practice in early childhood. Each chapter concludes by signposting further reading – book chapters, journal articles, websites – for you to build up greater depth of knowledge and we strongly encourage you to access these and extend your understanding of early childhood research and practice.

As a developing professional, it is important that you question, are willing to learn from others, and acquire critical and reflective thinking skills. In each chapter, you will find a number of learning features:

- **Reflective tasks** – to support your critical thinking about key aspects of professional practice.
- **Case studies** – to enable you to learn from stories and situations about real professionals and their practice.
- **Positive practice impact** – to provide specific examples of good professional practice in early childhood.

Structure of the book

We have enjoyed working together while writing this book, drawing on our diverse experience of work in early childhood and believe our collaborative approach has the potential to be a highly supportive and accessible resource for early childhood professionals. It can be read in-depth or dipped into when need arises. The chapters combine to provide a strong theoretical and practice-based framework of the role and context of the early childhood professional.

Chapter 1 begins by acknowledging the important capacity of quality ECEC to beneficially support young children's holistic development and future outcomes (Sim et al. 2018). This is considered particularly relevant for children living in socio-economic disadvantage; research evidence suggests that children's experience of quality ECEC can help them to overcome challenges presented by negative risk factors in their lives. We explore policy initiatives that have sought to promote quality early years provision. These range from the national *Sure Start* programme established at the end of the previous century to more recent initiatives, such as Early Years Pupil Premium funding, which aims to counter adverse effects on children who live in socio-economic disadvantage by enabling targeted support.

The development of early childhood provision is also influenced by theoretical views of children's learning and development that have promoted particular approaches to practice. We consider the views of some notable theorists in this chapter and explore their relevance to current early years practice and policy.

The chapter then explores the EYFS framework (DfE 2017), which advocates integrated approaches to early years provision through its set of statutory requirements. Reflective tasks encourage you to consider areas of these requirements and strategies that early childhood professionals might employ to enable their effective enactment in practice. The chapter also considers the four guiding principles of the EYFS framework (DfE 2017: 6): 'unique child'; 'positive relationships'; 'enabling environments'; and 'children learn in different ways and at different rates'. Case studies from practice provide useful examples that help to illustrate how these principles can be incorporated within early childhood professionals' approaches to early years practice.

Chapter 2 opens with reference to the 1989 United Nations Declaration on the Rights of the Child, ratified and applied in the UK since 1992. With reference to the 2010 Equality Act, we explore children's rights and their individuality, asserting that each child is unique. The aim of the chapter is to encourage you to reflect on how you can work with children and others to make sure that every child has equal opportunity to achieve their full potential, whatever that might be. This means promoting equality for all children in every aspect of the professional role and embraces effective partnership working with the child's family.

We consider the dangers of making assumptions about children and their families and there is opportunity for you to engage in deep reflection about your own understanding of equality practice and how you personally view difference and diversity. Our own personal values and beliefs can – often unintentionally – affect our attitudes to our practice. These can sometimes reveal themselves in the ways we find ourselves more supportive of some children and families than of others. Thus, self-awareness and self-questioning are hallmarks of the early childhood professional. These skills contribute significantly to creating early childhood settings that have the potential to be truly inclusive places where all – children, families and staff – feel equally valued and welcome and where diversity is celebrated.

Observation of and listening to children are critical to building up a picture of each child's unique behaviour and development. The Mosaic approach developed by Clark and Moss (2011) has broadened our understanding of the range of ways (such as in their drawings, their use of space, their choice of play) that observing and listening to children allows professionals to construct knowledge of the child. The Mosaic approach is outlined and promoted as a helpful tool for early childhood professionals in enabling them to meet the needs of each child. Observation and listening should always focus on what the children *can* do and not on what they *cannot* do.

The issue of children with special educational needs or disabilities (SEND) is considered, although it is beyond the scope of this book to detail the range of SEND that you might encounter in your work. The role of the Special Educational Needs and Disabilities Cooordinator (SENDCo) is discussed and shown to be crucial in implementing and coordinating a setting's SEND policy. Early Years Pupil Premium (EYPP) grants and the offer of funded places for vulnerable two-year-olds are considered and shown to be beneficial to those young children facing particular challenges. These additional provisions aim to ensure that disadvantaged children are as ready for school as their peers (Gibb et al. 2011).

In **Chapter 3**, we explore the significance of positive relationships with young children and their families. We think specifically of the development of the key person (KP) role, initially promoted by Goldschmied and Jackson as long ago as 1994 as vital to work with children under three. Since 2008 and the introduction of the EYFS framework, it has been a statutory requirement for all children, across the birth to five years age range, in registered settings delivering the EYFS to have a named key person. The concept of the KP role is discussed and shown to be a triangle of trusting relationships that embraces the child, the parent(s) and the early childhood professional. Some of the challenges relating to the KP role are also outlined.

Developing positive relationships with children involves 'tuning in' to them (Purvis and Selleck 1996). It is through effective and trusting relationships that children learn most effectively in their earliest years. This builds on the seminal work of researchers such as Trevarthen and his colleagues (2003), who observed the earliest interactions between primary caregivers and their babies, where each imitates and responds to the other. Young children need caring adults who will respond to their cues, noting their particular interests, likes and dislikes, moods and feelings. This is particularly important with very young children who cannot yet use recognisable language.

The needs of those children who find relationships with adults challenging is discussed briefly, including those on the autism spectrum. However, this is a complex and specialised area and the limitations of discussion here are acknowledged. For all children, the role of the early childhood professional in developing and maintaining positive relationships is promoted as that of 'thoughtful agent' (Appleby and Andrews 2011: 59). This includes taking a reflective approach to all aspects of the professional role, based on a deep understanding of the children's needs, and ensuring that these needs are met appropriately. Being a thoughtful agent with children also involves self-awareness, self-care and an understanding of professional boundaries.

Professional boundaries become even more important when facing the challenges of the professional role. Such challenges include tensions that may arise in partnership work with parents or in managing the difficult behaviours of a child. The concept of 'co-caring' (Lang et al. 2016: 40) is outlined, as this aims to ensure consistency of approach in the home and the early childhood setting so that the child's healthy development takes priority over any of the challenges. A co-caring approach suggests that where the relationships between early childhood professional, child and parents are strong, any tensions can be negotiated positively.

Chapter 4 provokes the reader to apply a rights-based lens to explore the characteristics and traits found in environments that enable and empower children. Children who have access to high-quality early years provision have their opportunities improved by being supported to build on what they already know and can do; and having opportunity to communicate with those who are respectful, able and competent to listen to children's voices and unique expressions. A key characteristic of high-quality provision is interacting with the child first and then the child as a learner in all environments to which they have access.

It is a statutory requirement across early childhood provision in England to provide access to outdoor spaces and activities (DfE 2017). Skilled and knowledgeable professionals should be accountable for and able to justify choices for resources and activities offered to children. Therefore, it is vital to recognise how resources, skills, training, partnerships, relationships, spaces, attitudes, curricula and communication all contribute to and construct the environment. For an environment to be enabling, there are many aspects of professional practice that need to be recognised and 'responsibilised'. The chapter encourages those who are or will be in the future working in practice to define what an enabling environment is, what it feels like and what it is made up of.

All stakeholders who use a setting are considered to be contributors, investors and capable learners in defining an enabling environment. Stakeholders are perceived as equal partners, which, of course, includes children. Throughout the chapter, reflective questions encourage you to understand the possible impact each stakeholder might have on others. Environments that promote children as capable, active participants who construct and express meaning about their reality during social interactions and practices are valuable experiences that reinforce children's identities as active and capable actors.

Spaces and places that trust children to take risks are explored to consider how both inside and outside environments support unique learning and enquiry. The Forest School philosophy and approach is discussed: engagement outside with nature so that physical, cognitive and emotional aspects of each child are enhanced and celebrated. The main message of the chapter reminds those working with young children who is accountable and responsible for resources and their deployment, and how to make a positive impact on learning potential and environments that enable.

Chapter 5 is concerned with the concept of quality within early years provision. The chapter highlights how quality provision impacts on the lives and

XVI INTRODUCTION

experiences of children, expanding opportunities with beneficial effects for their development and future outcomes (Mooney 2007). Dahlberg et al. (2006) advocate that the concept of quality needs to be questioned, as it is a subjective and values-based concept. Although the concept of 'quality' indicates something that is self-evident, tangible and understood (Dahlberg et al. 2006), this contrasts with a more layered concept that reflects a richer variety of assumptions and values about the nature of childhood and ECEC provision (Penn 2011).

For this reason, different definitions of childhood are explored to determine how pedagogies and practices impact on the lives of children. The importance of considering children's voices and views about how poverty impacts on their daily experiences and lives (Sheridan 2007; Sylva 2010; Wall et al. 2015) is discussed in the chapter, as an indicator of quality for provision and intervention aimed to tackle the disadvantage children living in or with poverty experience. The quality of provision, pedagogy and the environment (see Chapter 4) are posited as critical to children's active participation, based on democratic and inclusive processes (Hayes and Filipović 2017).

Children living in and with poverty are socially and economically disadvantaged, and this can impact on their educational experience, with implications for their potential attainment (Hillman and Williams 2015). To reduce the effect of disadvantage, the quality and stability of ECEC provision is considered as a pivotal resource (Otero and Melhuish 2015), particularly for children under three years of age, according to research based on neuroscience, psychology and economics, which notes the significance of children's earliest experiences for their developmental outcomes (Pascal and Bertram 2013). However, the meaning of quality is different, depending on the perspective of the stakeholders (Sylva and Taylor 2006), and this plurality will be considered in the chapter, thus reinforcing the need for quality provision and to understand what quality means.

In **Chapter 6**, children remain the stakeholders at the core of practice, but it is you – the professional – who is the focus as we investigate global trends over recent decades to professionalise the early childhood workforce. We ask what it means to be a professional and raise challenges that may be encountered on the professional journey. In particular, to set professionalisation in context, we provide a brief overview of research and practice in England, beginning with findings from the initial phase of the Effective Provision of Pre-school Education (EPPE) Project (Sylva et al. 2004) and concluding with brief discourse on current professional routes to working with children from birth to seven years.

Moving beyond the specific context in England, we consider the skills, knowledge and attributes required in the early childhood professional role. Building on previous chapters, specialist knowledge, pedagogical style and effective collaborative relationships are shown to be key components. An important study by Chalke (2015) identified three expressions of early childhood professionalism: the *head* – expressed in sound knowledge; the *heart* – articulating passion in the role; and the *hands* – exemplified in everyday quality practice. These three expressions are discussed and shown to be crucial in enabling early childhood professionals to manage the tensions of the role.

The chapter continues by acknowledging such tensions and challenges, including potential barriers to being viewed as professional arising from a historical view of work with young children as 'care' rather than 'education' and the further legacy of an under-qualified, poorly paid and heavily (female) gendered workforce. However, Urban (2011) sees changes in recent decades as a framework of opportunity for the early childhood workforce to be viewed differently – *professionally*. In particular, he cites the development of graduate routes. Yet, Nutbrown (2013), Hevey (2013) and Grenier (2013) highlight continuing inequalities in the current early childhood workforce between those with Qualified Teacher Status (QTS) and those with Early Years Teacher Status (EYTS), when both routes require similar academic and professional rigour. Such inequalities pose a threat to professionalism but can also be seen as opportunities for early childhood professionals themselves to define and ensure professionalisation.

The chapter concludes by identifying continuing professional development (CPD) – addressed further in Chapter 9 – as a key characteristic of professionalism. Commitment to our own professional journey mirrors the early learning process where the dispositions of learning are equally as important as the content and methods of learning. One form of powerful CPD is undertaking action research and creating a research culture in the setting. You are invited to consider what action research might look like in your own context, as it provides valuable opportunities to reflect on your role and make changes to practice.

Theoretical perspectives and policies promoting collaborative practice and partnerships are explored in **Chapter 7** to unpick how processes, relationships, communication and interactions support children's unique learning and development journey. The chapter provokes reflection as to who is accountable and responsible for supporting each unique child's interests, needs and aspirations (Whalley 2013). However, moving beyond accountability and responsibility, an important question concerns how early childhood professionals, children, agencies, parents and families work together. The EYFS framework recommends a multi-disciplinary teamwork approach so that collaboration offers those working in the best interest of children a bigger picture into children's lives and circumstances (DfE 2017). Its focus makes Chapter 7 complementary to Chapter 3, where professional relationships with children and their families are discussed. However, this chapter emphasises the importance of a holistic approach so that broader dimensions of the child in context can be considered via real and co-constructed partnerships (Gambaro et al. 2015).

Working with professionals across sectors and disciplines offers valuable insights, whilst presenting challenges, given different ways of working, diverse professional identities and the various professional intentions, perspectives and approaches. This chapter aims to look at commonality, differences and clashes of perspective between different professionals and between parents and professionals, so that what is being done on behalf of children can be enhanced, celebrated and made truly collaborative rather than perceived as conflicting (Edwards 2010). Of course, in any joined-up services and collaborative journey there will be highs and lows, misunderstandings and challenges towards meeting the best interest of children (Melasalmi and Husu 2016; Villumsen and Kristensen 2016).

The practice and concept of safeguarding underpins professional practice across disciplines and, therefore, is a theme that this chapter considers. Terminology used to safeguard children is identified as inconsistent due to each sector's differing perspective. For this reason, the chapter argues the need for those working across sectors to be reflective and open to discussion so that plans for children, professional language, and approaches to working can be transparently challenged for the purpose of clarity and shared goals (DfE 2017, 2018b).

The chapter is underpinned by the message of attending to children's holistic development via strong collaborations, as recognised by pioneers of early years provision. Friedrich Fröebel's kindergarten movement (1840) promotes the importance of play, indoor and outdoor environments and relationship with mother/parents; Maria Montessori's Casa dei Bambini/Children's House (1907) promotes provision based on observations of children to achieve holistic development via structured resources and sensory experiences. Other examples of provision based on collaborative relationships include Margaret and Rachel McMillan's open-air nursery for socio-economically disadvantaged children in Deptford (1914) and Rudolf Steiner-Waldorf kindergartens and schools focused on strong and respectful relationships and partnerships aimed at supporting children's emotional and spiritual development. Since the late 1940s, Loris Malaguzzi's educational philosophy has promoted respectful partnerships and dialogues.

The theory of reflection is explored in **Chapter 8** to unpick the many dimensional characteristics and traits that make up the act and art of reflection. The act of reflection can impact personally, professionally or academically, and will require engaging in much mental effort and cognitive processing when planning for change. Reflective thinking and processes occur every day, although to be aware of and control them is another matter. To tune into one's own thinking and then engage with it, to harness it and shape it, requires strength of mind and consciousnesses.

Once engaged in the act of reflection, there is then an art to reflect on the right thing for the right reason at the right time. The art of reflection provokes thinking about our thinking, enabling the reflector to focus on their thoughts, decisions and outcomes, either experienced or observed. The act and art of reflection are, therefore, rather like a ripple effect that spills outwards after the pebble of thought hits the water. Schön (1987) uses this metaphor to question if reflection is taking place in shallow waters or reaching into a murky bottom. This can provoke the reflector to ponder on the levels of thinking and reflection that are taking place. Are long- or short-term solutions being sought when making changes? Why? Are changes made the right ones? How will the reflector know or be sure?

Schön's theory of reflecting in and on action provokes the reader to engage with the act of reflecting in the here-and-now to consider if changes are needed. Reflecting in action impacts during the experience. Reflection on action follows an event which cannot be changed because it has passed, although the experience can be used to learn from in the future, to make changes if and when needed. Dewey's (1966) experiential learning theory provokes readers to consider how the act and art of reflection are borne from experiences and learning during real-life trial and error. Dewey's theory provokes celebration of lifelong learning and experiences so that learning is observed as an ongoing and evolving journey that continuously shapes thinking, knowing and knowledge. The work of other key theorists (Kolb et al. 1984; Moon 1999; Bolton 2010) is also discussed in the chapter so that the reader can consider how internal and external dialogue, thoughts and experiences clash to formulate new meaning to realise how fresh thinking and ideas can be used to impact on future outcomes.

Professional development is the focus of the final chapter, **Chapter 9**. Professional development is a powerful concept that can bring about change and have a powerful long-term impact with those we work for or with, in relation to all aspects of early childhood pedagogy. Professional development is at once an individual and genuinely social process (Moyles 2006; Cable and Miller 2011; Nutbrown 2012; Siraj and Hallet 2014; DfE 2017). Professional roles and responsibilities can be demanding to develop and evolve for many reasons, including time, opportunity and resourcing. Work in early childhood is multi-faceted and there is always so much to do and learn about. Motivation to want to develop is pivotal, alongside opportunity and support to do so from our team and employers. However, responsibility to know our role, current research and policy by reading and using the internet can be independently undertaken at any time. Early childhood professionals need to make informed decisions and changes; leading within everyday practice requires professional dedication, trust, transparency and dialogic discussion.

Thus, high-quality practice is promoted as a professional responsibility and duty owned by all who work with and for children. The impact of two-way reflective communication contributes towards enabling environments that are evolved collaboratively. There is an acknowledged duty for all professionals to undertake a learning journey. Nutbrown (2012) alludes to this with the term *pedagogical processes*. Pedagogical processes include training, mentoring and continuing professional development within the workplace. Chapter 9 therefore intersects with Chapter 8, which discusses the characteristics of the pedagogical process and its reflective nature, aimed at continuously improving routines, thinking and practices. Within the revised EYFS framework (DfE 2017), practitioners are required to use reflection to observe, evaluate and plan appropriate provision for children to meet their unique needs.

Although quality is an essential pillar of practice and the ultimate rationale for professional development (see Chapter 5), establishing a secure definition of what quality means is complex. It should not be assumed that because a qualification has been achieved or a professional development programme has been completed, an individual will understand how to interact appropriately with children and adults, how to bring about change, or how to challenge practice. The concept of quality requires clarity and needs to be contextualised via dialogue with all stake-holders so that its essence is unpicked, co-constructed, includes mutual engagement, and is fully understood by all concerned. This has implications for the nature, aims and scope of professional development, challenging individualistic and strictly outcome-driven interpretations.

1 Supporting children's learning and development

A range of important policy initiatives have led to an expansion of funding and provision of Early Childhood Education and Care (ECEC). This growth stems largely from international research, which indicates the potential benefits of early childhood education and care on children's developmental and educational outcomes. This, in turn, has led to a greater focus on reflective professional practices within early years education. In this chapter, we focus on the early childhood professional's role to support young children's learning and development and consider factors that influence this role, such as the requirements of the Early Years Foundation Stage (EYFS) framework (DfE 2017) and theoretical perspectives on children's learning and development.

Introduction

Since the end of the twentieth century, there has been mounting recognition of the importance of ECEC. The early years are now considered to be a significant stage in children's overall education, which can have long-term beneficial effects for their future learning and development (Taggart et al. 2015). This focus on ECEC has important implications for the early childhood professional's role of supporting children's learning and development. Early Childhood Education and Care is shaped by a number of influential factors, including theoretical perspectives of early learning and development, findings from research, and the EYFS framework (DfE 2017), which outlines the aims, requirements, and expected outcomes of ECEC that are applicable across all provision for children from birth to five years of age. In this chapter, we look at key aspects of the EYFS framework, including the learning and development requirements and the three characteristics of effective teaching and learning. We start by considering some influential policy drivers affecting early years provision.

Early years education and care: policy context

Government investment and greater prominence afforded to ECEC are largely attributed to its perceived capacity to promote children's development and future employment outcomes (Stirrup et al. 2017). Additionally, ECEC is seen to support opportunities for maternal employment and associated increases in family income (Palaiologou 2016). In view of these factors, it is important to explore *how* children's learning and development can be supported effectively by early childhood professionals so that beneficial outcomes associated with ECEC can be realised (Sim et al. 2018). As we consider this role, it is useful to note that research has identified the positive effects of high-quality early years provision on children's cognitive and social-behavioural outcomes, particularly for those children from the most disadvantaged backgrounds (DfE 2013a). Notable studies include the longitudinal research project 'Effective Provision for Pre-School Education' (EPPE), which highlighted the beneficial effects of good-quality pre-school provision on children's future outcomes (Sylva et al. 2004).

Children's outcomes and life chances are subject to various influences or 'risk factors'. These include their background environment, such as poverty and income; crucial family features, such as health; and important family processes, such as parental aspirations (HM Treasury and DfES 2007). The relationship between risk factors and poorer outcomes is complex and adverse outcomes may not be inevitable; however, there is an increased likelihood of a child experiencing unfavourable outcomes by the presence of negative or challenging risk factors (HM Treasury and DfES 2007). The likely impact of disadvantage on children's long-term outcomes was emphasised in Frank Field's (2010) report, which highlighted differences in cognitive ability and behaviour between children who are from poorer and more advantaged backgrounds. Issues raised in Field's report regarding the impact of socio-economic disadvantage on young children's outcomes continue to be documented. Law et al. (2017a) report a higher occurrence of language difficulties amongst children from socio-economically disadvantaged backgrounds than in the wider population. This is significant, as language difficulties are associated with poorer educational outcomes (Law et al. 2017b). Children's language development is integral to their readiness for formal schooling and broader areas of their learning; oral language proficiency represents one of the key predictors of successful educational outcomes (Hillman and Williams 2015). Although adverse effects of disadvantage on children's educational attainment and health cannot be fully eliminated by high-quality early years provision, their current and future outcomes can be improved (Taggart et al. 2015). A child's experience of quality ECEC can act as a protective factor, which helps them to overcome challenges posed by negative risk factors that could adversely affect their future outcomes (HM Treasury and DfES 2007). (The subject of quality provision is a prime concern for early childhood professionals and we consider this further in Chapter 5.)

Bronfenbrenner's (1979) ecological model of human development provides a theoretical framework for the provision of integrated services for young children. It demonstrates that family, school and the wider community all play a role in the child's development. In this model, the child is positioned at the centre of four systems that are represented as a set of nested structures, as Bronfenbrenner thought that children's development is shaped by their interaction with each of these structures (we consider this model further in Chapter 7).

The important role of ECEC has been recognised in a number of government policy initiatives since the 1990s. Announced in Parliament in 1998, the national *Sure Start* programme aimed to enhance children's educational, social and economic outcomes by providing local services within areas where high numbers of children under four years of age were living in poverty. Sure Start Local Programmes (SSLPs) offered a targeted range of integrated services to support children's social, emotional and cognitive development and health at an early age. The SSLPs operated to a set of key *Sure Start* principles, which included the active involvement of parents and carers in the development, management and delivery of service provision, as their involvement was considered to be crucial to ensure that provision for children and their families would be appropriate and accessible (Eisenstadt 2002). The SSLPs were replaced by the Sure Start Children's Centres (SSCCs) programme in 2003, which was viewed as an effective means of increasing the reach of services, although there remained a greater focus on service provision in areas of disadvantage. Expansion of SSCCs continued until after 2010 when centres began to be closed or to have more limited or dispersed service provision, which is attributed to constrained local authority budgets and the removal of ring-fenced funding for the SSCCs (Smith et al. 2018).

A continued emphasis on integrated approaches to enhance children's development at the earliest stage of their lives (Centre for Excellence and Outcomes 2010; Marmot 2010; Allen 2011) has supported further policy initiatives within early years provision premised on the understanding that ECEC can help to combat the negative effects of socio-economic disadvantage (Pascal and Bertram 2013). Policies include the introduction in 2013 of funded provision for disadvantaged two-year-olds and in 2015 Early Years Pupil Premium (EYPP) funding for eligible three- and four-year-olds. Both policies aimed to provide targeted support for disadvantaged children to counter the adverse effects of living in socio-economic disadvantage. However, there are concerns that some eligible two-year-olds are not benefiting from the 15 hours of funded provision to which they are entitled, and that high-quality provision that is associated with improved child outcomes is not consistently available (Stewart and Waldfogel 2017). (These initiatives are discussed further in Chapter 2.)

Although Ofsted observe that the attainment gap between the most and least advantaged five-year-old children had started to close by 2016, they also note that children in disadvantaged circumstances are less likely to access high-quality early years provision. While acknowledging the complexity of socio-economic disadvantage and recognising that there are no quick solutions that can be applied, Ofsted (2016) calls for broader efforts to ensure that additional funding for children in disadvantage circumstances has the required impact on their outcomes. To help manage complexities in practice, Cable and Miller (2011) suggest a need for early childhood professionals to readily engage with new initiatives and seek solutions to challenging issues by critically questioning, discussing and learning these with others.

An important aspect of your role as an early childhood professional is to continuously evaluate the aims and impact of practice in your setting on children's learning and development. As Callanan et al. (2017: 91) report, 'settings with good practice had embedded a culture of self-evaluation as a means of driving continuous improvement'. They found that staff in these settings reviewed planning and assessment processes on a regular basis and all staff were supported to reflect on their own and others' practice in order to foster children's improved outcomes.

Reflective task 1.1

Reviewing pupil progress

Read the following observation of a meeting where staff discussed children's progress across the EYFS and consider the staff's approach to reviewing the children's progress and planning their provision.

'*The pupil progress meetings at a primary school were focused on individual children, their achievements and potential barriers to making good progress. The emphasis of these meetings was primarily on what help can be provided rather than 'Why are children not making progress?' The information provided came from staff, not senior leaders. Staff indicated what their children could and couldn't do and hypothesised as to the reason why. This mature state of discussion required high levels of understanding and information from staff. This deep understanding of children and their families was matched by their high expectations. This led inexorably to the identification of problems as well as agreement on the children's next steps in learning and development.*' (Ofsted 2014: 44)

Think!

- How might you review children's attainment?
- How might you promote high expectations of their attainment?
- What resources could you draw on to help address a child's barriers to learning?

Early years pedagogy

The potential benefits of high-quality ECEC on children's outcomes focuses attention on approaches used by staff to support learning and development, which are conditional on '*what is intended to be taught*' and '*how it is facilitated*' (Wall et al. 2015: 4). *How* learning and teaching are approached can be described as *pedagogy* (Siraj and Hallet 2014).

The knowledge and skills of the early childhood professional are crucial to their effectiveness to support a child's learning and development (Pascal and Bertram 2013). You will be expected to model an informed approach to practice and adapt your practice to new contexts, according to children's individual needs. Your practice will be largely influenced by theoretical views about children's learning and development, findings from research, policy directives (including the EYFS framework: DfE 2017), contextual factors of your workplace and the views of others, including your engagement with social media. Your reflective practice will also facilitate deeper understanding of effective pedagogical approaches (this is considered further in Chapter 8).

Early years practice is influenced by a range of theoretical views. Although space does not allow a detailed exploration of learning theories here, it is useful to consider some theorists whose work has been particularly influential in the field of early years practice. These include Rousseau (1712–1778), who identified the benefit of outdoor play opportunities that enable children to engage freely in sensory experiences and playful games in natural settings. Rousseau thought children should be educated in a positive learning environment where the adult has a detailed knowledge of children in their care and encourages their interests and curiosities. Fröebel (1782–1852) emphasised the central importance of children's playful experiences and promoted the use of natural materials in practice. His views influenced the pioneers of early years practice in the first half of the twentieth century in England, including Susan Isaacs (1885–1948), who established a nursery in the 1920s at the Malting House School in Cambridge and drew on her observations of children's play to inform provision. However, it is the theories of Piaget (1896–1980) and Vygotsky (1896–1934) that are frequently cited as key influences on early years pedagogy and curriculum and support a prevailing child-centred and play-based approach to contemporary practice (Wall et al. 2015).

Piaget formed a constructivist theory of learning from his observations of children. He theorised that children progressively construct knowledge through their active engagement with their environment. He thought children relate their playful experiences to their existing schemas, which are categories of knowledge that support children to make sense of the world. Piaget thought that if knowledge could not be accommodated into an existing schema, then a new schema is formed (Aubrey and Riley 2016), and that children's cognitive development occurs in four stages:

1. Sensori-motor (from birth to approximately two years)
2. Pre-operational (from two to seven years)
3. Concrete operational (from seven to 11 years)
4. Formal operational (11 years to adult)

Piaget's theory of cognitive development implied that children need to demonstrate a certain stage of readiness in order to undertake new learning; however, this view was later criticised, as it was thought that the stages were too fixed and that the stages could overlap (Allen and Gordon 2011). Nevertheless, Piaget's view of the child as an active participant in their own learning was particularly influential on early years practice during the second half of the twentieth century, and has helped to promote opportunities for children's active exploration of indoor and outdoor environments during the formative stages of their development. An emphasis on the importance of children's play activity within a stimulating environment is supported by the notion of an 'enabling environment' (DfE 2017: 6) in early years provision, which is one of the principles of the EYFS framework (this is considered further in Chapter 4).

Towards the end of the twentieth century, support for Piaget's theories declined as socio-constructivist theory became more widely supported in early years policy and practice. Vygotsky (1978) highlighted the relevance of the social and cultural context in which learning occurs and emphasised the importance of children's interaction with adults and more capable peers, who he referred to as 'more knowledgeable others' (MKO). The term 'zone of proximal development' (ZPD) was used by Vygotsky to explain the difference between a child's actual achievement when working alone and their potential achievement when supported by a MKO (Epstein et al. 2011). Vygotsky promoted the value of children's interactions with others and suggested language was a tool that supported children's thinking and learning. This view was supported by the *Researching Effective Pedagogy in the Early Years* (REPEY) project (Siraj-Blatchford et al. 2002), which explored characteristics of effective practice and underpinning pedagogical understanding. Developed during the course of the landmark *Effective Provision of Pre-school Education* (EPPE) project (Sylva et al. 2004), which we consider further in Chapter 5, REPEY found that highly effective settings encouraged the process of sustained shared thinking (SST). The REPEY project used the term SST to explain how children's creative and critical thinking skills were promoted during effective child–adult verbal interactions.

The REPEY project suggested that SST was particularly powerful when also encouraged by parents in the home and the research highlighted the value of open-ended questioning, which prompts children to speculate and experiment in their learning (Siraj-Blatchford 2010). The ZPD and SST are important pedagogical approaches that an adult can use to support, scaffold and extend children's thinking and learning (Hallet 2016).

Vygotsky's theory also emphasised the significant role of play in children's learning, echoing the earlier insights of Rousseau, which he thought helped them to operate at a level in advance of their development. (His views about the importance of children's verbal interaction and their engagement in play are embedded in the EYFS framework, which we look at in the next section of the chapter.) Vygotsky's work has been extended by other social constructivist theorists, including Bruner, who suggested that children's learning is supported by adults 'scaffolding' a task (Allen and Whalley 2010: 88) and Rogoff, who developed Vygotsky's work on the ZPD with her concept of 'guided participation' (Allen and Gordon 2011: 49). These theories all emphasise the crucial role of the adult in supporting a child's learning and development and the importance of the social-cultural context in which learning occurs.

Reflective task 1.2

Providing opportunity

Reflect on opportunities you provide that:

- are connected to children's social-cultural experiences;
- encourage children to:
    - explain something to a peer or adult to clarify understanding;
    - ask questions;
    - share ideas with peers or adults;
    - hypothesise.

As you reflect on these points, consider if there are any areas of your own or others' practice that you feel could be developed further.

Your approaches to supporting a child's learning and development in practice will also be affected by particular values that are incorporated in your setting's practice, such as adherence to the principles of the 1989 United Nations Convention on the Rights of the Child (UNCRC), which has drawn attention to children's agency in early years practice and their opportunities to express their views and be respected (Einarsdóttir 2014; Pascal and Bertram 2014). International perspectives on early years provision, such as the innovative nursery provision developed by Malaguzzi in the Reggio Emilia area of Italy, also exert influence on approaches to practice. Malaguzzi (2011: 2) promoted the concept of a child's 'hundred languages', which supports them to express themselves using diverse forms of communication such as computers, dance or construction materials. (Both the principles of the UNCRC and ethos of Reggio Emilia practice are considered further in Chapter 2.)

A further influence on pedagogical approaches to supporting children's learning and development is *practice-based research*. Allen's (2011) report advises that early interventions that are used to support children's development should demonstrate clear evidence of their effectiveness. Following Allen's guidance, the Education Endowment Foundation (EEF 2018) has developed an online *Early Years Toolkit* that summarises educational research on effective pedagogical approaches and early years interventions in terms of their supporting evidence, cost and impact on children's learning. The Toolkit covers areas of practice, such as self-regulation strategies, parental engagement and early literacy approaches. However, there are challenges in determining effective strategies in practice that are applicable across the broad mixed-market of early years provision (Hillman and Williams 2015). The scope for large-scale intervention research is limited and opportunities for trials into practice might preclude the involvement of smaller private and voluntary settings that dominate provision in the sector, especially without the support of structures, such as local authorities, to assist in the process (Hillman and Williams 2015). This view suggests the need for a range of ongoing enquiry into practices.

Reflective task 1.3

Part 1: Pedagogical inquiry

- Reflect on your experience of pedagogical inquiry into practice.
- Consider how your understanding of pedagogy might inform your current or future role of supporting children's learning and development.

Part 2: Pedagogical approaches

You may wish to undertake this activity with a colleague or mentor.

- Record particular pedagogical approaches that you might take to facilitate children's learning and development – an example is provided below as guidance.

Example: I currently work in a reception class. I believe children excel in their own environment when the delivery of teaching is focused on what they enjoy, so I shape this around their interests. I think that when children are allowed to learn through meaningful life experiences, they are able to retain the information they are processing.

Your views:

- Note any factors that you think have influenced your understanding of these pedagogical approaches – a further example is provided as guidance.

Example: I am influenced by Maria Montessori's views on the learning environment for children; she believed in relating this to everyday life and realistic situations to enable children to learn. The teacher is known as a facilitator in this educational theory, organising the environment to allow children to learn at their own natural pace. I see this way of teaching and learning in my everyday work. I believe allowing children to learn through play in EYFS can help their social and educational development.

Your views:

The EYFS statutory framework

The early childhood professional's role to support children's learning and development is shaped by the requirements of the EYFS statutory framework (DfE 2017), which offers a common framework across all early years provision for children from birth to five years. Here, we explore the EYFS framework's aims, requirements, principles and characteristics of effective learning.

Statutory from September 2008, the EYFS framework brings together elements of education and care and acknowledges the findings of the EPPE Project – that children achieve the best outcomes when they attend early years settings that recognise socio-emotional and cognitive development as complementary to each other (Siraj-Blatchford 2010). The EYFS framework was revised in 2012 to include recommendations from the Tickell Review (DfE 2011a). Changes included a more manageable process of assessment of children's achievements at the end of the EYFS. Amendments were also made to the previous six areas of learning and development, which were replaced with three prime areas and four specific areas of learning and development. These aimed to support a greater focus on children's school readiness and future progress. Additionally, changes were made to the EYFS Welfare Requirements, which became the 'Safeguarding and Welfare' requirements to reflect a stronger emphasis on safeguarding, including a requirement for providers' safeguarding policies to cover the use of mobile phones and cameras. The EYFS framework was updated again in 2014, though at that time changes were made only to the 'Safeguarding and Welfare' requirements. A further update in 2017 clarified that all 'Learning and Development' and 'Safeguarding and Welfare' requirements in the EYFS framework were indicated by the word 'must', whereas 'should' is used when other provision ought to be considered by providers. The 'Safeguarding and Welfare' requirements were also amended to include reference to new or updated government guidance on the subject. Additionally, a new paediatric first aid requirement and Level 2 literacy and numeracy qualification requirements were included.

Aims of the EYFS framework

The EYFS framework seeks to enhance early years practice and improve outcomes for all children by promoting the following aims (adapted from DfE 2017: 5):

- quality and consistency of practice;
- a secure foundation through opportunities for learning and development based on individual children's needs and interests;
- partnership working between practitioners and children's parents and carers;
- equality of opportunity and anti-discriminatory practice that ensures each child is included and supported.

Your interpretation of these aims will be influenced by your knowledge and experience, as well as a range of contextual factors, including the children's home backgrounds, parental views, local policies, the setting or environment and staffing.

Positive practice impact

Alex, manager of an urban nursery

The following extract illustrates working closely with parents and children to improve learning outcomes.

'*Parents need to feel part of the learning – they are children's first educators so it's important they feel engaged and we're in tune with them. I explain our values to our parents – to be nurturing; to be fun; to be brave; to be inspiring! We do this in a range of ways.*

'*We're constantly reshuffling the environment to suit the needs of our children. We do a lot of activities to support the development of language and communication.*

'*I'm very keen on giving children choice and to involve them in their learning. If a child says to me they saw a volcano on television, then we will be making volcanoes. You have to treat children as individuals and allow them to have challenges. As long as they're not putting themselves in harm's way, why not?*'

Requirements of the EYFS framework

The EYFS framework sets standards that must be met by all early years providers. In particular, it outlines requirements for learning and development and for safeguarding children and promoting their welfare (DfE 2017: 5). Providers are required to allocate each child a 'key person [who] must help ensure that every child's learning and care is tailored to meet their individual needs' (DfE 2017: 10).

The 2017 EYFS framework's learning and development requirements cover seven areas of learning and development, as shown in Table 1.1, which are interconnected and frame educational programmes for children in early years settings. As noted, they consist of three prime and four specific areas of learning and development.

Table 1.1 2017 EYFS framework's learning and development requirements

Prime areas	Specific areas
• Communication and language • Physical development • Personal, social and emotional development	• Literacy • Mathematics • Understanding the world • Expressive arts and design

Source: DfE (2017: 1.3 and 1.4).

The prime areas of learning and development are considered to be particularly significant to provoke children's curiosity and enthusiasm for learning and to build their capacity to learn, develop relationships and thrive. They are strengthened and applied through the four specific areas of learning and development (DfE 2017). The EYFS framework advises practitioners who work with the youngest children in the EYFS to focus on the three prime areas, as these are considered to form the foundation of successful learning in the four specific areas.

Reflective task 1.4

Applying the EYFS framework

- Consider ways in which you might support the learning and development of children under three years of age in terms of the focused areas of practice listed in the 2017 EYFS framework.
- Record ways in which the seven areas of learning and development are represented in your setting across the provision for all children using the following table:

Representation	Prime areas	Specific areas
Assessment documents		
Planning documents		
Display boards		
Information for children, parents and carers		
Information for Ofsted		
Setting website		
Setting policies		

There are two further EYFS learning and development requirements (DfE 2017):

1. The early learning goals, which specify the knowledge, skills and understanding that children are expected to have gained by the end of the academic year in which they become five years old. Following the Tickell Review (DfE 2011a) of the EYFS, the number of early learning goals was

reduced from 69 to 17 to support a more manageable and meaningful assessment process.

2. Assessment procedures for measuring children's progress and reporting to parents or carers. It should be noted, however, that the EYFS framework emphasises that assessment and planning should not be an excessively bureaucratic process that requires practitioners to spend long periods away from the children. There are two formal points of assessment in the EYFS framework: the Progress Check for two-year-olds and the assessment at the end of the EYFS using the EYFS Profile. Information on children's development at these formal points of assessment should be shared with parents and carers; the EYFS Profile must also be shared with the child's Year 1 teacher. At the time of writing, a national baseline assessment process is planned to be introduced in 2020 to assess children's attainment on entry to school. The assessment would be undertaken within children's first half-term in the Reception year (DfE 2019).

The EYFS framework also outlines the use of formative assessment. This involves regular observation of children's activity and engagement, which informs practitioners about children's achievements and interests and guides planning for a child's next steps in their learning. A child's ongoing assessment can be referred to as a 'learning journey', as it records their progression over time. Pedagogical documentation, which includes observations and photographs of children's activities, can be collated across different learning contexts to provide an evidence base of children's developing competence and knowledge (Wood 2011).

Practitioners can be more attuned to children's learning by observing their schemas. The term 'schema' was used by Piaget to describe categories of knowledge that help children to make sense of the world. Atherton and Nutbrown (2013) note that observations of children's schemas, which they describe as repeated patterns of behaviour, help practitioners understand children's forms of thinking. According to Arnold et al. (2010), children's exploration of schemas can also help practitioners to understand children's current emotional events in their lives. They suggest that children use schemas for comfort and to help them explore and make sense of more complex events and changes. Analysing assessment information on schemas and other sources of evidence can help early childhood professionals to plan meaningful learning environments that aim to promote children's learning (Wood 2011).

Opportunities to assess and plan appropriate provision should involve children, as this acknowledges them as active participants in their learning experiences. The assessment process not only involves meaningful understanding of children's progression in their learning and development to inform appropriate provision but also requires a *collaborative* approach. Assessment needs be undertaken carefully and respectfully; Atherton and Nutbrown (2013) suggest that practitioners' interventions should be sensitive and timely.

Reflective task 1.5

Assessment activities

Reflect on the processes in your setting for the following assessment activities. As you reflect, think about how you might ensure care, sensitivity and respectfulness in these processes. Here are some examples for you to consider:

- formative assessment;
- involving children in assessment of their learning and development;
- the progress check for two-year-olds;
- tracking a child's progress in your setting;
- sharing assessment data with parents and carers;
- any particular local arrangements for EYFS assessment that apply to your setting;
- keeping informed of any changes in the EYFS Profile or other assessment processes that apply to your practice;
- how assessment informs planning.

Principles of the EYFS framework

The EYFS framework is a principled approach to practice. It details four overarching principles that steer early years practice to support children's learning, development, safety and welfare. These principles demonstrate how early childhood professionals should be responsive in their practice and are explored further in Chapters 2, 3 and 4.

The four EYFS principles are:

1. every child is a **unique child** who is constantly learning and can be resilient, capable, confident and self-assured
2. children learn to be strong and independent through **positive relationships**
3. children learn and develop well in **enabling environments**, in which their experiences respond to their individual needs and there is strong partnership between practitioners and parents and/or carers
4. **children develop and learn in different ways ... and at different rates**. The framework covers the education and care of all children in early years provision, including children with special educational needs and disabilities. (DfE 2017: 6; emphasis in original)

Reflective task 1.6

The EYFS framework's principles in practice

Think about examples from practice that could relate to one or more of the four principles. Reflect on the context of your example and then consider the likely impact of that experience on children's learning and development. An example from practice is provided for support in the following table; you may find it helpful to repeat this task using examples drawn from a different EYFS age group or context.

EYFS framework principle	Example from practice (Context)	Example from practice (Evaluative comments)
Unique child		
Positive relationships		
Enabling environments	*Example:* I noticed that children were putting sea life animals into the water tray, so I noted this down to follow up on this interest the next day.	*Example:* The next day I noticed that children started to talk about fish and sharks at the water tray and were creating stories around them. By following up on their interests, the children's experience of water play was meaningful and encouraged their talk.
	Your example:	*Your example:*
Different ways and different rates		

Characteristics of effective learning in the EYFS framework

The EYFS framework (DfE 2017: 10) advises that practitioners should consider the different ways in which children learn in their pedagogic approach to practice. The framework identifies three characteristics of effective learning that practitioners should use when reflecting on their role to support learning and development:

1. **playing and exploring** – children investigate and experience things, and 'have a go'
2. **active learning** – children concentrate and keep on trying if they encounter difficulties, and enjoy achievements
3. **creating and thinking critically** – children have and develop their own ideas, make links between ideas, and develop strategies for doing things.
    (DfE 2017: 1.9; emphasis in original)

Characteristic 1: Playing and exploring

The EYFS framework emphasises an age-appropriate and play-based pedagogical approach to early years practice through a combination of adult-led and child-initiated activities. Opportunities should be made for 'planned, purposeful play' (DfE 2017: 1.8). This perspective is influenced by the findings of the REPEY project (Siraj-Blatchford et al. 2002: 12), which identified a balanced approach of extending child-initiated play, together with the provision of teacher-initiated group activities, as effective for learning. The provision of play in educational settings is a contested subject. The EYFS framework's guidance on the notion of 'planned, purposeful play' (DfE 2017: 1.8) is recognised by Wood (2014a) as a means for children to reach educational aims rather than play being valued in its own right. Wood (2014a) suggests that the practitioner needs to maintain an open stance to the pedagogy of play; they should not allow opportunities for play to be limited by policy aims but rather enable children to build identity, friendships and meaning. As an early childhood professional, it is important to reflect on ways in which opportunities for play can be facilitated to support children's learning and development and to communicate your pedagogic approach to play with others, whilst also keeping an open perspective on this dynamic and contested activity.

Case study 1.1

Jesse, a teacher in an urban nursery school

Read the following case study and consider how the teacher is planning to support children's learning opportunities through mark-making activities that enable children to express their ideas and feelings by using different mark-making tools.

'The children have had a particular interest in mark-making and have been trying to write letters, numbers and their names. We provided a range of mark-making opportunities in the indoor and outdoor areas based on children's interests and we observed children's comments about marks they produced. We have taken photos of children's mark-making, which the children have shared with their parents. We have also encouraged parents to support their child's mark-making activities at home.'

Think!

Reflect on how:

* mark-making activities can enable children to communicate their ideas and feelings in a range of ways;
* the use of digital technology could support children's engagement and interest in mark-making activities;
* children could be encouraged to experiment within mark-making activities;
* parents can be supported to share their children's mark-making at home with the early years setting and vice versa.

Characteristic 2: Active learning

Pedagogical approaches to practice should recognise children as active learners. There should be opportunities for children to be immersed in active exploration and be motivated in relevant and provocative learning environments to support holistic areas of their learning and development (Atherton and Nutbrown 2013). Observation of children helps to identify children's learning dispositions, which describe their motivation and attitudes to learning. This can then inform planning of a motivating environment. Carr and Lee (2012: 131) suggest the use of 'learning stories' to describe children's dispositions. These make learning 'visible' (2012: 98) and emphasise children's achievements in holistic areas of their learning and development. Learning stories can be developed with digital images of children's play; these offer narrative accounts of children's play experiences, which enable them to review their experiences and share them with their peers and family.

Reflective task 1.7

Supporting children to tackle challenges

Consider ways in which children were supported to tackle challenges in this example of Ofsted observations of EYFS practice:

'We observed children during all of our visits who were engaged in activities that centred on rising to a challenge and/or solving a problem. These open-ended tasks, such as figuring out how to transport sand from one area of the yard to another using buckets and pulleys, or finding multiple ways to make ice creams that were 10 cubes high, enabled children to formulate solutions, test them out and learn from their mistakes. It taught them that making mistakes helped them to find the right solution on subsequent attempts and that there was often more than one way of completing the task. Setting challenges appeals to children's enquiring and inquisitive minds and allows them to develop all of the characteristics of effective learning.' (Ofsted 2015a: 12: Setting challenges)

Consider how you might:

- support children to tackle a challenging activity;
- encourage children to be resilient and persist with a challenge;
- encourage children to realise that making mistakes is part of their learning; and
- encourage parents and carers to realise that children's mistakes are part of their learning.

Characteristic 3: Creating and thinking critically

The process of sustained shared thinking, considered earlier in the chapter, supports the development of creative thinking. By engaging in effective and supportive interactions with a child and demonstrating genuine interest in what they are doing, you will be extending the child's thinking and supporting them to co-construct meanings (Wall et al. 2015). Between the ages of 24 and 36 months, advances generally occur in children's communication and language, their cooperation and social skills, and their thinking and memory. At this important stage of their development, the early childhood professional can support the child through provision of meaningful activities that encourage them to make links in their learning (Mathers et al. 2014). (The subject of sustained shared thinking is discussed further in Chapter 5.)

Reflective task 1.8

Developing ideas and engaging with learning

- Consider ways in which the early years setting might provide opportunities for children to develop their ideas and make links in their learning.
- What strategies might be used to help parents engage in supportive interactions with their children?

Summary and moving on

In this chapter, we have considered an increased interest and investment in the provision of ECEC and an accompanying policy focus on its potential to positively impact on children's futures. This focus has implications for your role to support children's learning and development. By developing further understanding of ways in which children's learning and development can be facilitated, you are more effectively prepared to manage the competing demands of your role, to critically assess innovative approaches, and to make a positive impact on children's experiences (Stephen 2010). One of the key aspects of your supporting role is the early identification of children's specific needs. This is considered further in the next chapter, where the subject of appropriate provision for children's needs and interests will be discussed.

Further reading

Conkbayir, M. and Pascal, C. (2014) *Early Childhood Theories and Contemporary Issues: An introduction*. London: Bloomsbury.

Education Endowment Foundation (EEF) (2018) *EEF Early Years Toolkit*. Available at: https://educationendowmentfoundation.org.uk/evidence-summaries/early-years-toolkit/ (accessed 29 December 2018).

MacBlain, S. (2018) *Learning Theories for Early Years Practice*. London: Sage.

Siraj-Blatchford, I., Sylva, K., Muttock, S., Gilden, R and Bell, D. (2002) *Researching Effective Pedagogy in the Early Years*. DfE Research Report RR356. Available at: https://dera.ioe.ac.uk/4650/1/RR356.pdf (accessed 5 January 2019).

2 Supporting children's individual needs

This chapter explores how early childhood professionals can ensure all children are included in their settings and considers ways in which positive attitudes to diversity and difference can be promoted. Relevant legislation and statutory frameworks supporting inclusive practice are outlined, including discussion of the Early Years Pupil Premium, provision for children with special educational needs and disabilities (SEND), and provision for vulnerable two-year-olds. Inclusive practice is concerned with practitioners' attitudes and behaviours and this chapter highlights how early childhood professionals help create settings where all children and families feel welcomed, valued and respected. (This can include collaborative working with other professionals.) Detailed exploration of the range of individual needs with which children might present is beyond the scope of this chapter but reflective tasks and case studies are offered to facilitate further thinking about inclusive practice.

Introduction

Fair and respectful treatment of all children is enshrined in the 1989 United Nations Convention on the Rights of the Child (UNCRC) and ratified by 192 countries across the world. The UNCRC was endorsed in the UK in 1991 and has applied since 1992. An emphasis on meeting the needs of all children has been enshrined in legislation and policy initiatives across the nations of the UK for some years (Welsh Assembly Government 2008; Department of Education Northern Ireland 2013; The Scottish Government 2014; DfE 2014, 2017). In this chapter, we consider the importance of forming positive relationships with children by focusing on their individual needs. Fundamental to this is recognising that every child is unique and on an individual learning journey (DfE 2017). For all professionals in early childhood settings, this involves actively seeking knowledge and understanding each child and their family context.

The principles of meeting individual needs are set in the wider context of *equality practice* (Lane 2008). There are many complex issues here but Lindon (2012) suggests that equality practice is not simply focusing on each particular child but also includes the image of the world that children are gaining, beyond their current experiences. This actively promotes equality of opportunity and anti-discriminatory practice – crucial to improving outcomes for children (DfE 2017). By thinking about the individual child, as well as the collective needs of children, the early childhood professional promotes an open, safe, secure and enabling environment and ensures all children feel included in the setting. Through systematic observation and monitoring, a better understanding of individual children is built up and their interests and needs are met through the selection and use of resources that provide opportunities and experiences for children; these should positively reflect cultural diversity, equality and inclusion in planning and provision (Devarakonda 2013).

Ensuring that each child's needs are met involves partnership working with parents, colleagues and other professionals across children's services. Positive dispositions, self-awareness and effective communication are paramount here, as are skills in working collaboratively and cooperatively with others to promote children's well-being, learning and development. Any sharing of information should be rooted in sound and current understanding of relevant legal requirements, national and local frameworks, policies and guidance.

Promoting equality for all children: Law and practice

Since the 1980s, in the UK and globally, legislative changes and increasing social and cultural awareness have led to an important emphasis on valuing and celebrating diversity. Equality for all children is now a key principle in early childhood provision and is premised on UK and European legislation, with a raft of policies designed to combat discrimination and protect children's rights. The Equality Act 2010, for instance, ensured that children are protected by law from discrimination on grounds of age, disability, gender, race, religion/belief, or sexual orientation. However, vigilance is still needed. Whilst a review of the state of children's rights in England (Williams et al., 2017) found indicators of positive progress especially with looked-after children and in cases of child mental health, in some situations the government is not doing enough to ensure the safety and well-being of the most vulnerable children.

As key practitioners in the children's workforce, you have a professional responsibility to understand something of social history, of the key changes in the law and how these have informed and shaped policy and practice in the context in which you are working. This will include understanding the changing demographics that impact on your setting and you should ensure that this is reviewed frequently, especially when new families join. This will include working knowledge on the dynamic area of wider legislation, policy and practice relating to equality and inclusion. By keeping abreast of current research relevant to early childhood provision, you will be demonstrating a reflective and responsive approach to changes in practice, which seeks to improve outcomes for all children.

Reflective task 2.1

Legislation and policy – UNCRC

Take a few moments now to look at selected Articles drawn from the UNCRC, seen in the following table, and note your own responses and your own belief/value stance about the statements. Reflect on how you might demonstrate these in your own practice.

Article	Own reaction – value stance	Way of demonstrating in practice	Area for further research
2.1. Respect and ensure the rights of each child without discrimination of any kind, irrespective of the child's or his or her parents' or legal guardians' race, colour, sex, language, religion, political or other opinion, national, ethnic or social origin, property, disability, birth or other status.			
12.1. Ensure the child is capable of forming his or her own views and has the right to express those views freely in all matters affecting the child, the views of the child being given due weight in accordance with the age and maturity of the child.			
23.1. Recognize that a mentally or physically disabled child should enjoy a full and decent life, in conditions which ensure dignity, promote self-reliance and facilitate the child's active participation			
29.1. The education of the child shall be directed to: (a) The development of the child's personality, talents and mental and physical abilities to their fullest potential			

The language of equality

Essentially, it is in 'supporting and adapting content, pedagogical approaches, resources, time and the learning environment' (Brock and Thornton 2015: 194) that professionals ensure children's individual needs are met. Yet, the words and language we use when working with children and families are also of enormous importance in any consideration of equality practice. It is also important to observe reactions to spoken and non-verbal language and, where necessary, adjust these in the light of these reactions even when there is no deliberate intention of being impolite or excluding any individual.

Specific definitions of terms commonly used relating to equality are evolving and so are not always firmly agreed; indeed, they are often contested (Borkett 2019). A useful starting point – especially when undertaken as a group exercise with peer discussion – is to check your own understandings. Look at the key terms linked to equality in Reflective task 2.2 and define these from your own understanding.

Reflective task 2.2

Definitions of equality

What do you understand by the following terms relating to equality? There are many different definitions for these terms but a website from *Action for Children* is signposted at the end of the chapter that may help you to clarify these for yourself.

Equality practice

Promoting equality

Anti-discriminatory practice

Anti-bias practice

Inclusive practice

Social inclusion

Attempting to determine absolute definitions relating to equality practice can side-track the core task for the early childhood professional, which is to ensure the child's best interests lie at the heart of all aspects of practice (UNICEF 1989). Law, policy and rhetoric are all very well. The real task for early childhood professionals lies in translating these into everyday reflective practice that demonstrates total commitment to the underpinning ethos and meaning of them.

Case study 2.1

Dawn and Jeff, co-leaders of a village pre-school (voluntary setting)

This case study illustrates some of the challenges of promoting equality for every child.

'We have led the local pre-school for over four years now and meet in the local village hall. We are a popular group with local families and always have a waiting list. Historically, we have not had any requests to cater for children with additional needs. Recently, however, two families have applied for places for their children: one child has a significant medical condition and the other has mobility challenges. Some of the parents of our current children have expressed concern about whether we have a big enough staff team to manage this. There are also concerns about the limited access we have to the outdoors, so we have bikes (etc.) in a section of the hall.'

Think!

- How might Dawn and Jeff best prepare themselves as leaders to create an inclusive setting for these new children?
- What action will they need to take in leading the staff to feel ready and skilled to manage inclusion on a daily basis?
- How might they address the concerns expressed by the parents?

A significant challenge to the development of inclusive practice can occur when practitioners are resistant to the policy requirements intended to ensure equality and inclusion in their setting. Polat (2011) contends that overcoming such resistance to inclusive practice requires a culture that recognises the normality of diversity and moves towards a celebration of difference. With the sweeping demographic changes that have taken place over the last few decades, early childhood professionals should take up the challenge to ensure that colleagues, children and parents adopt and maintain positive attitudes to diversity and difference. This will not only ensure that every child is included in everyday practice but also that they learn to value diversity themselves.

The child's many languages

Children gain knowledge and understanding through ideas, concepts and competences and each child will respond differently to the people, places and resources they experience (Hutchin 2013). This applies to work with young babies and continues right across childhood. The things that interest a child at any particular time are extremely significant to them and should not be ignored; these are the starting points in supporting children's learning and development. Ideally, we should delight in those starting points and share the child's enthusiasm for their interests. Drawing on her extensive experience of teaching young children and the processes of young children's learning, Paley (1991) positions delight in such uniqueness at the heart of early childhood practice.

There is an ever-present danger of making assumptions about children (Edgington 2004) and the key tools for tuning into children are *observation* and *listening*. Effective organisation of a key person system is critical here and is addressed further in the next chapter. Systematic observations are foundational in early childhood and provide a window through which we can understand children and their actions. They allow the application of developmental theory to actual practice, and thus facilitate professionals' reflective thinking. Seminal research in 2002 by Siraj-Blatchford et al. found a positive correlation between the knowledge the adult has of the child and the quality of their support for the child. In turn, this results in more effective learning.

Observations focus on what a child *can* do and *is* doing – not on what they cannot do. This is the basis for forward planning (Palaiologou 2012). Careful collection of information from observations offers in-depth insights into a child that are not readily available any other way. Listening to children also shows value for them. Children have a right to have their voices heard, and observations and conversations can provide a positive context to listen to children's attempts to communicate in word and action. This can open the way for more effective interaction with children, as their interpretation of events is often different from those of the adult involved. Remember, communication includes far more than actual words: a child's body language, facial expressions, the spaces they use in the setting, the activities accessed, creative engagement and their responses to events and situations all enable us to build up a picture of the child. Such an understanding of the child's 'hundred languages' of expression (Malaguzzi 2011: 2) comes from the approach to early childhood provision in Reggio Emilia, Italy, as discussed in the previous chapter.

Observations and careful listening provide professionals with a bank of knowledge to create an accurate picture of a child's behaviour and development. Observations can also provide valuable clues about the reasons for children's behaviour in certain situations. In the context of the contemporary multi-professional workforce, this information may be shared and opportunities taken for collaborative working. (This is discussed later in the chapter.)

Within the UK, Clark and Moss (2011) have developed Malaguzzi's concept of the 'hundred languages' of the child in the Mosaic approach to listening to children. This has helped broaden the tools available to build up a fuller picture of children's needs, interests and dispositions. Consider the following with a child in your present setting:

- join in conversation and listen attentively to the words and phrases the child uses;
- note body language;
- watch/track how the child uses the space;

- look carefully at the child's creative responses;
- consider allowing the child to use a camera to take photographs of the activities/spaces enjoyed most in the setting. What do the child's photographs tell you?

Reflective task 2.3

Observations and listening

- What place should observations have in your future practice?
- How might observations inform your planning for individual children – and the overall programme?
- Can you think of ways you could use observations effectively to help you learn more about children?
- How might you capture some of the child's 'hundred languages' in your observations?

The child in the family

It is important to take a holistic view of identity and the individual child and understand that the formation of identity is a complex and dynamic process. Although central to early childhood, identity is often modified as life experiences continue to shape and inform us as individuals (Kolb 2014). Nevertheless, the significance of the family in shaping a child's personal identity has long been recognised (Hillman and Williams 2015). Lindon (2012) has outlined some of the crucial factors for children in developing a sense of self:

- our own name – and how people use and react to it;
- our place within our immediate family – parents, siblings and other close relatives;
- how we look and how people react to our looks;
- what we can do and cannot do – and the extent to which this matters to people;
- a growing sense of 'what we do in our family/community';
- experiences of cultural traditions – our home language, mother/father roles, religious faith and other significant beliefs/values within daily life.

Reflective task 2.4

A sense of self

Consider Lindon's (2012) factors and reflect on your own experiences as a child. In particular, consider how your experiences have contributed to your sense of self.

Within early childhood settings, there is strong evidence (Siraj-Blatchford et al. 2002; Whalley et al. 2007) that effective partnerships with parents can have a positive impact on children's learning and development. The Pen Green Centre for children aged under five developed a model that represents dialogue about a child between staff at the centre and the significant adult(s) in the child's home (Whalley et al. 2007). Staff observe the children in the centre and parents/carers are asked to share their observations of their children at home, which, in turn, inform the staff's provision for the child. Staff, too, share their observations with parents, and so influence the child's provision at home. This is particularly important, given that the influence of parents and the home environment is much more significant than what happens in a setting (Desforges and Abouchaar 2003). Figure 2.1 demonstrates the working of the Pen Green Loop.

Reflective task 2.5

Pen Green Loop

- What might such a 'loop' of information look like in your setting?
- What challenges might you identify in creating such a partnership model for collecting information?
- What steps could you take to overcome these challenges?

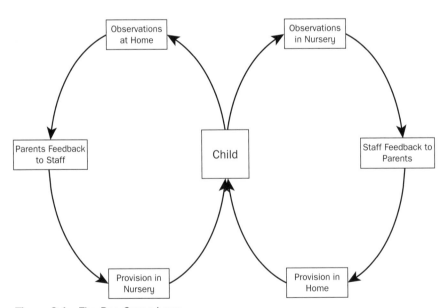

Figure 2.1 The Pen Green Loop

Source: Reproduced with permission from the Pen Green Centre for Children and their Families & Kingswood Children's Centre.

At the Pen Green Centre, children experience a continuity of care, as parents and staff in the centre work closely together. This creates a trusting and secure environment where all children can flourish as they learn and grow; it enables staff to work out strategies for removing barriers and to work with parents for the benefit of the child.

Personal values and beliefs

In promoting equality in early childhood settings, it is useful to examine how our own experiences affect and shape our views and beliefs. Although written some time ago, a seminal paper by the noted sociologist, Peggy Macintosh (1988), continues to offer a helpfully contemporary – if challenging – way into reflection, whatever our background, and is signposted at the end of this chapter as recommended further reading. Our own attitudes to 'difference' have a significant influence over our practice and we may find ourselves seeking to be more supportive of some children than others, whether this is intentional and conscious or not (Lane 2008). Therefore, when seeking to establish inclusive practice, it is important for early childhood professionals to reflect openly and honestly on their own perspectives on difference and diversity.

Current inequalities

There is increasing international evidence (Almond and Currie 2011; Heckman 2011) that high-quality early childhood education and care play a vital role in improving outcomes for children. Arguably, in recent decades, the priority and financial investment given to early intervention and to raising the quality of provision and status and professionalism of practitioners can be justified. However, inequalities continue (see, for instance, Field 2010; Pascal and Bertram 2013; OECD 2018) and this should be of concern to all early childhood professionals.

In particular, we know that families from minority ethnic groups do not always access or gain maximum benefit from the available provision and services to which they are entitled (Blanden et al. 2014) and therefore the children from these families often miss out on early learning opportunities. This is a complex issue but providers may not always fully take into account the diverse cultural and linguistic requirements of such children. Despite legislation and rhetoric, such as the Equality Act 2010, documented cases of racism in education settings continue (Andrews 2015; Sanghani 2016), with evidence that the pressure felt by black and minority ethnic (BME) children can all too easily lead to marginalisation, disaffection with learning and gross under-achievement (Houston 2015). Early childhood settings have the potential to be truly inclusive spaces where all children are valued equally and differences celebrated. Dahlberg and Moss (2005) take this further and argue for new discourse for early childhood provision. They posit an emerging paradigm of settings as places of deeply ethical practice where respectful, responsible relationships with each other and the environment become fundamental to all aspects of provision and ensure all children are fully included.

Case study 2.2

Carla, early childhood consultant

Look at the following case study and reflect on the issues raised in this situation.

Carla works as an early childhood graduate in a consultancy capacity across a small chain of private nurseries. The majority of the nurseries cater for the needs of white British children and families and the nursery environments and programmes reflect this. However, the neighbourhood of two of them is much more multi-cultural. The nurseries currently operate as individual settings, although all the staff teams come together twice a year. There is a prevailing attitude that a setting should only be concerned for the children using it. Carla is keen to support all the nurseries to celebrate diversity more effectively.

Think!

- How might Carla work across the nursery teams to create a more inclusive ethos?
- What are the challenges here?
- What professional development opportunities might Carla access for herself and/or develop for the nursery staff team?

Children for whom English is an additional language (EAL)

Language is a vital part of a child's identity and many children face the challenge of acquiring English alongside their home language. However, it is essential to recognise that all children are individual and may have needs additional to their language requirements. Children with EAL need opportunities to develop and use their home language in play and learning, whilst also ensuring good opportunities for them to learn English (DfE 2017). Effective strategies to support all children, such as the use of visual clues, are particularly relevant support for children with EAL. Marsh and Hallet (2008) identified the following pointers of good practice when working with children with EAL. You may like to refer back to these when you reach the next case study:

- creating a positive ethos that celebrates the individual;
- reflection of 'differences' in activities, stories, resources and pictures;
- opportunities for the child to use the home language;
- a strong partnership with parents, using an interpreter or digital translation technology if necessary;

- planned opportunities for talk with and between children;
- establishment of good models of standard spoken and written English;
- recognition and understanding of the stages of second language acquisition;
- introduction to new vocabulary in meaningful contexts;
- the use of rhyme, rhythm and repetition in stories and songs and the use of regular, repeated routines throughout the day.

Special educational needs and disabilities (SEND)

Further inequalities have arisen when families of children with SEND have not been able to access the services they need (Timpson 2014). Building on the Equality Act 2010 and the statutory requirements of the EYFS framework, the Children and Families Act 2014 introduced a new Code of Practice (DfE 2014) in England for children and young people with SEND aged from birth to 25 years, placing on local authorities:

> ... a duty to ensure integration between educational provision and training provision, health and social care provision where this would promote well-being and improve the quality of provision for disabled children and young people and those with SEN. (DfE 2014: 6)

Such a duty applies to all state-funded schools and early childhood providers.

Local authorities, health and care services now commission services jointly. For some children, this joined-up approach culminates in an Education, Health and Care (EHC) plan. Such plans replaced the former Statements of SEND but, with early intervention and support mechanisms in place as soon as possible after needs have been identified, many children should not need a formal EHC plan. In carefully observing and tuning in to children's individuality, monitoring what they can do and what their interests are, early childhood professionals are well placed to identify any additional needs. The standards set out in the EYFS framework (DfE 2017) include support for children with SEND, and early childhood professionals will often have a key role in cooperating with the local authority to implement the local offer once this is identified. This includes ensuring that children with SEND engage in all the activities provided, alongside those children who do not have such needs. Intervention and provision involve a graduated approach to develop plans of support – initially with low-level strategies before moving to more specific interventions, including the involvement of wider services and, where needed, an EHC plan. All interventions must be carried out in partnership with parents and carers and settings must admit a child where the setting is named on an EHC plan.

The Code of Practice (DfE 2014) sets out an 'assess – plan – do – review' approach to supporting children with SEND that is essentially an effective model for *all* children. In partnership with parents and carers, and taking full account of the child's individuality, a programme is planned that establishes clear *outcomes* aimed to result in a benefit or positive difference to the child as a direct result of strategic intervention. Effective monitoring of how well the child is progressing needs to be in place, together with agreement on action if the child does not make progress. Each step of the process needs to take full account of the views and wishes of the child and the parents. As the father of a child with disabilities himself, Slowie (2014) believes this is rooted in a vision where all involved see children and young people with learning disabilities through their parents' eyes.

The SEND Coordinator

The Ofsted Early Years Inspection arrangements (Ofsted 2019) include a judgement on how well settings help all children to make effective progress, including those whose needs or circumstances require particularly perceptive intervention or additional support. Furthermore, all settings should identify a Special Educational Needs and Disabilities Coordinator (SENDCo). The SENDCo is responsible for implementing and coordinating the setting's SEND policy, with due adherence to the Code of Practice (DfE 2014), and for overseeing inclusive practice. Typically, the SENDCo supports other staff in the early identification of children's individual needs and works closely with families to facilitate access to and review of the appropriate professional support for their child's disability or emerging special educational need.

Local services may include the support of an educational psychologist, physiotherapist, speech therapist, occupational therapist, behaviour support and/or learning support. If you become a professional, it is important that you understand the role of these wider services and can work collaboratively with them when required. Integrated working is central to effective early intervention; it places the child at the centre of the process, requiring everyone who is involved in supporting a child to work together effectively. Blanden et al. (2014) highlighted that integrated working is an important feature of early intervention, which seeks to ensure children and their families receive the timely support they need (we will return to this theme in Chapter 7).

Early childhood professionals should have a good understanding of the SENDCo role, which includes support for colleagues in assessing individual children's needs to ensure children feel both emotionally and physically safe. This includes focusing on those children who have been affected by changes or difficulties in their personal lives. The 2014 SEND Code of Practice promotes a graduated approach within the early childhood setting 'based on a cycle of action that can be revisited with increasing detail, increasing frequency and with the increased involvement of parents' (Council for Disabled Children, 2015: 1). Early childhood professionals should also develop skills in recognising when and how to refer children to colleagues for specialist support. The creation of an approachable and welcoming atmosphere will encourage parents to take an active role in exchanging information about their child's well-being, learning and development. The early childhood professional will also support families in accessing the support they and their child need.

Case study 2.3

Katya, SENDCo at a full day-care setting

Look at the following case study and see how Katya applied the SEND Code of Practice in her setting.

'*I have worked at the setting for five years now and was appointed SENDCo two years ago. Our local authority provides excellent regular training for SENDCos. I am passionate about meeting the needs of every child. This year, when Billie – aged three – started with us, her key person (KP) sensed from the outset that she had additional needs. Billie attends three mornings a week but made no attempt to engage with other children or staff, rarely spoke, and would only play on the large equipment, bikes and slide. She seemed unable to join in carpet time activities. Her KP and I met with her mum and she, too, shared her concerns. Billie liked to be on the go all the time and found it hard to sit still except when watching her favourite show on children's TV.*

'*With Billie's mum, we identified the outcome we were working towards: her inclusion, belonging and engagement in the group. Initial strategies included eye contact and exchange of words with her KP and parallel play with another child. The KP created some pictures of the TV characters Billie enjoyed and used these as a basis for one-to-one time with her. The KP would describe what the character was doing in the pictures and leave a "gap" for Billie's response. Eye contact with the KP was established within two sessions and, by the second week, Billie was anticipating which picture was coming next by using short two-word phrases. The KP then invited another child to come and look at the pictures with Billie and soon eye contact was established with the other child. After a few paired sessions with the pictures, the KP suggested that the two children go on the bikes while the rest of the group were having a story.*'

Think!

- How has Katya led on this with an 'assess – plan – do – review' approach?
- How is a graduated approach to intervention being demonstrated?
- Is there anything you would do differently if you were Katya?

Early Years Pupil Premium

In 2011, Pupil Premium (PP) grants were introduced to schools in the UK to raise the attainment of disadvantaged pupils from Reception to Year 11. Defining 'disadvantage' in this context is challenging but generally refers to those children and young people whose life chances are not equal to those of their peers because of poorer housing, employment opportunities and family income and circumstances. Evidence suggests that children from such backgrounds begin to fall behind the majority of their peer group from an early age (Allen 2011; OECD 2018) and PP was introduced as an endeavour to equalise life chances and to break the cycle of poverty (Goulden 2010).

The PP eligibility criteria for children and young people of school age include adoption, being looked after under local authority care, children whose parents work in the armed services and entitlement to free school meals. From April 2015, PP was extended to three- and four-year-olds in funded early education. Early Years Pupil Premium (EYPP) aims to improve the quality of education for the youngest disadvantaged children (Education and Skills Funding Agency 2018), with eligibility for EYPP similar to that for children in schools. Ofsted (2019) now reports on whether schools and early childhood settings are using PP/EYPP grants effectively. Again, it is important to note that children eligible for EYPP are not all the same and the approach to provision should always be individualised.

Focus on two-year-olds

Funded early education for disadvantaged two-year-olds was first piloted in 2006, aimed at improving outcomes linked to both social and cognitive development for disadvantaged children so that they are as ready for school as their peers (Gibb et al. 2011). Since 2013, this offer has been substantially scaled up and, currently, every two-year-old meeting the eligibility criteria (Gov.UK 2018) has a legal entitlement to 15 hours per week in early education. These criteria are similar to those for EYPP, and children who have EHC plans are also included in the offer. Early evaluations of this extended provision for two-year-olds painted a mixed picture (Georgeson et al. 2014). In many communities, this offer is making a substantive difference to young children and families but there are a number of concerns around how well the needs of these vulnerable two-year-olds are being met in the different settings. There is an emerging consensus that pedagogy for children under three is specialised, requiring a specific skill set different from teaching and learning with the three-to-five age range. Many of these two-year-olds also have additional needs that are not always identified or met.

Positive practice impact

Moira, SENDCo at a voluntary pre-school

Moira illustrates why knowledge of the learning and developmental needs of younger children is essential in order to meet their needs appropriately.

'Our playgroup is well-established and we meet in a community hall. Many of our children are from families originally from the Indian subcontinent. We have always taken children at 30 months but our local authority (LA) asked if we would take some younger two-year-olds who were eligible for the funding offer. Thankfully, the LA also put on a series of six days' training and all on the staff team were able to attend this, which prepared us well.

'One of the two-year-olds who started with us was Tariq, who did not speak either to other children or to us. At least Amina, our bi-lingual staff member, was able to converse with and reassure his Mum. Even after an extensive settling-in period with his Mum present, Tariq looked constantly bewildered and would just make a crying sound, expecting us to know what he wanted – just as his family did at home. With the increased funding, I was able to designate one of our experienced staff, Pam, as Tariq's key person. Amina was able to draw Mum in and gradually a rapport was built between her and Pam. From her observations, Pam began to interpret his "shouts". She would say things like: "Oh, you'd like to go on the bike now", or "I see – it's your coat you want". She encouraged Tariq firstly to point to the pictures of activities we had and then to repeat the nouns – "bike", "coat", etc.

'We then needed to establish whether Tariq had additional speech and language needs. Through our Area SENDCo, I was able to have Tariq assessed in the pre-school by a speech and language therapist, with Mum, Pam and Amina present. This assessment suggested that Tariq was processing both English and Urdu, had average levels of understanding for his age and was beginning to use English more meaningfully. She suggested some simple activities – a shopping basket and story sacks – that would support Tariq's acquisition of English.

'We also wanted to support Tariq in using his home language and, as we have a number of other bi-lingual children in the setting, Amina now regularly leads the story session in Urdu. By the end of term, we were seeing that Tariq was beginning to engage with some of the other children. This situation required effective teamwork.'

Two-year olds: Reviewing progress

Since 2009, the health and development review for children of this age has been part of the Healthy Child Programme (DHSC 2009; Blades et al. 2014). With the 2012 revision to the EYFS framework, a progress check for children between the ages of 24 and 30 months became a statutory requirement. Since 2015, a joint approach – early education and health – has been introduced, incorporating each of these assessments into an Integrated Review for all children aged 24 to 30 months. The DHSC has led on this initiative with the DfE (Gov.UK 2015) and, in working collaboratively, the overarching aim of the Integrated Review is to provide a holistic assessment of the child and promote positive outcomes, identifying progress, strengths and particular needs. Where additional needs are noted, assessment is intended to facilitate early intervention. Each local authority can select the model used for the Integrated Review, and it is important that early childhood profession-als are aware of locally agreed procedures and can contribute effectively, from a strong knowledge base of the individual child to the joint assessment.

Babies

As this chapter draws to a close, a focus on younger children is a timely reminder that, from the outset, the EYFS framework has applied to children from *birth* to five. In some full-day care and home-based settings, babies as young as three months will settle in, and important research such as that of Goouch and Powell (2013) has focused on baby room provision. With current demographic, employment and legis-lative trends, services for babies and toddlers continue to be a key consideration in the sector (Dalli 2014). A study by Ranns et al. (2011) suggested that, whilst the more highly qualified (graduate) early childhood professionals were having a significant impact on the quality of learning experiences for three- and four-year olds, there was less evidence of impact on the quality of practice with children under 30 months. It is critical that early childhood professionals have a rich bank of knowledge about development across the whole birth to five age range to ensure effective working with colleagues and other professionals to meet children's needs.

Reflective task 2.6

Working with the youngest children

- What is your current professional experience of work with two-year-olds?
- What is your current professional experience of work with babies and toddlers up to the age of two?
- How can you build up knowledge and understanding of your present or future role in supporting the youngest children, from birth to two years?
- How/when might the term 'additional needs' be applied to babies and very young children?

Summary and moving on

This chapter has explored the multi-faceted issue of providing for individual chil-dren's needs. We have explored how equality and inclusive practices aim to sup-port and include all children and how working closely with parents and carers is core to this, as is a commitment to working with other professionals. Reflection on your own experiences and values is part of the professional role. In the next chapter, we move on to consider the importance of respectful relationships in the early years. This applies in all of the following relationships: child-to-child, child-to-practitioner, practitioner-to-practitioner, practitioner-to-parent and in working with other professionals.

Further reading

Action for Children (2019) *Diversity and Inclusion Resources*. Available at: https://www.actionforchildren.org.uk/resources-and-publications/information-guides/diversity-and-inclusion/ (accessed 29 January 2019).

Department for Children, Schools and Families (DCSF) (2011) *Supporting Children Learning English as an Additional Language*. Available at: https://dera.ioe.ac.uk/6695/ (accessed 18 December 2018).

Macintosh, P. (1988) *White Privilege and Male Privilege: A personal account of coming to see correspondence through work in women's studies*. Working Paper #189. Wellesley, MA: Wellesley Centers for Women. Available at: https://www.wcwonline.org/Publications-by-title/white-privilege-and-male-privilege-a-personal-account-of-coming-to-see-correspondences-through-work-in-women-s-studies-2 (accessed 30 September 2018).

Nutbrown, C., Clough, P. and Atherton, F. (2013) *Inclusion in the Early Years*, 2nd edn. London: Sage.

3 Promoting positive relationships

The focus of this chapter continues the theme introduced in Chapters 1 and 2 of the early childhood professional developing respectful relationships with the children and their parents or carers. The nature of such relationships, particularly the role of the key person (KP), is discussed to show how positive rapport might be established from the outset of a child entering a setting. Suggested links between effective interactions and a child's learning are offered, focusing on the theme 'Positive Relationships', which is a key principle embedded in the Early Years Foundation Stage (EYFS) framework. Early learning in New Zealand's Te Whāriki approach and in the Reggio Emilia approach in Italy, both of which have relationships at their core, are also explored.

Introduction

Children learn best when they are healthy, safe and secure, when their individual needs are met and when they have positive *relationships* with the adults caring for them. (DfE 2017: 16; emphasis added)

But what do we mean by 'relationships'?

The concept of 'relationships' is complicated (Hinde 1979) but can be viewed as interpersonal connectedness (Tronick 2005) or a kind of attraction or mutual liking (Degotardi and Pearson 2014). There is strong evidence to suggest that it is primarily through interactions and relationships that children in their first five years of critical development cope and adapt (Rockel 2014; Dalli 2016). It is essential that professionals working with young children have a secure understanding of their role in forming relationships and demonstrate a commitment to ongoing reflection on this aspect of their practice. Building caring relationships that respect individual differences is at the heart of being an early childhood professional.

Positive relationships

Essentially, your role as an early childhood professional will include building and maintaining relationships with the children in the setting, with their families, within your staff team and with other professionals with whom you come into contact. The focus of this chapter is on relationships with the children and families. (Other dimensions are covered in Chapter 7; however, many of the skills required in building relationships are transferable and the two chapters can be viewed as complementary.)

Since the EYFS framework was introduced, 'Positive Relationships' has been a promoted theme, described as: warm, loving and fostering a sense of belonging; sensitive and responsive to children's needs and interests; supportive of children's autonomy and independence; and consistent in setting clear boundaries (Early Education 2012).

Arguably, establishing trust is a central attribute in ensuring positive relationships (Johnson 2010). Trust can take a long time to build but only seconds to destroy, which is an important reminder of the huge responsibility held by all who work with the youngest children and their families. Rolfe (2004) asserts that the child–educator relationship is critical in contributing to a child's emotional security. You might reflect on this in relation to your own work in early childhood settings.

Reflective task 3.1

Building trusting relationships

'Trust' is defined as: a 'firm belief in the reliability, truth, or ability of someone or something' (*Oxford Dictionaries* 2018).

In his theory of life-span development, Erikson (1950) described development between birth and 18 months as a stage of constructive tension between trust and mistrust, in which the balance needs to be towards the young child's positive experience of trust. Experiences of mistrust for such young children can be any change to routine for which they are not carefully prepared.

Think!

- In what ways might you foster such trust in relationships with children and families in a school or early childhood setting?
- How do you see the early childhood professional role in ensuring that children's experiences of mistrust are taken seriously and addressed in such a way that a sense of trust prevails?

The key person role

Since the mid-1990s, the key person (KP) system has become embedded into early childhood practice in England. Concern had long been expressed from researchers such as Bain and Barnett (1986) about the inconsistency of adult attention to young children in day care. In response, the role of the KP developed from the seminal work of Goldschmied and Jackson (1994, 2004) and, later, that of others such as Elfer et al. (2012) and Jackson and Forbes (2014). The KP system draws on John Bowlby's theory of attachment (1953) and the mother–child dyad, that unique uninterrupted closeness of the two, as a model for practice with young children in out-of-home settings. However, Mary Ainsworth's follow-up work (for example, in 1968) showed that children are also able to form healthy secondary attachments to key *others*, including in out-of-home settings.

The KP system can be critical in enabling young children to make positive transitions from home into a setting and from different sections and groups within the same setting. Since 2008, in England it has been a statutory requirement for all settings delivering the EYFS programme to assign a named KP to each child. The relationship established between the KP and the child aims to 'ensure that every child's care is tailored to meet their individual needs' (DfE 2017: 3.27). Partnership with the child's parents or carers is inseparable from the KP system and the parent is always part of the triangle of relationships (Degotardi and Pearson 2014). (We will look at this further later in this chapter.) However, the KP was never intended to be a replacement or substitute parent – rather, to be a knowledgeable, understanding and consistent presence in the out-of-home setting, providing professional care for a child in partnership with the parents.

Reflective task 3.2

The key person role

- Do you have any experience of the KP role? If so, reflect on this.
- What do you believe are the opportunities in being a KP?
- What specific challenges do you identify in the KP role?
- If you are or become an early childhood professional, it is possible that your role will move from *being* a KP yourself to *leading and managing* the KP system in all or part of your setting – ensuring that all in the team understand what is involved. One early childhood leader described this as becoming a 'Key Grandma' (Whalley 2017: 106). What do you think is meant by this?

The KP system is not without its critics and one challenger (Grenier 2011) suggested that it was all too easy for the role to be reduced to that of surveillance and monitoring of individual children. Robson (2012) questioned whether attachment, as a construct, is culturally specific and, therefore, cannot be generalised, citing Rogoff's (2003) research, which indicated that young children reflect their own cultural practices in relationships with others. Although not critical of the KP system directly, Dahlberg et al. (2013) contested the commonly held belief that, for young children, the out-of-home setting should be a substitute for the real home. They described the benefit of its *not* being a home, as out-of-home settings offer the children a different, complementary experience in which they are able to learn how to establish and manage relationships with small groups of other children and adults.

A further, very practical, concern was highlighted in a study conducted by Page et al. (2015), where some practitioners with very young children (babies and toddlers) expressed anxiety about false accusations if they showed affection through physical contact. Given contemporary discourse around safeguarding, such concern is perhaps unsurprising. Dalli (2016) identified that practitioners working with babies and toddlers spend more time with the children, including intimate bodily contact, than those working with older children. Whilst the issue of showing children physical affection remains problematic, for many practitioners across the birth-to-five age range, appropriate touch and physical contact remains a very important part of forming positive relationships with young children. Indeed, a study by Sieratzki and Woll (2005) found touch to be the basis of intensely reciprocal relationships with babies – which offers an important counter-argument to the concern expressed by the participants in Page and co-workers' (2015) study.

Reflective task 3.3

Challenges of the KP role

Once you become an early childhood professional, or if you are currently in practice, it is important that you engage critically with these issues around the KP role. As we emphasised in Chapter 2, the core task will be to ensure that practice in your setting operates in the best interests of every child. Think about the potential challenges for the KP role outlined in the previous section, using the task below. If possible, discuss this with colleagues and parents of young children to gain their perspectives.

The KP role is ...	*In the child's best interests, the KP role should ...*
... surveillance and monitoring (Grenier 2011)	
... culturally defined (Robson 2012)	
... restricting children from developing wider relationships with other adults and children (Dahlberg et al. 2013)	
... eliciting concerns about showing affection/using physical contact with children (Page et al. 2015)	

'In tune' with young children

Despite these concerns, the essence of the KP role is to 'tune in' to children, something we explored briefly in Chapter 2. The concept of caring adults 'tuning in' to the children in their charge is not new and was first highlighted in the mid-1990s (Purvis and Selleck 1996). Trevarthen (2011: 16) defined the concept of 'mutual attunement' – proto-conversations or a rhythmic dance, similar across cultures – to describe the earliest kind of interactions between a primary carer and young baby. Each imitates, responds to and influences the other, demonstrating a pleasurable, reciprocal relationship: 'the dance of dialogue … I do this and you do that back' (Read 2010: 17). Whilst fully respecting the parents' role as primary carers, early childhood professionals should also seek to form such close and dependable relationships with the children in their care. In turn, this will foster children's cooperation and motivation and should lead to positive outcomes for them.

Reflective task 3.4

Mutual attunement

Read (2010) described three key elements to being 'in tune' with the children in an out-of-home setting:

- positively reflecting something back about who the child is – a source of joy and love;
- getting on the child's wavelength and being deeply respectful of the child's developing sense of self;
- gaining mutual pleasure in each other – developing an empathy that results in an understanding of each other.

Think!

- How can early childhood professionals ensure there are good opportunities to 'tune in' to the children in a setting?
- What are the barriers to 'tuning in'?

Young children are looking for caring adults who will respond to their cues. For all children, this will focus on observing and listening to them carefully, noting their interests, moods or feelings. Before babies and toddlers can speak, such tuning in to their cues will also include smell and touch (Johnson 2010). Essentially, though, being 'in tune' with the children in your care means you will respond to the actual needs of the individual child rather than to your idea of what the child might need. Of paramount importance is that the child's well-being is respected and responded to appropriately (Bradford 2012).

Case study 3.1

Chloe, three years nine months in pre-school nursery

Chloe seems very settled in her nursery setting. She plays with a number of other children, though Scott (similar age) is the one she plays with the most. Scott, however, has been involved in a road traffic accident and, although his injuries are not serious, he is going to be missing from nursery for a few weeks.

Think!

- How might the KP and staff team respond in this situation?
- How can staff ensure they are meeting Chloe's needs?

Children who find relationships challenging

In Chapter 2, the focus was on the early childhood professional's role with children who may have additional needs, and there is an important reminder here to acknowledge those children who find relationships challenging – for a variety of reasons. Most of these children will require an early intervention approach and possibly specialist help. For example, children on the autism spectrum often experience difficulties in their interactions with others. Children at the severe end of the spectrum may find spoken language hard to understand and even those at the milder end of the spectrum may find it difficult to use or understand facial expression, tone of voice or humour (National Autistic Society 2016). Similarly, those at the milder end may show distress reactions to touch, sound and smell. Other children may find relationships difficult because of intense emotional trauma. Such children can find it difficult to trust an adult and therefore cannot easily interact with and respond to them.

Reflective task 3.5

Building knowledge and experience

- What knowledge and experience do you have of working with children who find relationships and social interactions very challenging? How might you enhance your knowledge and experience in this area?
- What do you know about early intervention and support for children who find relationships challenging? Where can you find out more?

Thoughtful agents: Maintaining professional boundaries

One of the key factors in enabling the early childhood professional to 'tune in' to children is the time and capacity to reflect on and think deeply about practice (this is the focus of Chapter 8). An alternative understanding of the KP role is that of 'thoughtful agent' (Appleby and Andrews 2011: 59), one who takes a reflective approach to all aspects of practice with children, based on their needs, and seeks to develop this effectively. Maintaining a reflective stance to relationships with children offers an appropriate balance to the emotional demands of being a KP (Elfer and Dearnley 2007), especially in caring for very young children. Indeed, as we will discuss further in Chapter 6, Page (2011: 310) asserted that such care might be seen as 'professional love', with practitioners who care deeply for their children – engaging both head and heart – in their role. As a 'thoughtful agent', you will be seeking always to act and respond in the best interests of the child – balancing your feelings with thoughtful reflection.

Case study 3.2

Duane, early childhood professional working with two- and three-year-olds

Duane is an experienced practitioner but new to the toddler room. His full-day care setting has a policy whereby, as children settle in, the team notes if they gravitate naturally to any particular member of staff. Duane found that Maxwell, aged 20 months, seemed to relate to him from day one and so he became his KP. Two months in, Maxwell still likes to be beside Duane or carried by him for much of the day. Duane finds himself looking forward to spending time with Maxwell at work and has grown very fond of him.

Think!

- How can Duane ensure he is being a 'thoughtful agent' with Maxwell?
- Might this be an example of 'professional love'?
- How do you think Duane is balancing his thinking with his feelings in his role as KP?

Being a 'thoughtful agent' also involves self-awareness, self-care and an understanding of the ethical dimension of one's work. Although, to date, there is no formal code of ethics for early childhood professionals in the UK, there is a shared understanding of placing the utmost importance on the protection and well-being of children, families and staff (Early Education 2011). Remaining alert to unethical practices, then, is the responsibility of everyone in early childhood settings. This includes an understanding of the professional boundaries that are essential in maintaining safe and appropriate relationships with children. The term 'professional boundaries' in the context of relationships between staff and children is not easily defined but can include the extent to which a relationship builds trust and does not lead to any abuse of power. It can also mean ensuring that the relationship is focused on the *child's* needs and not used to meet the *practitioner's* needs. This is a complex area and setting policies such as confidentiality, staff codes of conduct and staff appraisals should be in place to monitor such professional boundaries.

Reflective task 3.6

Maintaining professional boundaries

The following guidelines are based on those offered more generically to people working in care with children and young people across the age range (Melyn 2009). They can be used to reflect on your present or future role and how you might establish and maintain professional boundaries.

Guidelines	*Reflection on how you might manage this in your current/ future role*
Be positive: learn to separate personal issues from your professional responsibilities with the children	
Be aware that your own mood and feelings can affect the children	
Be careful about the language you use – both in words and through touch, gesture, physical closeness and eye contact	
Respect the children's right to personal space – including their right to silence or solitary play	
Find out as much as you can about the children that will enable you to work for their best interests. However, don't seek non-essential information about the child's family	

Use your line management system to share any concerns. This ensures that the setting demonstrates unity and consistency of approach in developing professional relationships

The concept of agency has wider application, too. In developing relationships with children, the early childhood professional role includes promoting children's independence and agency. Of course, the EYFS framework covers the enormous journey from the significant needs of the young baby to the confident child starting school but, at each stage of development, children need opportunities to explore and make sense of their surroundings, learning about their influence and control over things that happen (Touhill 2013). In supporting children to be independent, early childhood professionals take into account the wider context of the child's community.

Encouraging agency in young children also enables them to forge effective relationships with their peers – learning to collaborate and respect the 'other'. Some children find this particularly challenging and, again, the key here is to know and be 'attuned' to the individual child. As we discussed in Chapter 2, with all children, it is important to recognise, respect and build on their individual qualities and potential (Early Education 2011).

Case study 3.3

Miran, aged 30 months

Miran's family is from Syria. Miran was born in the UK and Arabic is his home language. At the pre-school, which he has been attending each morning for three weeks now, Miran uses no recognisable words in either Arabic or English. He does not show any obvious distress in the group and goes towards the activities set out when he arrives. However, he does not yet appear to interact with or relate to either the children or any of the staff.

Think!

- How might the staff team have prepared for Miran starting in the group?
- How can the KP allocated to work with Miran stay attuned to his needs?

The triangle of relationships: Interaction with parents

All children belong to distinctive families and communities. In building up relationships with the children, you will have a responsibility to learn as much as you can about the child's world. In the previous chapter, we discussed the importance of working with parents to meet children's needs; the KP system has always viewed parents and carers as part of the triangle of relationships (Goldschmied and Jackson 1994).

In the previous chapter, we considered the Pen Green Loop (Figure 2.1), emphasising the well-established practice of building and maintaining respectful, sensitive and trusting relationships with parents (Whalley et al. 2007). This is now embedded into early childhood frameworks for learning and development across the world, including in the EYFS framework (DfE 2017). Indeed, research evidence (NSCDC 2004) suggests that the effectiveness of this triangular relationship is crucial for the long-term social, emotional and cognitive development of children. If the KP system is led and managed carefully, the parent or carer should feel fully part of the 'triangle' – commonly viewed as a partnership of *trust* (Barnardos 2016) with parents (see Figure 3.1).

Relating to parents, then, is 'an important bridge to build' (Read 2010: 43), especially as young children start in settings for the first time. Parents of babies and toddlers can be especially anxious about this initial separation from their very young child and, as Page's (2011) study indicated, many parents are looking for a deeply caring relationship to be established between key practitioners and their child. We have already referred to Page's earlier research (2008) in which she asserted that the work of early childhood professionals involves not only care and education but also *love*. (This is not without its challenges and in Chapter 6 we will consider this notion in the context of professionalism and professional identity.)

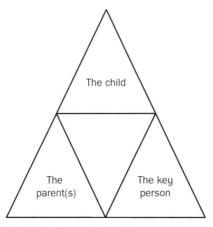

Figure 3.1   The triangle of trusting relationships

In terms of relationships with parents, there is scope for KPs to love the children in their care, though too close a relationship may be perceived as edging staff towards a parental role (Page 2008). It can also feel threatening to parents if they see a special relationship between their child and another adult, especially when they may be struggling with guilt at leaving their child (Elfer et al. 2012). Yet again, maintaining professional boundaries is critical here and the strength of the KP system outweighs the potential pitfalls – especially when a reflective approach is adopted by the early childhood professional.

Parents need to feel that they can share any news or concerns about their child with a trusted professional in the setting, so a close relationship with the KP or significant others is vital. The triangular model of the KP system (Figure 3.1) might also be viewed as an emotional container for some of the strong feelings that can arise between families and staff and ensure a shared approach to acting in the child's best interests. For parents, the KP becomes the *specific* person they get to know rather than a less personal *team* of staff in their child's setting as they hand over or reunite with their child (Elfer et al. 2012). As noted earlier, as an early childhood professional you may well become a KP or have responsibility for overseeing the system – but, in any case, ensuring that positive relationships with parents is established from the outset is paramount. Even before a child starts at the setting, initial contact – however this is done – creates important first impressions that are often an indicator of the effectiveness of a future relationship.

Case study 3.4

Sara, a first-time mum, prepares to return to work

'I was a first-time mum preparing to leave my nine-month-old daughter with a total stranger. It felt terrifying and I got mixed advice from friends and the health visitor: some advocated a nursery setting and others a childminder. In the end, I visited both. At the nursery, one person met me at the door and then immediately introduced me to another person – whose name I missed – and then I felt bombarded by information even before we'd looked into the rooms. I felt as if I was being talked "at" rather than "to" – though, to be fair, I was asked if I had any other questions before we left. By contrast, as soon as I met Charlotte in her home, I felt relaxed and she had the knack of gently relating to my daughter – through smile and gesture – even whilst she was fully attentive to me and my questions. I knew almost straightaway that this was someone both I and my daughter would get on well with. It was a huge weight off my shoulders: I could trust Charlotte and know my child would be fine with her.'

Think!

- This is just one woman's experience but, putting yourself in Sara's shoes, what does this say to you about 'first impressions' in the parent–practitioner–child relationship?
- Reflect on how parents might perceive your setting when they make an initial visit. What do you need to think about?

Although first impressions are very important, there are many skills involved in working with and relating to parents and in maintaining effective partnerships with them. Drawing on research, Degotardi and Pearson (2014) highlight two key elements in effective relationships between educators and parents:

- *Authenticity* – where the educator demonstrates a genuine interest in the parents, in getting to know them, showing interest in and appreciation of aspects of the parents' lives beyond the child and setting (Hedges 2012).
- *Reciprocity* – not simply sharing knowledge with parents on a regular basis, important though this is. It involves an intentional commitment to find out what is happening to the child at home, valuing and welcoming the parents' contributions. This involves skilled questioning and careful listening, which Brooker (2010) identifies as foundational to respectful reciprocity.

Reflective task 3.7

Authenticity and reciprocity

Think about the characteristics of *authenticity* and *reciprocity* in relationships with parents. If you are working in a setting, conduct a self-audit reflecting on any areas for development in your practice. If you are in training, how might you develop these characteristics in your practice? Look back at the Pen Green Loop (Figure 2.1) to support your reflection.

Partnership with parents: Opportunities and challenges

As with all relationships, there may be challenges along the way. You may be in a setting where the majority of parents are working and often pre-occupied at drop-off and reunite times, or you may be in a setting where children under three are in receipt of a funded place, given their particular needs or vulnerabilities. You may not fully understand a particular child's home language or culture. Treating parents equally does not mean treating them all the same, and part of the skill required by the early childhood professional is to treat all parents with equal *respect* whilst acknowledging and accommodating differences. It is important, for instance, to

Case studies 3.5

Partnership with parents

The following case studies highlight some of the challenges in both establishing and maintaining positive relationships with parents and carers.

Rachel, first-time mum

Rachel's daughter, Sadie (aged eight months), was about to start in a full-day care setting three days a week as Rachel was returning to her paid work. Sadie had been a fretful, wakeful baby and Rachel had responded to this by 'baby-wearing', carrying her in a sling around the home and outdoors for the greater part of each day. As the baby room team met with Rachel and Sadie to prepare for her settling-in, Rachel raised this issue. She was concerned about how Sadie would cope if she was not carried around the baby room.

Abi, manager of an urban children's centre

Abi, the manager of a children's centre, operated an open-door policy for parents. In the space of a week, she had one parent complain that their two-year-old child slept for too long at the centre and then was not tired in the evening and another parent asking why their two-year-old was not sleeping at nursery as she kept falling asleep on the way home.

Claire, home-based childminder

Claire, a childminder, was asked by Fran, the mother of Fraser, who had just had his third birthday, to 'do the flash cards' with him every day as she was 'determined he'll be able to read before he goes to school'.

Think!

In each of these cases, ask yourself:

- As an early childhood professional, how would I remain both respectful and trustworthy in my response?
- What professional issues might such scenarios open up for me?

consider how early childhood professionals can build partnerships with parents who may seem less inclined to be involved. It is particularly critical to learn what parental involvement means in different cultures and seek to understand the specific goals parents hold for their children, which may differ from those of your own cultural group (McDermott 2008). This requires being 'in tune' not only with the children but with the parents and demonstrating *authenticity* and *reciprocity* in your relationships with them.

The parent–educator relationship is rarely without tensions. Lang et al. (2016: 40) conducted a study of parents and educators and promoted the concept of 'co-caring' to describe parent partnership, finding that consistency in approach in the home and setting was important for children's healthy development. However, disagreements on practices can arise that can undermine the strength of such co-caring. In particular, these can leave parents feeling de-skilled or undervalued, or having little or no place in their child's learning. Rather than seeing such disagreements as a huge obstacle, Lang et al. showed that where the relationship between parent and educator is strong, such differences can be negotiated positively.

Positive practice impact

Anya, room leader for two-year-olds in an urban nursery setting

Anya illustrates the importance of building trusting relationships with parents and involving them in the transition process.

Anya's nursery has places for children in receipt of funded places. As soon as the funding is confirmed, ahead of the child starting at the setting, Anya makes a home visit to the family. One such family consists of Flo, a mum, who has a challenge with mobility and finds it difficult to walk very far, and Freddy, her two-year-old son. Living in a second-floor apartment, Flo has difficulty getting out to the park with Freddy. Hence his allocation of a place at Anya's nursery.

At the initial visit, Anya listens very carefully to Flo's concerns and anxiety that Freddy is 'too young' to be away from her each morning. Anya expresses genuine empathy for Flo and explains that while he is settling in, Flo is welcome to be part of this process. Anya explains that she will be the KP for Freddy and Flo, to whom they can both relate. Anya shows pictures of some of the nursery activities and shares information about occasional events for parents. Anya says she will liaise with Flo's social worker to ensure transport arrangements are in place to and from the nursery. By the end of this initial home visit, Flo is feeling much more confident about Freddy taking up the place.

Relationships as a pedagogical tool: Social pedagogy

At the start of the chapter, we asserted that it is primarily through interactions and relationships that children learn in their earliest years (Rockel 2014). Drawing on seminal theories, such as Vygotsky's (1978) social constructivism, Bandura's (1977) social learning theory and Rogoff's (1991) notion of guided participation, early learning is seen to be informed by the social and cultural contexts in which it takes place (Robson 2012). These links between learning and relationships are often termed 'social pedagogy' – expressing the critical importance of meaningful inter-action between educator and young children as they begin to make sense of their worlds and 'learn to be' (Tayler 2015: 160).

Dalli (2014), highlighting insights from Fox and Rutter's (2010: 26) neurological research, promotes the idea that the brain is not simply a cognitive organ but is a 'social brain' strongly connected to affective and other environmental conditions. The NSCDC (2007: 1) identified that the most significant method of early learning is through the 'serve and return' nature of the child's engagement in relationships. This builds on the analogy of games like tennis where each player concentrates on and responds to the cue from another. As children 'serve and return' with the significant adults in their lives, Meltzoff et al. (2009) believe there are three social skills that children are using to learn and develop:

- imitation;
- shared attention;
- empathetic understanding.

It is also through these processes that children make sense of their environment (Dalli 2014). Such findings provide increasingly convincing evidence of a relational pedagogy – 'the lived in-between space and time of the learner and teacher' (Papatheodorou 2009: 11) – as an appropriate approach to working with young children.

Reflective task 3.8

Skills for learning

Think about children you know – in your own setting, within your family – or have read about.

- How might they be developing skills in *imitation, shared atten-tion* and *empathic understanding* as tools for learning?
- What evidence could you use to support this?

The caretakers of both the Reggio Emilia approach to pre-school practice and provision in northern Italy and the *Te Whāriki* (meaning 'the weaving') pre-school curriculum in New Zealand are quick to emphasise that any attempts to duplicate these approaches outside their cultural context are probably doomed to fail (Lee et al. 2013). Nevertheless, there are important emphases in both these approaches that offer useful insights to discussions of relational or social pedagogy.

Johnson (2010) suggests that a deep awareness of the child within relationships has been built into both these approaches to early childhood provision. In the Reggio Emilia approach, children are viewed as taking charge of their own learning, using the educator as a tool to lend help, information or experience where necessary. Central to this mode of learning is 'the development of reciprocal relationships of love and trust between adult and child and between the children themselves' (Learning and Teaching Scotland, LTS 2006: 11). Such interaction is viewed by Reggio educators as fundamental to the learning process and they see their roles as creating such a reciprocal relationship of learning and teaching. Rinaldi (1998, cited by LTS 2006: 13), currently President of Reggio Children, described such a relationship as 'a metaphorical dance between teacher and child', as together they share in the learning process. The timing and pace of the 'dance' is always set by the child.

New Zealand's *Te Whāriki* curriculum reflects its bi-cultural society, drawing on both Maori and British social and cultural understandings, and promoting diversity that upholds Maori rights (Lee et al. 2013). That in itself is deeply relational – indicating respectful reciprocity – and the first of four principles of *Te Whāriki* is ngā hononga (relationships). Relationships with people underlie this principle but relationships with place and things are also included. Sustained and shared thinking (Sylva et al. 2010) is one aspect of relationships with people where both educator and learner are intentionally engaged in co-inquiry (Robinson and Bartlett 2011). The further emphasis on place and things is also noteworthy: children often use 'place' – real or imagined – as they are learning through play. Children build up a relationship with their environment, including the setting; in their play, they might go 'on an aeroplane' or 'to the shop'. Similarly, for children, objects and materials can 'cross boundaries' (Lee et al. 2013: 47), connecting home and setting – through photographs or food, for example – and become important tools in their learning.

Reflective task 3.9

Global insights

You may already be familiar with insights from Reggio Emilia and the *Te Whāriki* curriculum. If so, continue to find out more and reflect on these. Focus on what you might apply in your own understanding of relationships – with people, places and things – in early learning. If you are unfamiliar with these insights, further reading on this principle is signposted at the end of the chapter and you are strongly encouraged to reflect on this.

Currently, in England, there is significant emphasis on the three prime areas of the EYFS framework: personal, social and emotional development; communication and language; and physical development (DfE 2017). The KP role, in building a close and meaningful relationship with the child, carries particular responsibilities for monitoring and supporting children's learning in these areas. Learning in these prime areas is foundational to all the other areas and can 'begin to develop quickly in response to relationships and experiences' (Early Education 2012: 4). *Development Matters* (Early Education 2012) offers practical guidance on how the theme, 'Positive Relationships', supports early learning holistically. The focus is on what adults can do and the section on 'Characteristics of Effective Learning' is particularly helpful. You can use this document as a useful tool to support you as 'thoughtful agent' (Appleby and Andrews 2011: 59) with and for the children in your care, but – as we have already identified – the driving question remains: what is in the best interests of the child?

Summary and moving on

This chapter has focused on the role of the early childhood professional in developing positive relationships with both children and their families and also of supporting children as they learn to interact with each other. The role of the KP – viewed as a partnership between child, educator and parent – has been shown to be core to this process and the concept of the educator as a 'thoughtful agent' has been explored. One of the KP's tasks is to support the child's development in the EYFS framework, particularly in the three prime areas. Insights from the Reggio Emilia and *Te Whāriki* approaches to early learning have been considered, especially as they place relationships at the heart of early learning and development.

Further reading

Degotardi, S. and Pearson, E. (2014) Relationships in early years settings: Definitions and challenges, in *The Relationship Worlds of Infants and Toddlers: Multiple perspectives from early years theory and practice*. Maidenhead: Open University Press.

Lee, W., Carr, M., Soutar, B. and Mitchell, L. (2013) Principle one: Ngā hononga/ relationships, in *Understanding the Te Whāriki Approach*. London: Routledge.

Rose, J. and Rogers, S. (2012) The communicator, in *The Role of the Adult in Early Years Settings*. Maidenhead: Open University Press.

Tayler, C. (2015) Learning in early childhood: Experiences, relationships and 'learning to be', *European Journal of Education*, 50 (2): 160–174.

4 Enabling environments

> This chapter builds on themes introduced in the previous chapters and considers the philosophy and pedagogical underpinning of an enabling environment. The aim of the chapter is to explore features of an enabling environment that promote children's sense of self, well-being and self-esteem. Enabling environments can create conditions for children's empowerment; they acknowledge children as capable, active participants in the construction of meaning in the world and their social practices. These are core requirements for effective learning. The chapter will consider how a rights-based lens can be applied to explore and identify dimensions of practice that contribute towards the development and review of enabling environments.

Introduction

We start by exploring characteristics of an enabling environment and consider what it might feel and look like to its occupants. We do this to encourage reflection on who might be enabled within the environment and how an enabling process may occur. Understanding and interpretation of an enabling environment in practice will be shaped by different influential perspectives of the child and how they learn and develop. As considered in Chapters 1 and 2, the Early Years Foundation Stage (EYFS) framework articulates a view of the 'unique child' who can be a strong, confident, capable and active learner. An enabling environment provides opportunities and experiences for the child that are responsive to their individual needs and acknowledge the importance of sound partnerships between parents and practitioners (DfE 2017).

Wyness (2000) and the OMEP (Organisation Mondiale pour l'Education Prescolaire 2010) recognise that adults need to listen to perspectives and ideas expressed directly by children in all matters that relate to their life experiences. Adults need to listen to children to be fully aware of their voices, perspectives and ideas in matters that relate directly to them (Engdahl 2015). Children are their own agents and it is the role of adults to be able to tune into a child's agency, identity, capabilities and voice. Loris Malaguzzi (1920–1994), a world-famous advocate for children, was the pedagogical leader of the Reggio Emilia early years philosophy and author of the poem, *The One Hundred Languages of Children*. The poem captures beautifully a philosophy of children who are competent and capable communicators, able to express their thinking, curiosity, reactions, feelings, interests and knowledge with those who are willing and able to listen. Indeed, children are enabled and enabling in many ways and use one hundred languages (Rinaldi 2012) to express themselves and their interests. They tell adults 'we know stuff too', although adults might not always be 'tuned in' or actively listening to them (OMEP 2010; Penn 2011, 2014).

The characteristics of enabling environments

The term 'enabling environment' is described here as a setting that offers a positive and supportive environment for decision-making and action, where children are empowered to be active agents in the learning process. It is vital that enabling environments are not only constructed and presented to children by adults but rather are co-constructed with children. Key findings from Sylva and co-workers' (2004) report, *The Effective Provision of Pre-School Education* (EPPE), indicate that effective enabling environments have sound evidence of two-way child/adult-initiated communication, strong parent partnerships, and staff with up-to-date knowledge and understandings of how to combine care and education when responding to young children's holistic needs.

Enabling environments are characterised by a specific pedagogical approach. Within an enabling environment, adults take the risk of trusting children, within the limits required for safeguarding and the promotion of well-being (Baraldi and Farini 2013). The main implication here is that children's decision-making is not dependent on approval offered by the adult. The permission for children to make choices, decisions and experiences is embedded in practice and planning by early childhood professionals who are both willing and able to listen to children's unlimited and unique expressions. The overarching and guiding principles within the EYFS framework (DfE 2017), which underpin early years practice, recognise that enabling environments need to be ready to welcome babies and young children and provide them with the opportunities to flourish as capable learners.

Capable children enter provision with their own starting points, life stories, personalities and dispositions; this reinforces the need for the setting's environment to see the child first and the learner second. To best achieve this, strong partnerships between practitioners and parents or carers are advocated by the EYFS framework (as considered in Chapter 3). It is vital that the position and voice of the child are equally established within partnerships; this is the ethical and pedagogical key to understanding that enabling environments are created *with* children as well as *for* children. The model shown in Figure 4.1 invites reflection on the impact and involvement of each stakeholder within early years partnerships.

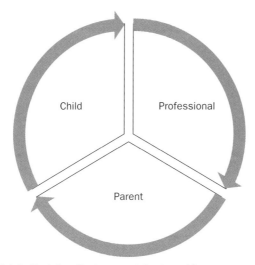

Figure 4.1 Model 1: Enabling Environment Partnership

Reflective task 4.1

Model 1

Reflect on Model 1 and the following tasks to consider if children enter early years provision as capable citizens and equal partners.

- Are the child + parent + professional equal stakeholders in this model?
- Are the child + parent + professional equal stakeholders in practice?

Development Matters in the Early Years Foundation Stage (Early Education 2012), the EYFS framework (DfE 2017) and the Preschool Learning Alliance (2017) all recognise enabling environments as indoor and outdoor spaces that nurture a sense of belonging, offer risk-taking opportunities to children, encourage individual exploration, celebrate diversity and difference, and recognise children as co-constructors of their own learning. An enabling environment is much more than a space; rather, it is a living amalgamation of spaces, people, identities, emotions, communication and shared experiences. An enabling environment is thus a complex system, where a variety of traits and characteristics can be woven together to create a well-organised, planned, safe and challenging learning situation. Enabling environments are where life happens, experiences are born and new skills are crafted by *all* participants in the interactions within the environment. Any space can be developed as an enabling environment but, at the same time, the most well-resourced setting is not necessarily enabling; everything depends on access, attitude and self-determination.

The dispositions of children and adults contribute to the actions and interactions that influence the levels of enabling that are on offer. Enabling environments are ultimately multi-dimensional spaces.

Enabling and enabled children and early years educators

Early childhood professionals choose to care for children and help shape their daily lives. They are especially focused on children's unique personalities and the development of their potential. Children are considered to be capable of being agents and advocates of change. The following case study is an example of an activity (a game) that aims to contribute to the development of an enabling environment in a Reception Class.

Case study 4.1

Reception class activity

The game is intended to promote children's voices, agency and participation. Planned activities by the early childhood professional focus on play opportunities and active participation using the theme of *treasure*.

First, the children are encouraged to share memories about what they know about treasure and what treasure means to them.

The game that follows consists of making, taking and finding treasure within a three-minute time frame. Children interact physically and verbally with the treasure, following their memories and interests so that each new game has a new twist. The goal of the game is for each child taking part to secure an area where individual treasure can be kept safely. Each child tries to collect as much treasure as possible from the class reserve treasure chest but only one piece of treasure can be taken from the chest per visit.

Children then store the treasure in their own area. The child with the most treasure wins the game. However, if the class treasure in the chest runs out, the focus to collect treasure changes. At this point, children can help themselves to other children's treasure. This is when the game becomes complex, noisy and, at times, emotive. A major rule of the game is that the adult cannot take part, offer guidance or get involved in any way during the agreed time frame so that children have their own space to problem-solve and negotiate without adult support or interference.

The game encourages children to develop both individual and group game plans.

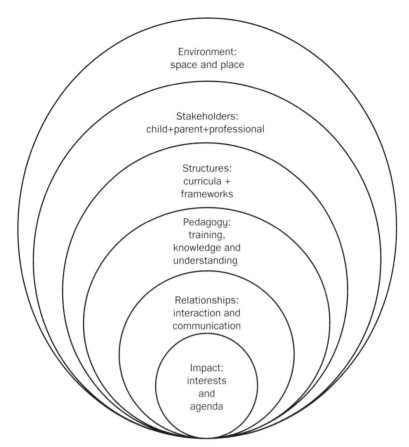

Figure 4.2 Model 2: Dimensions of Enabling

Co-constructing game rules and plans encourages children to listen to each other, take turns and negotiate. Children will have the opportunity to challenge each other's ideas, problem-solve, deal with trial or error, develop ideas and weigh up potential outcomes. Children have space to discuss previous tried-and-tested strategies and wonder if similar strategies could work again or not (Skemp 1989; Pound 1999). The game offers children time to think, space to work something out and opportunities to connect with self and others. The game also promotes decision-making where children articulate and defend choices made. Children share ideas that open up dialogic discussion, argument and strategy-building concepts. Communication and thinking skills evolve as the game develops week after week. Children are enabled to communicate with each other and to connect and remember experiences and game strategies. Sustained shared thinking and listening have time to develop and evolve.

Figure 4.2 offers an insight into some of the many dimensional layers found within environments that enable. Each layer within the model is by no means hierarchical or a definite category. Each aims to provoke reflection or self-assessment of characteristics and traits that can be related to each, to identify what does or does not contribute towards positive experiences and opportunities. For instance, the model might represent an onion that can be peeled off in layers to reveal yet another layer. This model relates to Chapters 8 and 9 where early years professionals are provoked to critique practice to bring about positive change or to lead. To make change effective, it is vital to be able to notice and consider how environments work and what they are made up of. Further layers can be added to the model along with personalised characteristics or traits for each setting or professional.

Reflective task 4.2

Models 1 and 2

Apply Models 1 and 2 (Figures 4.1 and 4.2) to:

- define the role of children throughout the game; and
- consider if the game contributes towards an enabling environment or not, and explain why.

Promoting each child's active participation and listening carefully to children during whole-group discussion, without leading or interrupting, can be a challenge. In the following case study, an early childhood professional who has regularly used a similar game with a Reception class reflects on their experience of challenge when using the game.

Case study 4.2

Reception class, Part 1

'*I immediately stepped in at the beginning when children were not taking turns, listening to each other or moving forward. I think I did this because of learnt behaviour and response patterns. Children had learnt to look to me for support and I jumped in and gave it to them, with no time delay, not waiting to see if they could sort it out for themselves. I felt I needed to control behaviour, which in hindsight was not always the best approach, not so enabling. Also, reflecting further, I was not following the rules of the game – although I still expected the children to!*'

As this case study illustrates, adults can generate a place and time to engage with or challenge children within enabling environments, based on the premise that this will lead to an enrichment of their lives, learning and experiences. Early childhood professionals create environments to empower the development of children's subjective participation and holistic development. The adult's interest resides in observing with great care what children are actually interested in and what they are hoping to achieve. Motivation and expectations about why children do what they do underpins the adult's reflection and is a key contributor to professional learning. (See Chapters 8 and 9 for further exploration of reflection, change and adult impact.)

A further reflection undertaken by the same professional indicates that this game offered insight into children's thinking at a deeper level than they had generally experienced with other planned activities:

Case study 4.2 (continued)

Reception class, Part 2

'Some of the children really shocked me. They shone, took the lead or were a bit more manipulative or supportive towards others. I hadn't seen that side of them. The strategies, conversation and shared emotions during the game, and particularly during the discussion afterwards, were at times electric.'

Reflective task 4.3

Model 2

Reflect on enabling environments and consider the following questions, applying layers from Model 2 (Figure 4.2) that relate to your responses. How might layers identified in the model impact and influence each other?

Dimensions of enabling	Enabling pedagogy	Enabling practice
What is empowering for children in your setting?	In what ways is your practice and the setting empowering? Offer two examples each of: (i) how you empower children; How the setting empowers children; and (iii) how children empower others	How do you know the environment is empowering?

| How are the resources and routines in the setting empowering? | What policy or theory informs your practice? | How do you measure the impact of an enabling environment? |
| How are parent partnerships enabled and enabling? | How do you know or find out if those in the environment are enabled? | Identify the specific skills, communication or pedagogical styles used to enable |

Inside or outside: Open the door

Indoor and outdoor environments are enabling when children are stimulated to develop 'self' holistically and their individual well-being, health and learning needs are met. Freedom, spaces, resources and well-thought-out opportunities need to be provided in order to ensure this (Maynard and Waters 2007). Skilled and knowledgeable professionals are able to justify choice of resources, how and why environments are being used to enable and empower, how and why staff are deployed, and how progress and next steps are being questioned with children via dialogic interaction and reflection (Canning 2014; Murray 2017; Ofsted 2017; White 2016).

Both indoor and outdoor spaces can be the context for the development of an enabling environment. However, it is important to remember that it is a statutory requirement across early years provision in England to provide children with access to outdoor spaces and activities (DfE 2017). This is in line with Burdette and Whitaker (2005) and Waite (2007), who recognise that outdoor provision enhances life skills, health and well-being, which boost well-being, emotional literacy, and personal, social and emotional development. The shift in thinking about how, when and where children learn was promoted by the New Labour government's manifesto 'Learning Outside the Classroom' (DfES 2006c). The key message in this document promoted an ethos of learning and play that continues today. However, it is useful to reflect on the concept and expectation of what a classroom is and where learning happens. High-quality opportunities for learning can happen within any environment.

Outdoor provision seems to be crucial to the development and enhancement of life skills, learning and well-being. However, not all settings are able to offer on-site access to outdoor provision due to a lack of access to suitable spaces. In these circumstances, staff will need to be creative in identifying the type of access to outdoor provision that can be made available. The phrase 'yes, we take the inside outside' is often intended to mean that this is enough to guarantee access to high-quality learning experiences. However, the physical act of moving resources between environments is not enough to ensure that carefully planned or well-placed resources that work effectively indoors will offer the same affordance when transferred outside (Waller 2007; Brymer et al. 2014).

There are many factors and pedagogical shifts to consider (as identified in Model 2) to plan, prepare and develop enabling environments. The phrase 'taking the inside outside' can be interpreted differently. For example, it might indicate the provision of structured activities within an outdoor environment that aim to prepare children for school readiness. But children's experiences are enriched as they transition between a range of environments and spaces offering exciting opportunities, which can be enhanced by knowledgeable early childhood professionals who challenge phrases such as 'taking the inside outside' (Waller 2007; Solly 2015; Ritson 2016). Rinaldi (2012) advocates that children benefit from early childhood professionals who have a sound pedagogical underpinning, know how children learn and know how the environment can be a resource for learning. Clark and Moss (2011), Penn (2012) and Conkbayir and Pascal (2014) all recognise that it is vital for those working with children to be able to develop the communication and observational skills needed to effectively immerse themselves into the spaces and realities that belong to children.

An example of the use of outdoor space that can be transformed into an enabling environment is provided by the Forest School movement. Forest School is a special approach with its own ethos. It focuses on outdoor and woodland education, celebrating freedom and spiritual connectedness (Forest School Association 2018). Similar to the theory underpinning enabling environments, Forest School is a philosophy that promotes individual interaction and engagement with nature. Children are perceived as leaders of their own learning, requiring specific skills and support to enhance outdoor living and exploration. These skills are supported by trained pedagogues who teach children to use equipment and resources safely, appropriately and creatively, and enjoy the outdoor environment to promote well-being. The Forest School approach follows the child's lead via observation and dialogic discussion to offer support for skills and opportunities if and when they are needed (Brymer et al. 2014; Solly 2015).

Emotional intelligence and emotional literacy underpin the Forest School philosophy and pedagogy. Interactions with nature and risks in the environment help to build self-esteem and confidence, and hands-on experiences within a natural environment enable children to develop skills at their own pace and preferred way (Dunn 1988; Knight 2012; Solly 2015). Due to its philosophy and methodology, Forest School demands an enabling environment to flourish, generate and enrich in a positive circular relationship; its philosophy and practice arguably best represent the essence of an enabling environment. However, it is important to recognise that being outside with children in a natural open space does not on its own represent a Forest School approach. A physical transition between inside and outside needs to be enhanced by knowledgeable early childhood professionals who are in tune with their own pedagogical identity and professional development needs (Moyles 2015; Solly 2015). (See Chapter 9 for further discussion around reflective practice to lead change.)

Children's experiences of Forest School enable exploration and learning and develop lifelong skills that follow individual disposition, curiosity, intelligence and drive. The Forest School philosophy that underpins practice celebrates and promotes enthusiasm for nature, emotional literacy, risk-taking and problem-solving skills, which in turn enhance self-esteem and confidence (O'Brien and Murray 2007; Constable 2014; Murray 2017). In fact, during outside exploration and 'being', children can be at one with the environment and in the environment. Steiner's theory and educational approach (1995, 1996) recognise that being outside, in nature, with a never-ending resource of open-ended opportunities supports children's spiritual and creative dimensions. Children are influenced positively whilst interacting with the natural environment and an adult who is able and trained to observe, interact at the right time, and offer a balanced approach with repetitive guidance and interaction when needed, which enables rather than disempowers (Siraj-Blatchford et al. 2002; Mathers et al. 2014; Wood 2014b). (Further reading on this subject is suggested at the end of the chapter.)

Outside being and learning

During outside exploration, multi-intelligences and literacies are stimulated to promote deep-level learning and understanding with all the core five senses on alert. Howard Gardner's theory of Multi-Intelligences (1993) captures this quandary, stating that traditional forms of testing for intelligence within an educational context are limiting. Only chosen criteria are being assessed and many more are not. A child's potential should not and cannot be defined by meeting a criterion that labels ability, especially if the criterion is not good or flexible enough to capture styles, interests, approaches and life skills already developed. Against any one-dimensional simplification of the reality of the child, Forest School, and enabling environments in general, aim to promote and celebrate the unique skills and knowledge of each child, creating opportunities to express them. Whilst an outdoor space offers opportunities for children's exploration, risk-taking, cooperation and reflection, its potentiality as an enabling environment changes with the children, adults and resources within it, as well as with the relationships between these actors. Outside environments are enabling when they aim to offer children interaction with nature and help them to learn how to assess risks so that, as much as possible, they can think and be responsible for outcomes.

Tovey (2007; Tovey and Waller 2014) argues that adults may prevent risks due to their own experiences, expectations or fear of their responsibility. Such fears limit the opportunities for the child to develop the skills and knowledge that are necessary to thrive in situations of uncertainty and demand decision-making. Early childhood professionals are required to encourage children to make calculated risks rather than being authoritative or overprotective – this is key to enabling environments. Appropriate and differentiated guidance should be offered to empower and enable children rather than promote risk aversion (Knight 2013; Solly 2015).

Positive practice impact

Nursery setting

The following extract portrays an early childhood professional's reflection on a childhood memory of risk-taking. It should encourage reflection and self-assessment to review how enabling you and your colleagues are, as well as on how to make an environment more enabling.

'When I was about five, I remember weighing up the risk of walking on a big blue plastic tub that held all the wooden bricks. I was standing on the coat peg bench and put one foot upon it, all was well. I remember knowing that one foot was solid and OK but the other foot might not be. However, I hadn't worked out what could possibly go wrong or what the outcome would be. Although somewhere in my mind I was telling myself this might not be safe. My second foot went on and I held my breath and, once my full weight was on the edge of the plastic tub, it toppled over. I remember trying so hard to keep my balance, but I couldn't control my balance or the tub – I fell and hit my head, it bled and I cried. Thinking about it now, I realise I am really good at balancing, problematising risks and hazards, and listening to my inner voice. I really do believe I learnt a lot about life from that experience and the risk, even though it wasn't the right risk to take ... or was it?'

Hands-on experiences that encourage children to learn and think how to deal with risks and when to take them (or not) need to be included within any pedagogical approach (Knight 2012; Tovey and Waller 2014). Sharing solutions and problem-solving require space for thinking and trial and error. Children need to know they will be safe if they get it wrong. Outdoor spaces offer more opportunities for children to explore, investigate and manage risks to prepare for daily life and challenges (Maynard and Waters 2007; Tovey 2007). Risky play within natural environments aims to engage, provoke, stimulate and embrace children in the here and now. Sensory exploration and open-ended landscapes offer endless opportunities and realities. Some of the most exciting games are outside and enable space and time for acquisition of empathy, understanding and knowledge at levels not accessible in environments that may be limited by regulations and gatekeepers (Bilton et al. 2016).

Reflective task 4.4

Risk-taking

- Reflect on how you think early childhood professionals can enable children's risk-taking within an enabling environment.
- What type of risk-taking might cause concern for early childhood professionals?

Within an enabling environment, the space for children to continue developing their voice and make informed choices should be nurtured so that children can act, explore and make choices and errors safely, within a genuine pedagogical framework of 'learning by doing', whereby the adults and children are facilitators of experiences. It is important that children have space and opportunity for interaction and engagement with their thinking and reflections during dialogic discussion.

However, the centrality of children's empowerment and the willingness of the adults to trust children do not remove the need for a sound and safe management structure, which is, of course, necessary to make sure that any pedagogical strategy is fully understood, compliant with statutory regulations and implemented by all staff. Similar to all effective educational environments, the enabling environment needs clear policies, roles and channels of communication.

At the same time, the need for effective working structures and distribution of roles and related accountability is accompanied by the value recognised in the voice of practitioners as well as stakeholders. Participatory forms of management, where leadership is exercised by different staff in different situations, is a defining characteristic of the structure of an enabling environment. The possibility to exercise leadership within the framework of the pedagogical mission of the enabling environment is directed towards fostering professional creativity (Craft 2011; Nutbrown 2012, 2013; Moss 2016).

Role of the adult

The pedagogical approach to defining enabling environments deserves further discussion, as it is influenced by multi-dimensional factors such as learning theories, policies and emotional intelligence through which early childhood professionals' interactions with children are attuned to their individual needs, ways of learning and ways of being (as discussed in Chapter 3). Pedagogical choices and enabling environments are entwined, offering the potential to generate a perfect combination that leaves children empowered, heard, listened to and engaged. An enabling environment is not about tick lists or reference to concepts such as 'child- or adult-led' or 'child- or adult-initiated' without sufficient critical engagement with these terms. Enabling environments are real-life meaningful spaces and experiences with respectful communication and interaction that 'see', 'hear' and 'engage' with the person, rather than conforming to a generalised role of 'learner' or 'teacher'.

Meaningful exchange also supports children to be *resilient*. Resilience is needed to enable and to be enabled. The concept of resilience means to have the ability to overcome challenge and risk, to recoil and keep safe (Watkins et al. 2007; Roberts 2010) (the concept of resilience is discussed further in Chapter 9). To enable or be enabled is a complex process and can be supported by role-modelling strategies and discussing feelings. Sustained shared thinking, listening and dialogic discussion are tools that enable and support the flourishing of resilience. Seligman et al. (1995) recognise that resilience is an interchangeable concept that evolves during life experiences, social relationships and connection with others, and advocates that skills to support and enhance resilience enable children to develop faster, be happier and be sufficiently resourceful to bounce back and respond during times of challenge. These skills are supported within enabling environments during meaningful exchange, interaction and dialogic discussion. Seligman et al. (1995) identify the following seven traits as key to support resilience:

- emotional awareness and regulation;
- impulse control;
- optimism;
- causal analysis;
- empathy;
- self-efficacy; and
- reaching out to others.

Children in an enabling environment are also learners, explorers, decoders, problem-solvers, scientists, creators, challengers, investigators, judges and risk assessors. They are the more knowledgeable ones in some instances. They are helpers and carers who are engaging with and embracing life. Who children are, what they have experienced and who they want to be can only be realised by facilitating meaningful dialogic interaction and sustained shared thinking and listening (Prout 2003, 2008; Siraj-Blatchford and Sylva 2004; Waller 2007). Creating an enabling environment is therefore underpinned by a pivotal choice: the choice is about doing *with* children, rather than *to* them (Freire 1985).

Dahlberg and Moss (2005) recognise that those working with children need to develop respectful listening to children. Alderson (2000) and Penn (2011, 2014) support a refocus and extension of the somewhat general phrase of 'listening to children'. Lundy (2007) argues that listening is one thing – hearing and responding to what a child is saying or expressing is completely different. Listening, hearing and acting upon what children express is an important area to be explored to consider how an environment and adult are both enabling and rights-based.

Reflective task 4.5

Doing things *for* and doing things *to*

- Reflect on how adults might do things *for* or *to* children and how levels of enabling might be influenced.
- Consider similarities and differences between the two phrases 'doing things *to* children' and 'doing things *for* children'.
- Use an example from practice, whether one you have been involved in or one you have studied, to demonstrate the difference between doing something with children rather than doing something to children.
- Consider what it means to listen to children. Does this differ from listening to adults?
- Identify some likely distractions during activities or routines that might prevent adults from listening to children.

Montessori and Malaguzzi are two twentieth-century scholars and practitioners whose theories impacted decisively on educational practices and whose pedagogical research has contributed significantly to knowledge and understanding of enabling environments. Montessori's theory recognised children as holders of specific rights concerning basic needs, health and education (Montessori 1912/2012). Malaguzzi (1995) developed the world-famous 'Reggio Model', which advocates children's basic rights and active participation within their own education (as discussed in Chapters 1 and 3). This model values children's voice, creativity and their unique one hundred languages of expression and unique ways to communicate (Malaguzzi 1995; Pahl 2007; Edwards et al. 2011). Malaguzzi's rights-based approach recognises that the pedagogical ethos and values when working with children require willing and insightful practitioners who can reflectively learn 'from' and 'with' children (Rinaldi 2005). The skills of embracing unique communication and decoding meaning through the one hundred languages of children are key so that children develop autonomy towards active citizenship. Children have one hundred ways to express themselves and learn (as mentioned in Chapter 1). Subsequently, there are never-ending possibilities for language and voice to be expressed that require early childhood professionals who are able to listen.

Such approaches are mirrored in the ethos and practice of enabling environments, where the child is recognised as an autonomous producer of knowledge and supported in the expression of that knowledge (Rinaldi 1998, 2005). Enabling environments are spaces where children are recognised as bearers of rights that must be recognised, including the right to make decisions and choices (Montessori 1912/2012). Finally, the enabling environment is based on the idea that the quality of learning is an outcome of the access and quality of experiences and opportunities for the child to explore and reflect on their actions. This is a core tenet of both

Montessori's approach and Malaguzzi's Reggio Model and is in line with Dewey's influential concept of 'learning by doing' (Dewey 1966) (see Chapter 8).

Enabling environments need to be inclusive so that all stakeholders are empowered, informed and included in decision-making, problem-solving and planning. This is reflected in Ofsted and the Department for Education's 2017 guidelines that focus on how setting leadership and pedagogy empower enabling environments to meet the needs of individuals and groups of children. Opportunities to access high-quality environments that acknowledge chiildren for who they are and what they can do are an entitlement and a right, rather than a gift bestowed upon them. All children have the right to access and co-construct provision and environments that effectively plan, observe and assess who they are and what they can do today.

Looking at the practice of enabling environments, the compatibility with the EYFS framework's principles is clear: enabling environments facilitate children to play, explore and learn by doing and sharing their knowledge, offering a positive atmosphere to develop resilience, capabilities, confidence and self-assuredness towards a setting for creative learning (Bruce 2012). The emphasis here is on the process rather than a pre-defined outcome. Learning is understood as a never-ending journey with no destination, where the quality of the journey depends on the quantity of opportunities and support offered to children as they learn and construct their social and personal worlds (Dewey 1966; Schön 1987; Bruce 2012).

Offering opportunities that enlarge the space for choices and experiences implies that an enabling environment is underpinned by inclusiveness and an approach that values the knowledge, interests and needs of all the children in the setting (Tovey 2007; Bruce 2012). Spaces within environments enable diverse levels of practice from all stakeholders who work with and for children.

Besides the physical space and the underpinning philosophy of its management, another aspect of an enabling environment is the organisational dimension. Enabling environments are generated within educational settings where resources and staff are deployed by knowledgeable experts who are accountable for their decisions. Staff are key to the success of any enabling environment and must share, own and be involved in developing the setting's pedagogical vision, strategy and rationale (Pascal and Bertram 2014). This is an organisational imperative; it is the reasoning behind why resources are chosen or made available to children and where staff are deployed, which must be understood by all staff.

The voice of the child within an enabling environment

An enabling environment is a space where the voice of the child is listened to and facilitated in its expression. A definition of the meaning of the 'voice of the child' can start from a reflection on the concept of 'giving a child a voice'. First, it is pertinent to ask the questions: 'who is giving a child a voice?' and 'does a child not already have a voice?' For instance, Alderson (2008) argues that children's voice is not something that should be given; rather, it is something children already have. Adult-defined discourse can hold power to the extent that 'voice' from children is often viewed as being *given by* the adult. This has implications in practice because the role of the adult becomes pivotal. If there is a generalised expectation for the adult to positively promote the voice of the child in order for that voice to flourish, it is important that staff understand how to facilitate opportunities for the expression of children's voice and to generate a culture where all adults share the idea that children have a voice that should be supported.

Lundy (2007) and Jones and Welch (2013) argue that structures or interactions within educational environments and practice can silence both voice and participation due to dominant rules or behavioural sanctions emanating from pedagogy and power hierarchies. However, the voice of the child is at the centre of the United Nations Convention on the Rights of the Child (UNCRC), ratified in the UK in 1991. Therefore, any educational or social policy now includes the principle that the voice of the child must be listened to with regard to decisions that affect the child's life and experiences (Wyness 2012a, 2012b). The recognition and promotion of the voice of the child is a presupposition of children's self-determination and enshrined in Articles 12 to 15 of the UNCRC. Adults need to listen to what is being expressed, shared and communicated by children. It is our individual experiences and education that influence patterns and levels of listening; these can be described as *listening filters* that can promote or prevent *real* listening to occur (Scollan and McNeill 2019).

Reflective task 4.6

Enabling colleagues

In this reflective task, we encourage you to reflect on how enabling you and your colleagues are, as well as on how to make an environment more enabling.

- Define an enabling environment and describe what it might look like.
- Share your definition with colleagues to compare similarities and differences.
- Identify the role children have in creating an enabling environment.
- How might your setting/team collectively promote an enabling environment?
- Apply Model 1 to assess how the contribution from each stakeholder might be assessed or evaluated in (i) practice, (ii) planning and (iii) record-keeping. Write a summary to communicate your reflections that captures the levels of stakeholder contributions.
- How does an early childhood professional's professional skills and values contribute towards the promotion of an enabling environment? (Refer to Chapters 6 and 9 for more on this.)
- Define your own rights-based lens that enables children to actively participate in their own learning.

The influence of adults affects children's 'real' and meaningful active participation. The extent to which a child can actively use their voice or participate within an enabling environment is influenced by adults who can effectively self-assess to critique their own impact and practice (Freeman 1998, 2007; Alderson 2000; Handley 2005). (This is discussed further in Chapter 9.) If a child is to take possession of their rights, possible tensions may arise when a rights-based lens is not understood or applied (Trevarthen 2011; Alderson 2012).

Enabling environments can be enriched when adults access space and time to listen to and interact with children so that children can speak and be heard within a rights-based lens. Jones and Welch (2013) propose an insightful reflection for early childhood professionals who wish to promote children's voice within environments that enable children to actively participate in their own learning and encourage early childhood professionals to consider what it means to be a commentator on children's lives. The concept of *commentator* (Jones and Walker 2011; Jones and Welch 2013) invites adults to reflect upon their own expectations of how children are perceived as active agents with opinions and valid contributions to make. The role of a positive enabling environment is pivotal in supporting the child to realise their potentialities.

Summary and moving on

In this chapter, we have considered how children are viewed as competent and skilful participants in the learning process. One of the key aspects of enabling environments is that adults encourage children to actively participate whilst recognising children are active agents and partners in learning. Enabling environments enhance children's agency to shape their own lives and to influence their social context.

Further reading

Brodie, K. (2018) *The Holistic Care and Development of Children from Birth to Three: An essential guide for students and practitioners.* Abingdon: Routledge.

Hodgman, L. (2015) *Enabling Environments in the Early Years: Making provision for high quality and challenging learning experiences in early years settings.* Salisbury: Practical Pre-School Books.

O'Brien, L. and Murray, R. (2006) *A Marvellous Opportunity for Children to Learn: A participatory evaluation of Forest School in England and Wales.* Norwich: HMSO. Available at: https://www.forestschooltraining.co.uk/_webedit/uploaded-files/All%20Files/Research%20papers/Marvellous%20opportunity.pdf (accessed 14 October 2018).

Solly, K. (2015) Environment, in *Risk, Challenge and Adventure in the Early Years.* Abingdon: Routledge.

5 Conceptualising high-quality early years provision

This chapter is concerned with quality in early years provision, which has become a key issue for early years research, policy and practice (Duhn et al. 2016). This focus on quality has been prompted by mounting evidence that highlights the significance of early years education for children's development and future outcomes (Mooney 2007). However, the notion of quality is a complex and contested concept that is subject to different interpretations. This chapter explores some perspectives on the concept of quality and considers various processes that might be used to evaluate the quality of early years provision.

Introduction

From the end of the twentieth century, increased investment in early childhood education and care (ECEC) has aimed to tackle the adverse effects of socio-economic disadvantage and sought to address perceived gaps in children's attainment when they enter school (Hillman and Williams 2015). This is premised on the view that there are positive benefits of quality ECEC for children's cognitive, socio-emotional and behavioural development and that children from socio-economically disadvantaged circumstances can benefit in particular from quality early years provision (Sylva 2010). The quality and stability of ECEC provision for children under three years of age is considered to be particularly important for their development (Otero and Melhuish 2015).

As discussed in Chapter 1, the Early Years Foundation Stage (EYFS) framework (DfE 2017) outlines the aims, requirements and expected outcomes of ECEC that are applicable across all provision for children from birth to five years of age. However, despite much research on the subject, there is no general agreement on a definition of quality, how it is constituted or how it might be experienced from different perspectives (Sheridan 2007). The concept of quality is open to different understandings that can be based on personal experience, the judgements of experts or measurable outcomes (Sylva and Taylor 2006). The chapter explores notions of quality and considers how particular aims, values and intended outcomes for ECEC might be perceived by different participants in the early years sector, as these will influence their perspectives on quality provision and how it might be evaluated. Processes that might be used to evaluate the quality of early years provision are also considered.

Perspectives on quality

The word 'quality' is commonly used in early years policy and practice documentation and features in several titles of early years literature (see, for instance, DES 1990; National Audit Office 2004; Mathers et al. 2012; Nutbrown 2012). A greater focus on quality in ECEC is premised on research findings from the areas of neuroscience, psychology and economics, which note the significance of children's earliest experiences for their developmental outcomes (Pascal and Bertram 2013).

Research suggests that significant brain development takes place in the first few years of a child's life and that there are important beneficial educational, socio-behavioural and economic effects to be gained from quality early years provision, particularly for children who live in socio-economically disadvantaged circumstances (Otero and Melhuish 2015; Wall et al. 2015). When children start school, a gap in attainment is already apparent; children from socio-economically disadvantaged backgrounds lag behind their more advantaged peers by approximately 11 months (Stewart and Waldfogel 2017). As discussed in Chapter 1, children are assessed against the early learning goals, which indicate the expected level of development at the end of the academic year in which they become five years old (DfE 2017). The gap in the level of development attained by five-year-old children eligible for free school meals and their more advantaged peers has narrowed since 2007 when there was a 21.2 percentage point difference in attainment; however, EYFS Profile assessment of early learning goals in 2015 demonstrated there was still a significant variation of 17.7 percentage points in attainment (Stewart and Waldfogel 2017: 25).

Longer duration of children's experience of quality provision (in terms of months, rather than hours per day) is thought to have a positive influence on children's outcomes (Sammons 2010). Access to affordable and high-quality ECEC is also considered to support working parents, particularly mothers, to participate more in the workforce (OECD 2017). However, while there is a general recognition that quality ECEC has a positive impact on children's learning and development (Penn 2011; Melhuish et al. 2017), experience of low-quality provision is seen to have an adverse impact (Siraj-Blatchford and Wong 1999; National Audit Office 2004). Due to the perceived positive effects of quality provision on young children's short- and longer-term outcomes, investment in extending ECEC has been encouraged at a global level by such institutions as the United Nations Educational, Scientific and Cultural Organisation (UNESCO) and the World Bank (Wall et al. 2015).

Apart from funded provision for all three- and four-year-olds, policy initiatives in England, such as the Early Years Pupil Premium (EYPP) and funded provision for two-year-olds living in disadvantaged circumstances, which were discussed in Chapter 2, have sought to support further opportunities for young children to benefit from quality ECEC.

Conceptualising quality

The potential beneficial impact of quality on children's development and future outcomes prompts further exploration of how quality ECEC might be conceptualised. The word is commonly used to imply that children are offered good or effective care and education. Therefore, negative perceptions of the quality of provision by Ofsted (Office for Standards in Education, Children's Services and Skills) inspectors or other visitors to a setting could have an adverse impact on that setting's reputation, which, in turn, might have implications for its capacity to sustain ECEC provision (The Red House Children's Centre 2016).

However, Dahlberg et al. (2006) suggest that the concept of quality needs to be questioned, as it is subjective and values-based. The widespread use of the word 'quality' indicates that it is something that is self-evident, tangible and known (Dahlberg et al. 2006), whereas it can be argued that quality can be perceived to be a layered concept that reflects a variety of assumptions and values about the nature of childhood and ECEC provision (Penn 2011). Citing the work of Dahlberg et al. (2006) on the concept of quality, Evans (2016) notes more emphasis is placed on the process of identifying quality than on explaining what is meant by the word.

Exploration of the concept of quality needs to incorporate a review of how perceptions of quality have been informed and shaped by particular aims and outcomes of ECEC provision (Campbell-Barr and Leeson 2016). Different interpretations of the concept might be made by staff, children, parents and other stakeholders in early years settings according to the issues that are of greatest concern to them (Alexander 2010). At a national level, Penn (2011) advises that if government aims for ECEC are focused on improving young children's educational achievement at school and future outcomes, then debate about aspects of the quality of early years provision will be focused on learning. However, other pertinent factors need to be considered; for example, a parent seeking suitable provision for their child might consider a nursery's capacity to promote healthy eating practices or to engage children in sustainability activities that aim to support their understanding of the likely impact of their decision-making on the environment (Edwards et al. 2016).

Children's views on quality of provision offer a further perspective. Sheridan (2007) highlights the importance of providing opportunities for children to express their views about their provision and participate in its development, as they have a right to do so accorded to them by the United Nations Convention on the Rights of the Child (UNCRC). Opportunities to enable children's active participation in quality evaluation of their provision recognise the importance of incorporating democratic and inclusive processes within evaluative methods and acknowledge the legitimacy of children's views (Hayes and Filipović 2017). Moreover, according to Podmore (2009), children's perspectives can actively contribute to the process of early childhood professionals' own self-evaluation and development of provision. Following the findings from research into children's perspectives on play in their setting, Ólafsdóttir and Einarsdóttir (2017) noted that staff at one setting developed the environment and introduced additional resources that aimed to enhance play opportunities for the children.

It is useful to turn to quality criteria proposed by Katz (1993: 6) when considering the perspectives of different stakeholder positions. These perspectives can contribute to determining the quality of early years provision. However, Katz warns they may not always be complementary and suggests that children's subjective experience of their provision can be ascertained through processes of observation and interaction, which provides a 'bottom-up' perspective of quality. They also help to identify particular features of the setting, such as staffing and resources, through the lens of a 'top-down' perspective.

The criteria offered by Katz are summarised in Table 5.1. They enable exploration of quality from the perspective of how provision is experienced by children, their families and staff based at the setting, as well as visitors to the provision.

Applying Katz's criteria to consider concepts of quality from different stakeholder perspectives helps to illustrate how early years provision can be influenced by broad aims and values about children's learning and development. You may find it useful to consider your perspective on quality in the following task and reflect on how your perspectives might be shaped by various influential factors. Some examples of such influential factors are given in Table 5.2 to support your reflection, though you may wish to add others that may be relevant to you.

Table 5.1 Quality criteria proposed by Katz (1993)

Stakeholder	Stakeholder position	Examples of stakeholder perspectives on quality
Observer, visiting adult	'Top-down'	• Ratios of adults to children • Staff qualifications and turnover • Physical space and resources • Features of adult–child interactions
Children	'Bottom-up'	• Engaging in meaningful and interesting activities • Feeling welcome and accepted • Being treated respectfully by others
Parents/carers, staff members	'Outside/inside'	• Respectful and supportive relationships
Staff	Inside	• Trusting, collaborative and accepting relationships

Source: Katz (1993: 6–8).

Reflective task 5.1

On quality

Reflect on your understanding of quality in early years practice. You may wish to consider your view on quality in relation to a particular early years setting.

- What factors have influenced your perspective of quality?
- How might these influences be demonstrated in everyday activities and experiences within your setting or placement?

Table 5.2 Examples of factors that might influence perspectives of quality provision

• Personal knowledge and experience	• Research reports
• EYFS framework and other statutory requirements	• Meetings and conferences
	• Visits to other settings
• Ofsted	• Visitors to your setting or placement
• Feedback from children, parents and colleagues	
• Personal study and professional development	• Media and social media networks

Two key approaches to conceptualising quality are discussed by Wall et al. (2015): *objective* and *relative* quality. From an objective perspective, quality involves particular characteristics of practice, such as pedagogical approaches that are felt to be commonly understood, which enable links to be made between provision and children's outcomes (Mathers et al. 2012). This objective approach is concerned with measuring the quality of features of provision and considering their overall effectiveness against identified learning goals (Wall et al. 2015). This process has been criticised for tending to be based on limited rather than multiple perspectives of quality practice, which may not be applicable across different socio-cultural contexts of provision (Mathers et al. 2012). In a study of research into quality, Fenech (2011) suggests that when objective processes are used by researchers to capture aspects of quality, their voices can be privileged as experts in determining realities about quality. At the same time, these processes can serve to diminish the perspectives of children, parents and early childhood professionals whose own contributions could provide important understandings about quality. Moreover, if key participants in early years provision do not feel included in evaluative processes that determine the quality of ECEC provision, then it is possible they will have little confidence in the way judgements about quality are made. This does not mean that objective processes have no place in conceptualising quality; rather, if they are applied appropriately, they can enrich understanding about quality provision and support further development of practice. However, it is important that early childhood professionals aim to support all relevant participants involved in provision at their setting to contribute their perspectives on quality so they have opportunities for genuine involvement in the processes of determining and developing quality provision.

Whilst acknowledging the need for accountability to children, their families and taxpayers who support funded ECEC places, Penn (2011) advises that notions of quality ECEC should be based on the unique context of the provision. A relativist approach to conceptualising quality suggests that definitions of quality should be locally determined so they are adapted to the specific context of the provision and acknowledge the perspectives of stakeholders who are concerned with practice at the setting (Mathers et al. 2012). This approach does not assume that stakeholders will all express the same aims and values for children's learning and development; rather, different perspectives will contribute to constructing a shared contextualised understanding (Siraj-Blatchford and Wong 1999). From a relativist perspective, quality is conceptualised as a dynamic concept that can only be recognised in a relative context, such as a particular socio-cultural context (Wall et al. 2015). However, this approach has also been questioned. Critics argue that if quality provision is determined locally, then national standards of quality cannot be established and links to outcomes cannot be formed (Mathers et al. 2012).

Campbell-Barr and Leeson (2016) discuss Modernist (objective) and Post-structuralist (relativist) approaches to the concept of quality. Modernist approaches are prone to using measurable indicators of quality and to identifying particular features of ECEC practice that support planned goals to be attained (Campbell-Barr and Leeson 2016). This approach has been questioned, as understandings of quality may be confined to features of practice that have been measured (Fenech 2011). Whilst acknowledging that Modernist approaches support our understanding of quality, Campbell-Barr and Leeson (2016) note that it is important to consider who is involved in determining constituent features and measures of quality and to recognise that some details about ECEC provision may be missed by such evaluative processes. Alternatively, Post-structuralist approaches are concerned with questioning dominant perspectives about the concept of quality and how it has been constructed (Campbell-Barr and Leeson 2016). From a Post-structuralist perspective, Moss (2016) suggests that evaluation of early education should be premised on critical co-construction of judgements about good practice that acknowledge the complexity and differences that exist within contexts of practice. By undertaking this process, a space is created in which new and diverse pedagogical understandings can be formed that relate to specific contexts of practice (Evans 2016).

Three indicators of quality provision have been suggested by Munton et al. (1995): *process, structure* and *child outcomes*. However, Gambaro et al. (2015) advise that using this last indicator as a measure of quality can be problematic due to the absence of a control group or baseline. Process quality indicators are a key aspect of pedagogy and relate to children's experience of early education, such as social interaction between the child and practitioner, children's inclusion in activities, and practitioners' sensitivity and attitudes towards children and their families (Umek 2014). Structural quality indicators related to environmental features are outlined in the EYFS framework's safeguarding and welfare requirements (DfE 2017: section 3). These indicators are considered to be generally measurable features of practice.

According to Gambaro et al. (2015), aspects of structural quality in the EYFS framework, such as ratios, physical space and staff qualifications, can vary between early years settings; however, Ofsted's inspection processes and the statutory requirements of the EYFS framework offer some consistency for early years provision.

Process indicators can be affected by structural dimensions of quality; for example, the process of adults' interactions with children can be influenced by staff-to-child ratios (Wall et al. 2015). When considering the impact of the physical and social context of early years practice on children's experience of early education, the Rumbold Report (DES 1990: 10) stated that: 'children are affected by the context in which learning takes place, the people involved in it, and the values and beliefs that are embedded in it'.

Case studies 5.1

Quality indicators

Look at the following case studies and, from your perspective as an aspiring or practising early years professional, consider how the activities detailed might act as quality indicators (structural and/or process). You may also wish to consider these examples from the perspectives of parents or visiting adults, or how they might be experienced by children.

Jo, manager of a pre-school

'We have a system of organising a settling-in consultation morning with parents of new children at about six weeks after they start at the nursery. This provides the opportunity for the key person (KP) and parents to discuss their child's progress. During these meetings, parents can also share their knowledge about their child. I think it is very important for children to have a trusting, secure relationship for their social and emotional development and for the KP to feel confident about children's needs and their routines, so that they can plan for their learning and development.'

Safah, room leader for two-year-olds (suburban nursery setting)

'I use gestures to support and extend children's understanding. When they are listened to and acknowledged by the people around them, they feel special and secure. They gain confidence, which allows them to explore the world and express themselves with their peers and with adults.'

Cara, a teacher in a maintained nursery (urban school setting)

'I recognise the benefits of outdoor play for children and have set up outdoor play resources in the garden area. The resources are well-maintained and we carry out a robust system of risk assessment *every day before children come out to play. I plan a team rota to ensure staff-to-child ratios in the outdoor area are appropriate and encourage members of staff to do observations outdoors, as continuous assessment will help us to provide challenging activities. I think it's important to have an explicit routine that everyone recognises and respects.'*

Martha, an early years teacher in an independent school

'*I planned a trip to the local park and asked parents for written permission for their children to go on the trip. During circle time, I talked with the children about the purpose of the visit and asked them what they expect to see on our visit. I reminded them about health and safety aspects of the trip. I did a risk assessment and marked any road crossings or hazards on the planned route and checked staff-to-child ratios. We took medical and dietary information and a first aid bag, as well as some snacks and drinks. Before we set off, the children were again briefed about safety on the visit.'*

Freya, family support worker in a suburban children's centre

'*Safeguarding and promoting the health and welfare of children are paramount. Record-keeping of accidents is vital for children's safety. I think it's important to keep up to date on health and safety policies and follow the centre's processes.'*

Think!

- Using the following table, reflect on some examples of practice that you consider would constitute quality provision in an early years setting where you work or are in placement. Consider your reasons for conceptualising these examples as aspects of quality and note any structural and/or process indicators that might be identified in the examples.

Examples of quality provision from own perspective		
Example of practice	*Reason for conceptualising example as an aspect of quality*	*Structural and/or process indicators that might be identified*

Evaluating quality

Quality measures that are used to evaluate quality of ECEC provision can incorporate structural and process elements of ECEC (Sylva 2010). The Rumbold Report (DES 1990) identified the difficulty in seeking to apply a universal set of regulations for evaluating early years practice due to the diversity of provision in the sector. ECEC provision is offered within a diverse range of contexts in the state and private, voluntary and independent (PVI) sectors that have varied goals, structures and philosophies (Hillman and Williams 2015). It is considered unlikely by Gambaro et al. (2015) that all features and complexities of ECEC provision can be captured by a single evaluative measure. However, all registered early years settings are required to follow the EYFS framework (DfE 2017), which outlines the aims, requirements and expected outcomes of ECEC provision and are subject to external inspection of their provision by Ofsted, an independent government department.

Ofsted (2019: 28) details the main principles for inspection and explains the 4-point scale that Ofsted inspectors use when evaluating standards of a setting's provision. Grades on this scale are:

- 'outstanding' (grade 1);
- 'good' (grade 2);
- 'requires improvement' (grade 3); and
- 'inadequate' (grade 4).

At the time of writing, the revised *Education Inspection Framework (EIF)* (Ofsted 2019) is due to be implemented in practice. Judgements for the revised EIF are:

- overall effectiveness;
- the quality of education
- behaviour and attitudes
- personal development,
- leadership and management

Grade descriptors for each of the main criteria that are used to make judgements on early years provision are included in the *Early Years Inspection Handbook* (Ofsted 2019). Ofsted (2019: 32) have introduced the term 'cultural capital' as part of their judgement on 'the quality of education', which they define as 'the essential knowledge that children need to be educated citizens'. 'Cultural capital' is a complex and contested concept and it will be interesting to see how it is interpreted within the inspection process.

Ofsted considers if leaders' and managers' self-evaluation of the strengths and weaknesses of their setting's provision is realistic and explore how the setting might uphold or improve its standards. Ofsted's analysis of the accuracy of the provider's perspectives on quality includes reference to parents' views on their children's provision and to children's progression at the setting. Following their inspection, Ofsted provides a report about the setting, which is structured accoring to the criteria before for determining standards of provision. Ofsted reports, including their graded judgements, are placed on the Ofsted website in the public domain. Gambaro et al. (2015) note that as Ofsted judgements rest not only on quality criteria relating to provision at the setting but also include evaluation of children's outcomes, the overall evaluation of the setting should be viewed with some caution, as settings whose intake includes more socio-economically advantaged children could be favoured by Ofsted's grading processes.

Reflective task 5.2

Ofsted judgements

Look at some Ofsted reports on early years settings that are published on their website and consider the judgements made about the setting's overall provision.

Explore references to dimensions of quality in the reports and reflect on how judgements made about these aspects of quality provide insight into the quality of provision at the setting. You may find it helpful to refer to the grade descriptors for the main criteria in the *Early Years Inspection Handbook* (Ofsted 2018) that are used to support inspectors to make their judgements. Some examples of dimensions of quality, adapted from Ofsted (2018), are given here for guidance:

- teaching, learning and assessment;
- progression in children's learning and development in relation to their starting points;
- children's personal and emotional development;
- children's readiness for the next stage of their education;
- effectiveness of leadership and management;
- engagement with parents; and
- effectiveness of arrangements for safeguarding children.

Environment rating scales

Further methods used to evaluate quality include observational environment rating scales, which are standardised assessment tools that aim to measure process elements of provision. Sylva (2010) explains that the word 'environment', when used in the context of environment rating scales, can include strategies implemented by practitioners, their relationships with children and social interactions, as well as how space and resources are used in the setting. The following are some examples of rating scales.

Infant/Toddler Environment Rating Scale – Revised edition (ITERS-R) (Harms et al. 2003) and **Early Childhood Environment Rating Scale – Revised edition (ECERS-R)** (Harms et al. 2003, 2005).

ITERS-R and ECERS-R were developed in the USA. ITERS-R is designed to evaluate quality in settings for children from birth to 30 months; ECERS-R aims to measure quality in settings for two- to five-year-olds. Both rating scales consist of seven sub-scales; ITERS-R has 39 items whilst ECERS-R contains 43 items.

The first six sub-scales for both ITERS-R and ECERS-R are concerned with quality of care; the seventh sub-scale relates to ways in which the setting works with parents and considers provision for their staff. The subscales are:

1. Space and furnishings
2. Personal care routines
3. Listening and talking (ITERS-R); Language and reasoning (ECERS-R)
4. Activities
5. Interaction
6. Programme structure
7. Parents and staff

Items are rated on a seven-point scale, ranging from 1 (inadequate) to 7 (excellent).

Early Childhood Environment Rating Scale Extension (ECERS-E) (Sylva et al. 2003; Sylva 2010)

This scale was developed by members of the Effective Provision of Pre-School Education (EPPE) research project team as an extension to ECERS-R to evaluate curricular provision in settings for three- to five-year-olds. The scale consists of 18 items arranged in four sub-scales, which are:

1. Literacy
2. Mathematics
3. Science and the environment
4. Diversity

Sustained Shared Thinking and Emotional Well-being (SSTEW) Scale for 2- to 5-Year-Olds (Siraj-Blatchford et al. 2015)

The SSTEW scale builds on ITERS-R, ECERS-R and ECERS-E, but focuses on the practitioner's role to support learning and development. It has five sub-scales that consist of 14 items. The five sub-scales are arranged in two developmental domains: social and emotional well-being (items 1–4) and cognitive development (items 5–14). The sub-scales are:

1. Building trust, confidence and independence
2. Social and emotional well-being
3. Supporting and extending language and communication
4. Supporting learning and critical thinking
5. Assessing learning and language

Reflective task 5.3

Sub-scales and quality evaluation

Consider which items you would include as sub-scales to evaluate quality

You may wish to research the published items that are included in the sub-scales for each of the environment rating scales above and compare the list of published items with your list of items. You may also find it helpful to investigate one or more of the following ERS:

Caregiver Interaction Scale (CIS) (Arnett 1989)

CIS is designed to measure the emotional tone, discipline style and responsiveness of caregiver–child interactions. It has four sub-scales and 26 items. The sub-scales are: positive relationships; punitiveness; permissiveness; and detachment.

School Age Care Environment Rating Scale (SACERS)
(Harms et al. 1996)

SACERS aims to assess out-of-school provision for 5- to 12-year-olds.

Family Child Care Rating Scale – Revised edition (FCCERS-R)
(Harms et al. 2007)

FCCERS-R aims to evaluate home-based care for children aged birth to 12 years and has seven sub-scales, as with ITERS-R and ECERS-R.

The EPPE longitudinal research project, which began in 1997 in England, investigated the effects of pre-school provision on three-year-old children's academic and social-behavioural outcomes. The EPPE project was later extended to become the Effective Pre-school, Primary and Secondary Education (EPPSE) project, which enabled evidence to be collected on the longer-term impact of pre-school education. The research team particularly focused on process elements of pre-school quality and used the ECERS-R, ECERS-E and CIS ratings scales to support their assessment. Evidence from the EPPE study indicates process quality as a sound predictor of children's later outcomes (Gambaro et al. 2015). Sammons et al. (2008) found that attendance at pre-school had a positive impact on children's cognitive outcomes at the end of Year 6 (at age 11) when compared with children who had no attendance. This impact was enhanced by quality of the provision: high-quality pre-school provision was particularly beneficial at the end of Year 6 for boys, children with special educational needs and those living in disadvantage (Taggart et al. 2015). The impact of quality pre-school provision was found to have a continued effect on attainment in secondary school at the end of Year 9 (at age 14) in the subjects of mathematics and science, though effects were weaker than had been discerned at younger ages (Sylva et al. 2012). The EPPSE study also reported that children who had attended high-quality pre-schools were more likely to achieve five GSCEs at the age of 16 at A*–C grades, including English and mathematics (Taggart et al. 2015).

The Study of Early Education and Development (SEED) is a major longitudinal study that aims to explore ECEC provision in England and how it might support child and family outcomes (Callanan et al. 2017). As part of the wider quality assessment aspect of the SEED research, environment rating scales are being used to collect information on process quality in ECEC settings, including ITERS-R, SSTEW, ECERS-R and ECERS-E (Callanan et al. 2017). Relevant rating scales are being applied in the SEED study according to the age groups that form the focus of the quality assessment; the environment rating scales support the setting of benchmark criteria for designating 'excellent' or 'good' provision for two-year-olds and for three-year-olds (Callanan et al. 2017).

Siraj-Blatchford and Wong (1999) note evaluation of ECEC quality has three main purposes:

- to support regulation of the quality of ECEC and ensure providers meet their statutory requirements;
- to contribute to research and inform development of policy; and
- to aid development of practice.

Reflective task 5.4

Evaluative measures

Consider how evaluative measures might support each of the three purposes listed by Siraj-Blatchford and Wong (1999). Identify an example, drawn from policy or practice at a local or national level, for each of the purposes.

Area of support provided by evaluative measures	Example drawn from policy or practice at a local or national level	Likely impact of example on ECEC at local or national level
Regulation		
Research		
Development of practice		

The impact of staffing on quality provision

The early childhood professional's role is considered more fully in Chapter 6; however, some reference should be made here to the importance of ECEC staff, as quality of staff is seen as a key aspect of quality ECEC. Findings from the EPPE research project suggested that children made more progress at settings whose staff had higher education qualifications (Sammons 2010). Following her review of early years workforce qualifications, Nutbrown (2012) advised that ECEC staff have the most influence on the quality of ECEC and emphasised the importance of effective pedagogical leadership for improving the quality of provision. Nutbrown (2012) recommended that graduate pedagogical leadership should be developed in all early years settings, particularly in provision for babies and in PVI settings. In their report on ECEC for children under three years, Mathers et al. (2014) also note that quality ECEC provision is supported by sound attributes and pedagogical approaches of setting leaders. However, they suggest that, whilst there is sound evidence of higher-quality provision for graduate-led provision for three- and four-year-olds, evidence relating to provision for younger children is less consistent. Mathers et al. (2014) consider that ECEC staff working with children under three years of age should have expert knowledge of child development theory, access to professional development, and opportunities to link theory to practice and to reflect and adapt their practice. Nutbrown's (2012) review of early education and childcare qualifications also reported that ECEC staff should have access to professional development and opportunities to discuss their practice and learn from each other. In their discussion of children's opportunities to engage in new forms of digital literacy practices, Wolfe and Flewitt (2010) note the importance of early childhood professionals having opportunities for suitable training and curricular guidance so they can effectively support children's development as proficient users of new media. It is further suggested by Goodfellow (2003) that ECEC staff should participate in critical reflection to ensure the nature of their professional practice is communicated by themselves and their employers to others, as this would support the recognition and value of the various dimensions of quality ECEC work.

Positive practice impact

Jo, manager of a private nursery providing full-day care

The following extract illustrates the benefits of continuing professional development:

'I continue to learn and keep up to date with current issues about theory and practice. I believe it is necessary to look at new ideas, experiences and challenges to become an effective manager. It helps to be aware of my strengths and areas for improvement. Information I have gained from

discussion with others and feedback from parents has helped to identify my learning needs and goals. I take on training courses and keep a learning diary that helps me to reflect on my learning from everyday experiences.'

Reflective task 5.5

Professional development

Consider activities that you undertake to support your own development of professional skills.

Think!

* How do professional development activities help to sustain and develop quality provision in an early years setting?

There is broad agreement that children's outcomes are supported by provision that is warm, stimulating, sensitive and responsive (Penn 2011; Mathers et al. 2014; Gambaro et al. 2015; Otero and Melhuish 2015; Hayes and Filipović 2017). In Chapter 3, we considered the importance of an early childhood professional building positive relationships with children, their families and the staff with whom they work. The language used by staff is an important aspect of their pedagogical interactions; McInnes et al. (2013) note that language that effectively supports children's development incorporates use of questioning strategies and involves shared problem-solving. The quality of staff interaction with children and the notion of sustained shared thinking was considered in Chapter 1; the EPPE research team found that staff in 'excellent' settings used opportunities to extend children's thinking by engaging in sustained shared thinking and by extending child-initiated interactions (Siraj-Blatchford 2010).

Case study 5.2

Reese, teacher in a Reception class in a maintained school

Consider how an early childhood professional might demonstrate quality interactions with children. An example is provided to support you with this task.

'Listening to children and communicating sensitively with them is important. I pay attention to what they say and respect their views. I have been using Makaton signs in my interactions with the children to engage their interest and extend their understanding. I use a variety of ways of giving children positive feedback and encourage turn-taking activities.'

Summary and moving on

This chapter has explored the subject of quality in the context of ECEC policy and practice and considered different interpretations of quality and how it might be evaluated. You have been encouraged to consider your own views on quality and factors that have influenced your views. This is important because, as Evans (2016) suggests, ways in which quality is discussed affect practices within ECEC and therefore the learning experiences of children and adults in the setting. Whilst acknowledging evidence of the importance of quality provision and its likely impact on children's short- and longer-term outcomes, we have also considered the notion that the framing of the concept of quality needs reworking (Penn 2011). This chapter identifies some perspectives on quality that consider it to be a multi-dimensional and dynamic concept that should democratically incorporate the views of all those concerned with ECEC provision in the process of constructing meanings of the term (Dahlberg et al. 1999). We have also explored ways in which quality might be evaluated and considered quality indicators that are used to regulate ECEC provision and inform those involved in practice, including researchers and policy-makers. The chapter concluded by considering the notion of quality in terms of staffing in ECEC, while the role of the early childhood professional is considered further in the next chapter.

Further reading

Callanan, M., Anderson, M., Haywood, S., Hudson, R. and Speight, S. (2017) *Study of Early Education and Development: Good practice in early education*. Research Report. London: Department for Education. Available at: www.foundationyears.org.uk/files/2017/01/SEED-Good-Practice-in-Early-Education.pdf (accessed 14 March 2017).

Gambaro, L. (2017) Who is minding the kids? New developments and lost opportunities in reforming the British early education workforce, *Journal of European Social Policy*, 27 (4): 320–331.

Otero, M. and Melhuish, E. (2015) *Study of Early Education and Development (SEED): Study of the quality of childminder provision in England*. Available at: https://www.gov.uk/government/publications/study-of-early-education-and-development-childminder-provision (accessed 3 December 2016).

Penn, H. (2011) *Quality in Early Childhood Services*. Maidenhead: Open University Press.

6 The professionalisation of the early years workforce

This chapter is set in the context of the global growth of professionalisation in the early years but applied in particular to the early childhood workforce in England. Definitions of 'professionalism' and the concept of 'professionalisation' are discussed and problematised, especially when applied to work with young children. Policies and legislation that have driven the agenda for professionalisation are considered, alongside key research that has informed this agenda. The reader is challenged to think about the professional skills, knowledge and attributes required in today's workforce, and case studies and reflective tasks are offered that aim to deepen understanding of what professionalism means in the changing social and cultural context of the early childhood workforce.

Introduction

With the unprecedented attention to policy and practice in early childhood in many countries over recent decades, the professionalism of early childhood professionals and the professionalising of the workforce have become key issues for both policy-makers and academics (Dalli and Urban 2011). As long ago as 2008, professionalisation strategies were noted across 27 European countries (Oberhuemer and Scheryer 2008), positioning early childhood education and care as the 'essential foundation for successful lifelong learning, social integration, personal development and later employability' (European Commission 2011). [Although the focus here is principally on the context in England, it is noteworthy that this global trend has continued, with research emerging from countries as diverse as Indonesia (Hakim and Dalli 2018), Greece (Gregoriadis et al. 2018), New Zealand (Cherrington 2018) and Croatia (Visković and Jevtić 2018).]

Miller and Cable (2011) have suggested that there is no universal understanding about what 'professionalism' in early childhood education and care (ECEC) means, though Parker-Rees (2018: 242–243) believes we are moving to 'a richer understanding of the relationship between local knowledge [of particular contexts]' and 'more generalised shareable knowledge' relating to early childhood professionalism. It is early childhood professionals themselves who are part of the emerging picture and contributing to its meaning in their work and settings. A key question for critical reflection at the outset of this chapter and pervading throughout is: *What does 'being professional' mean for me in my context?*

Professionalism in early childhood

Despite its widespread use in the media and everyday language, professionalism defies common agreement as to its meaning (Hoyle and John 1995). Perspectives on professionalism in early years provision vary considerably, and Friedson (2001) has argued that there is no single explanatory defining characteristic of professionalism; rather, it is a 'concrete, changing, historical and national phenomenon' (Brock 2015: 66), always influenced by the context in which it is located (Felstead et al. 2009). Arguably, to 'professionalise' is to turn a 'job' into a 'profession', which suggests a particular set of skills and knowledge, possibly linked to pay and progression (Osgood 2009). Professionalisation – the process of becoming a professional – then becomes related to proficiency with status, recognition and reward (Helsby 1996; Brock 2011). Professionalism also suggests commitment, integrity and high standards of behaviour (Osgood 2009).

Case study 6.1

Connor, trainee teacher

Take a moment to think about the differences between professionalism and professionalisation and how these might affect you. Connor's experience may help you to do this.

'I am currently completing a programme of initial teacher training and undertaking teaching practice in a nursery class in a school with three- and four-year-old children. I'm not sure I consider myself to be a "professional" at the moment – I feel I need to prove my competence as a teacher before I can do that. However, it is essential that I behave professionally in every aspect of the teaching practice. Teaching practice is demanding both in terms of time to prepare and being "on top" of all the unexpected things that happen during the day that I couldn't possibly have prepared for! I see myself as a role model for the children, so I need to think about my whole approach to the role. I set myself high standards – I like to be very early, well prepared, have time to discuss with the class teacher (etc.) and really concentrate on

each encounter with the children in the class. Even though I know I am still learning to be a "professional", I can still model professional behaviour.'

Think!

- Do you agree or disagree with Connor that he is not yet a professional? What are your reasons?
- Connor makes a distinction between being a professional and acting professionally. What do you see as the differences and the links between the two?
- Connor describes a component of 'acting professionally' as being a 'role model' to the children. What links do you make between professionalism and being a role model?
- Where do you position yourself in relation to being professionalised and/or acting professionally?

Professionalisation of the early childhood workforce in England: Research and practice

This chapter takes the perspective that 'being a professional' is influenced by the context in which an individual is situated. The EPPE project (Sylva et al. 2004) highlighted the link between the quality of provision in pre-school settings and the quality of the staff who work in them (see Chapters 4 and 5 for more on the EPPE Project). Hence, reforming the workforce was viewed by the government of the time as critical in raising the standard of provision. Arguably, within the children's workforce in England, the journey towards increased professionalisation has continued to be shaped to a large extent by government policy. However, increasingly, such 'governmentality' (Wood 2015) has resulted in government policy asserting what it means to be professional, rather than continuing to draw on the rich bank of research data emerging from both academics and practitioners. This results in early childhood professionals having to comply with externally set knowledge, skills and competencies and a limited opportunity to define professionalism for themselves.

Particularly since 2000, the early childhood workforce in England has undergone a period of unprecedented change (Brock 2011). Even before the EPPE findings were produced, a new role of 'Senior Practitioner' had been introduced, linked to the successful completion of a new type of degree programme in England: the Early Years Sector-endorsed Foundation Degree (EYSEFD) (DfES 2001). This was a vocational qualification designed to integrate academic study with work-based learning (Miller 2011). However, the Senior Practitioner role never developed as a recognised status within the workforce although, at the time of writing, the foundation degree continues to be an important gateway for many early childhood professionals, allowing academic study while remaining in employment. Foundation degrees also became a route towards a full bachelor's degree and onwards to the new professional status developed later. Today, there are thousands of practitioners who remain profoundly grateful for the motivation provided through the EYSEFD and other foundation degrees for personal and professional development (Knight et al. 2006).

A key finding of the EPPE project (Sylva et al. 2004) indicated that over 20,000 early childhood settings in the private, voluntary and independent sector in England were not led by a graduate (Miller 2011). In light of this, following consultation with stakeholders, the government identified the need for a new (full) graduate-led professional role in the children's workforce and introduced Early Years Professional Status (EYPS) (CWDC 2006; DfES 2006a), which embedded the notion of professionalism in its title. The focus of the new EYPS role was that of 'agent of change' (Miller 2008: 259), the graduate leader of practice who would raise standards and lead in the provision of the shortly-to-be-introduced Early Years Foundation Stage (EYFS) framework (DCSF 2008b). To achieve EYPS, candidates needed to have GCSE English and maths (grade A–C), a bachelor's degree (not necessarily in a subject related to early childhood), and meet a set of 39 prescribed professional standards in their practice and leadership of others' practice. By the time EYPS was replaced with a new professional role – Early Years Teacher Status (NCTL 2013) – there were over 13,000 EYPs across England (*Nursery World* 2015), and an important longitudinal study (Hadfield et al. 2012) found that EYPS had a highly positive impact on supporting workforce development in the early childhood sector.

At the time of writing, there are two principal graduate training programmes for roles in working with young children: Early Years Teacher Status (EYTS) for work with children from birth to five (NCTL 2013) and Qualified Teacher Status (QTS) for teaching children aged three to seven (DfE 2016). The reality of the highest qualifications for early childhood both carrying the title 'teacher' brings England in line with other countries such as New Zealand, where all qualified staff working with children from birth onwards are called 'teachers' (Dalli 2011).

In 2011, Professor Cathy Nutbrown was tasked by the government of the day to lead an independent review of ECEC qualifications in England. Nutbrown consulted widely with practitioners, parents and academics and, in her final report, noted the increasing professionalism of the sector and the significant welcome for this from both within and outside the early childhood workforce. The review was premised on a belief that:

> … learning begins from birth and high-quality early education and care has the potential to make an important and positive impact on the learning and wellbeing of babies and young children in their daily lives and in the longer term. (Nutbrown 2012: 2)

A number of recommendations were set out in the final report relating to the training and qualifications of staff in the early years. One of these recommendations proposed a 'new early years specialist route to QTS specialising in the years from birth to 7' (Nutbrown 2012: 72, Recommendation 16).

In direct contradiction to Nutbrown's recommendation, the government's response – *More Great Childcare* (DfE 2013a) – outlined two *separate* graduate roles, covering different age groups. The previously established initial teacher training/QTS route for teaching with three- to seven-year-olds had been retained and a new route leading to the award of EYTS was introduced to establish professionals who would be 'specialists in early childhood development, trained to work with babies and young children from birth to 5' (DfE 2013a: 44). Arguably, EYTS is comparable to QTS as a postgraduate status with professional standards to meet. However, EYTS does not carry QTS with it as, to date, the government has not accepted this is necessary and, at the time of writing, has no plans in place to end the lack of parity between EYPS/EYTS and QTS (Gaunt 2018).

Reflective task 6.1

Your professional journey

We have just provided something of a whistle-stop overview of the gradual professionalisation of the early childhood workforce in England in the twenty-first century. Using this, take time to reflect on your own professional journey.

- Chart your professional journey in the form of a timeline, high-lighting what have been or will be significant waymarks for you.
- What are your feelings about the journey you have made or are about to make? What have been or do you expect to be the high points and low points?
- What issues are current for you in terms of your own sense of professionalism?

Nutbrown registered particularly strong concern about the lack of QTS with EYTS, even though the requirement is to meet virtually the same teaching standards expected of a classroom teacher working with young children. Nutbrown believed this was 'insulting and misleading to those who undertake Early Years Initial Teacher Training [EYITT] courses' (2013: 3). This issue has generated ongoing academic and practitioner discourse and debate beyond Nutbrown. Grenier (2013), Hevey (2013) and others argue that the notion of 'teacher' here is being used to mean something different from the usually understood and accepted meaning, which is misleading for those both inside and outside the educational arena.

A number of higher education and other providers have offered training to aspiring EYTs since 2013 and, to date, many candidates have met the requirements for the status (DfE/NCTL 2018). However, by 2016, there was also an indication that many providers across the country were withdrawing EYITT courses given the low demand for places (Crown 2016), with students preferring instead to embark on programmes that award QTS. With the acute and rapid changes that are a feature of early childhood provision and practice (Rodd 2013), it is important that early childhood professionals keep abreast of and engage critically with any new proposals and take the opportunity to respond to any consultations put out by the government.

While reading the previous paragraphs, you may have been able to position yourself and your own professional journey, whether this is in its infancy and limited to your placement(s) or you have been practising for some years and may be considering the next step. Those steps outlined so far are not exhaustive; there are other routes, and professionalisation is personal to you. The following case studies illustrate something of the diversity in the early childhood professional role and may prompt further thoughts on your own role and progression possibilities.

Case studies 6.2

Abi, Sangita and Cazz

Abi is the manager of an urban children's centre. She had always wanted to work with young children and explored her options when leaving school. She completed an early childhood studies degree at university and then sought employment, discovering that she could only be employed as a – technically unqualified – nursery assistant. When, in 2006, she heard about EYPS, Abi applied to a local provider and met the Standards during the short pilot phase. Very quickly, she became a room leader in a children's centre, then deputy manager with responsibility for the under-threes and is now the overall centre manager. In reflecting on her own journey, she said: 'I wouldn't be where I am now without achieving EYPS and doing that made me think about things in practice perhaps that little bit more.'

Sangita completed her initial teacher training and Bachelor of Education in India before proceeding to a Master of Education programme and then working as a nursery (kindergarten) teacher for some years. She moved to England about eight years ago and, at first, struggled to get her qualifications recognised. In the end, the advice she received was to complete a level 3 qualification in ECEC. She then secured employment firstly in a nursery and then as a teaching assistant in a school. When she enquired about EYPS at her local university, she was accepted quickly to complete the short six-month route and now combines work as a lead childminder with that of tutor-assessor of level 2 and 3 qualifications for a local training organisation. Sangita said: 'Doing EYPS has changed everything: my way of working has changed, my planning, my style of observation, my way of thinking has changed.'

Cazz went straight to university from school and graduated with a 2:1 degree in childhood studies. After graduating, she wanted to explore a career either in a school or in a private, voluntary and independent (PVI) early childhood setting so, for the next year, she worked as a volunteer in Reception/Key Stage 1 in schools for six months and then as an unqualified member of staff in a local nursery for a further six months. After her time in the Reception class, Cazz knew she wanted to work in school. Her university also offered a postgraduate programme in initial teacher training (three–seven years) with QTS. Cazz met all the criteria for the programme so applied, successfully completed the year and was then able to secure a post as a Reception class teacher. Cazz looks back on all she learned about working with children and their families through her studies and placements and says these 'made me reflect so much on the skills that children need from us to feel emotionally supported and learn successfully'.

Think!

- What skills and attributes have Abi, Sangita and Cazz needed to make their own professional journeys?
- What are the similarities and differences between their journeys and your own?

One of the questions raised in the above case studies relates to 'skills and attributes' and we now move to thinking more specifically about these, together with other aspects of professionalism in the sector.

Professional skills, knowledge, attributes and more

Whilst there are voices – such as Raven (2011) – who contest the notion that professionalism can be quantified as competencies, skills and so on, there has been some important work done on identifying professional traits. Brock's (2012) research drew on the perspectives of a range of early childhood professionals and, from this, identified seven inter-related dimensions of professionalism:

1. *Knowledge* – including both a systematic body of professional knowledge and the knowledge gained through experience.
2. *Education and training* – accredited qualifications gained through further and higher education, followed by self-directed continuing professional development.
3. *Skills* – a specific skill set according to the context but including the ability to critically reflect and skills to articulate understanding.

4. *Autonomy* – developing a strong voice in the shaping of practice in your setting.
5. *Values* – strong beliefs in principles that give priority to the needs of children and families.
6. *Ethics* – holding ethical principles with high levels of commitment to the role.
7. *Reward* – personal satisfaction in the role, being valued and recognised as a professional.

Similarly, Dalli (2011: 40) identified specialist knowledge, pedagogical style and collaborative relations as key components of a 'ground-up' definition of professionalism when working with children in early childhood. Dalli believes professionalism is seen through the level of theoretical knowledge practitioners hold about child development and early learning and their commitment to continue on this learning journey. It is also demonstrated through the way practitioners relate to the children and nurture their holistic learning and development. Professionalism is also seen in the effective relationships established and built on with colleagues, parents and other professionals.

Case study 6.3

Katie, manager of a nursery

When asked to list the skills, knowledge and attributes she had needed for a 'typical day' in her work, Katie produced the following table.

Knowledge:	*Skills:*	*Attributes:*
• Being up to date with legislation, such as the EYFS framework, SEN Code of Practice, etc. • Good understanding of child development • Knowledge of my team and how individuals learn and take on board information • In-depth knowledge of our policies and procedures	• Listening • Communication • Social skills • Delegation • Organisational skills • Motivating others • Observational skills and where to take the child's learning next (having ideas) • Working with parents and carers	• Patient • Enthusiastic • Caring • The ability to be imaginative • Being able to support others • Turning negative situations into positives, with both adults and children • Sharing ideas

Complete a table of your own based on a 'typical day' in your own role and setting, whether in placement or in a professional capacity. Reflect on how the knowledge, skills and attributes contribute to your sense of professionalism.

On a typical day, I have needed the following ...

Knowledge:	*Skills:*	*Attributes:*

Chalke (2015) took this further and offered another perspective, identifying three expressions of early childhood professionalism through:

- **the head** – expressed through knowledge, reasoning and thinking about early childhood pedagogy and practice;
- **the heart** – owning and articulating passion, feelings, values and beliefs; and
- **the hands** – exemplified in actual day-to-day practice.

Chalke further identified an overarching theme of early childhood professionalism – that of effectively managing the tensions of the role. Chalke (2015: 67) believes it is through this 'holistic silhouette' of expressions that practitioners will construct their own individual professional pedagogy and meet the challenges of contemporary early childhood practice.

Reflective task 6.2

Head, heart and hands

Take each of Chalke's three expressions in turn – the head, heart and hands – and list the elements and aspects of practice that contribute to your own personal model of professionalism.

Challenges to professionalism

Throughout this book, we have referred to you – the reader – as an *early childhood professional* and in this we strongly affirm the professionalisation of the workforce. However, as you have reflected on the contents of this chapter, you have probably identified some of the challenges to this – the tensions to which Chalke refers. In this section, the aim is not simply to catalogue these challenges but to set them in context and encourage a positive approach to addressing them. Urban (2011: 17) noted the move towards 'systemic professionalism' in early childhood but suggested this was not a conclusion but a framework of opportunity. Such a framework requires you, as aspiring or current practitioners, to engage openly and deeply with making sense of the early childhood professional role. Indeed, you are the ones best placed to ensure the professionalisation of early childhood provision continues to be a 'work in progress' and not a 'missed opportunity' (Lloyd and Hallet 2010: 75).

Historically, many people viewed those working in the sector as simply caring for children, which, in itself, was not generally seen as a significant profession (McGillivray 2011). Miller (2011) went further and painted a picture of a workforce that was under-qualified, poorly paid and heavily (female) gendered. This is part of the inherited legacy and challenges to professionalism still encountered in today's children's workforce, though – undoubtedly – the emphasis on new graduate roles and enhanced public understanding have been instrumental in raising recognition of the key positions played in early childhood practice. However, clear career pathways and structures relating to pay and conditions – all inherent in comparable roles such as that of teacher and social worker – were markedly absent from EYPS (Whalley 2011) and the lack of parity between EYTS and QTS may mean less pay, status and professional recognition (Grenier 2013).

In an earlier section of the chapter, we noted that early childhood workforce policy can be very controlling and government-led (Wood 2015). Osgood (2012) argued that this has created the notion of the early childhood professional as a competent technician rather than an autonomous creative thinker. Osgood believed such a narrowly defined construction of professionalism to be limiting and unhelpful to the process of professionalisation. Potentially, such government attention on creating a graduate profession actually masks the structural disadvantages in pay, status and recognition. A study by Powell and Goouch (2014: 16) found that many practitioners working with young babies in day care discerned a sense of 'oppressive interference' from policy-makers, which they felt disempowered them – although the study findings also suggested that practitioners may be complying and colluding in their own sense of powerlessness by a tacit acceptance of such 'interference'. A positive and *hopeful* attitude combined with a commitment to being reflective and willing to challenge such oppressive interference (Freire 2004) are key aspects of the professional role. Reflect now on the importance of such *hope* and challenge being expressed in practice using the following task.

Reflective task 6.3

Cultivating positivity and hope

Outlining such stark challenges to being a professional may feel a little overwhelming. Many of these challenges have political dimensions, which are beyond your control. However, it is still helpful for you to engage constructively with them.

- Where do you position yourself and your role having read the previous section? Note your feelings as you reflect on the challenges of perceived interference from policy-makers.
- How might you cultivate 'hope'? In particular, how can you move from a hopeful *attitude* to putting it into *practice* in order to move on the process of professionalisation?

Long before graduate roles were introduced to the sector, Moyles (2001: 81) asserted that working in early childhood settings required 'passion, professionalism and paradox'. Moyles' study – like the later one by Chalke (2015) – identified that practitioners generally hold a strong element of passion for the role. This might be seen to compromise professionalism – the paradox – and potentially exploit the goodwill of the practitioner, which then perpetuates low status and so on. However, Moyles concluded that passion is actually embedded in and essential to professionalism and practitioners need to hold strong feelings about their role and the children and families with whom they work. Despite the major regulatory changes in the children's workforce since Moyles' study, arguably those three elements remain in healthy tension within the role. The following case study illustrates this.

Case study 6.4

Laura, manager of a private nursery

'I have worked in the same nursery for over 10 years. Now I have become a graduate leader and manager of my setting, I can see that – possibly – my love for my role (mainly as baby room leader during that time) and especially for the babies and toddlers in my care, meant that I never really saw myself as a professional. I looked after babies, I loved my job and that was the end of it. It was just a chance glance at a flyer for a foundation degree in early years at my local college that gave me the kick I needed. I found that I loved studying too and completed not only the foundation degree but a full childhood studies degree, attaining graduate status. Yet, I have never lost my love and passion for the children. They remain the focus of all I do – only now I take professional pride in what I do.'

Think!

- Reflect on the elements of passion, professionalism and paradox in Laura's story. How do these mirror your own?
- Why do you think Laura might not have felt like a 'professional' prior to her degree studies?

Many early childhood professionals use the word 'passion' when referring to their work and, indeed, this is an important tool in coping with the tensions and paradoxes of the role and for inspiring professionalism (Moyles 2001). Page (2011) went further and suggested the need for a theorising of love, care and education in early childhood practice. In her study with mothers who were considering their options for provision for their children as they returned to work, Page believed that what mothers wanted was a deeply loving response to their young children, especially at the point of transition from home to day-care setting. Page (2011: 310) defined this as 'professional love', which does not compromise the professional dimension of the role. More recently, Lumsden (2016) promoted the idea of establishing a professional organisation for early childhood – a 'Royal College' – that could lead on a *holistic* approach to early childhood policy and practice and go some way to addressing the ongoing challenges faced on the journey towards professionalisation.

Reflective task 6.4

Passion, professionalism and paradox

- Consider the elements of passion, professionalism and paradox in your own role or the role you are studying for.
- Do you believe there is a place for Page's notion of 'professional love' in early childhood provision?
- What do you think might be gained from Lumsden's idea of a distinctive professional organisation in the sector?

The importance of continuing professional development

We have used the notion of a professional 'journey' throughout this chapter and the importance of continuing your own learning journey is pivotal to maintaining a professional stance. Professional development is the focus of Chapter 9, but a commitment to ongoing learning is integral to a sense of professionalism. Anning and Edwards (2010) suggested that children learn to love learning through being with adults who also love to learn. They believe that the process of professional development mirrors the early learning process. For children and adults alike, the dispositions for learning are of equal if not greater importance than the 'what?' and 'how?' of learning. Anning and Edwards (2010) assert that there are essential dispositions for the inquiring early childhood professional:

- the capacity to see the educational potential in all experiences shared with children;
- the capacity to respond to the demands they have identified in work with children;

- critical enquiry and reflective learning; and
- ways of seeing and being seen which draw on the expertise of the early childhood professional.

Such dispositions can be developed through reading, attending training, embarking on higher-level accredited study, working with a critical friend or mentor, the professional appraisal process and career development.

Reflective task 6.5

Continuing professional development (CPD)

You should maintain a record of your CPD activity as routine. Some may not apply to you at the present time but take a few moments to record here noteworthy aspects of recent professional development and think how these are enhancing your stance as an early childhood professional.

CPD activity	*How is this enhancing your stance as an early childhood professional?*
A book or journal article you have read	
A training event	
A module on an accredited study programme	
Working with a critical friend or mentor	
Undergoing staff appraisal or supervision	
Career advancement	

Rodd (2013) and others have identified a further aspect of professionalism as *action research*, aiming to narrow the gap between research and practice through professional learning that fosters reflection. Rodd goes further and suggests that early childhood professionals are best placed to initiate and contribute to a research culture in their settings, rooted as they are in day-to-day practice with children and families. Action research involves inquiring into one's own practices or practices with the children. It is a systematic, reflective and collaborative process that examines an aspect or area of provision for the purpose of planning, implementing and evaluating change (Garner et al. 2009). Historically, early childhood professionals in England are not as confident about action research as their counterparts in other countries where this aspect of the professional role is embedded within the pedagogue's tasks (Bottle 2007). Borgia and Schuler (1996) believe that action research is a key element of professional development, as it allows early childhood professionals to reflect on their work and make changes to practice.

Borgia and Schuler (1996) identified five 'Cs' to be the components of action research:

1. *Commitment* – allowing time, perseverance and resilience for the process of the research.
2. *Collaboration* – ensuring that within the power relations, all colleagues are equal.
3. *Concern* – paying attention to authenticity and validity in the research process; being willing to use a critical friend to ensure this.
4. *Consideration* – allowing space and time for reflection as meanings are sought. This includes a focused and critical assessment of one's own behaviour within the research.
5. *Change* – action research will always result in change, whether to practice, understanding, behaviour or responses.

Reflective task 6.6

Action research

- How can carrying out action research enhance a sense of professionalism?
- What would help you to undertake action research, for example working in collaboration with more experienced colleagues?
- In what way, if at all, might the five 'Cs' help you?

Encouraging professionalism in others

When asked how they encouraged the professional development of others, a group of early childhood professionals gave the following responses (reproduced with the consent of the research participants):

'As nursery manager, I make sure I access relevant information in jour-nals and websites and then make sure my colleagues know about this. I'll often share it at team meetings.'

'I'm room leader in the toddler section and encourage all in my team to attend training courses. I'm an avid reader and buy and then lend books to colleagues. Recently, I found some excellent information sign-posting resources on visual impairment. As we have a toddler in our group with visual impairment, I've been able to share this with the team.'

'I have a strong rapport with the teaching assistant who works with me in the reception class. I'm encouraging her to think about starting a foundation degree as I feel she has the potential to develop her own career.'

The task of supporting others to be professional and to engage in professional development is part of the early childhood professional role. As noted in the previous section, one of the most effective ways of supporting the professional development of others is by attending to your own CPD and role-modelling your enthusiasm for learning to others. In this way, you are engaging in guided participation (Rogoff 1991). This is comparable to children's experience of early learning in a well-supported and safe environment with adults who take a genuine interest in them and their learning. You are also helping to create a community of practice (Wenger 1996) where all involved – other staff, children and parents – are engaged as 'co-educators' in the learning process (Whalley et al. 2017: 84).

Positive practice impact

Petra, leader of a community pre-school playgroup

Petra illustrates the ability to identify and encourage agency and auton-omy in others who, in turn, will become more aware of their own profes-sional selves.

'I find that most of the professional development I undertake, I want to undertake because I see this as a way to improve my practice in my current role. I believe I encourage others in three ways:

- *Through **encouraging them to share my vision**. I have the privilege of learning with the children and with their parents and wider fami-lies. We see one of our important roles as building our setting's "com-munity" into a supportive network. I believe we are stronger together and want to build us all into a "learning community".*
- *Through **allowing them time**. My committee and I share a commit-ment to non-contact time for all and also pay all the team to meet*

weekly for a staff meeting. At our meetings, we don't just discuss practical issues like planning but also discuss our own reading, short courses, current study and so on. I also organise three in-house training sessions per year.

- *Through **the way I lead**. I asked my staff about this and some mentioned that I act as inspiration by studying myself. Others said I offer reassurance and encouragement that they "can do this" and another said I helped to break down her resistance to further learning. One of the most important things, though, is the financial help we give. I set aside a substantial budget for CPD each year.'*

Summary and moving on

In this chapter, we have explored what it means to be a professional in the early childhood workforce. We have set this within the context of a global and national process towards professionalising the sector and identified a number of challenges to this process. Through this, we have identified that it is you – as future or practising early childhood professionals – who are both the key stakeholders and the key shapers of such professionalisation and noted that a commitment to CPD is part of that journey. Encouraging others' CPD is also core to the early childhood professional role.

Further reading

Brock, A. (2015) What does professionalism mean for me?, in A. Brock (ed.) *The Early Years Reflective Practice Handbook*. Abingdon: Routledge.

Chalke, J. (2013) Will the early childhood professional please stand up? Professionalism in the early childhood workforce in England, *Contemporary Issues in Early Childhood*, 14 (3): 212–222.

Dalli, C. (2011) Pedagogy, knowledge and collaboration: Towards a ground-up perspective on professionalism, in C. Dalli and M. Urban (eds.) *Professionalism in Early Childhood Education and Care: International perspectives*. London: Routledge.

Hordern, J. (2016) Knowledge, practice, and the shaping of early childhood professionalism, *European Early Childhood Education Research Journal*, 24 (4): 508–520.

7 Collaborative practice in early years settings

Collaborative practice with parents, colleagues and other professionals within and beyond the setting is an important aspect of the early childhood professional's role to support children's well-being, learning and development. Building on the theme of positive relationships between early childhood professionals, children and their families, which was explored in Chapter 3, this chapter considers theoretical perspectives and policy initiatives that have advocated collaborative practice to support children's cognitive, behavioural, socio-emotional and physical development. We explore the process of collaborative practice in early years settings and consider how early childhood professionals engage in a collaborative approach to promote collective accountability for early childhood education and care (ECEC).

Introduction

A collaborative mode of working enables early childhood professionals to combine their knowledge, expertise and skills to offer an integrated approach to support young children and their families. A range of professionals might contribute to an integrated approach, including: practitioners in settings that provide ECEC, children's centre outreach workers, midwives, health visitors, speech and language therapists, general practitioners, paediatricians, police officers and social workers. Collaborative practice is embedded in the EYFS framework, which advises that,

> ... practitioners should address any learning and development needs in partnership with parents and/or carers, and any relevant professionals. (DfE 2017: 2.2)

Providers are required to ensure staff have training opportunities to develop their understanding of children's learning and development (DfE 2017), which may include support from and collaboration with other professionals. This supports early childhood professionals to make effective assessments of children in their care and to be aware of a child's potential need for help at an early stage (DfE 2018a).

In this chapter, we consider the importance of a holistic approach to working with young children, one that incorporates broader dimensions of their lives (Gambaro et al. 2015). Collaborative practice facilitates access to a range of professional knowledge and skills in order to support a particular short- or longer-term issue affecting children's learning and development. However, the capacity to collaborate efficiently and responsively with others requires additional layers of expertise, as well as the specialist knowledge and skills that are associated with particular professional roles (Edwards 2010). The chapter explores how early childhood professionals can most effectively engage in the process of collaborative working with parents, colleagues and other professionals to support ECEC, including potential barriers to collaborative practice. This chapter can be seen as complementary to Chapter 3, which focuses on relationships with children and families.

Collaborative practice: Terminology

The provision of 'joined-up' services that offer support can be practised in various ways according to local and national organisational contexts (Melasalmi and Husu 2016; Villumsen and Kristensen 2016). However, although an integrated

Table 7.1 Terms used to denote different forms of collaborative working

Term	Explanation of term
Integrated working	Health and education professionals inform each other about children's strengths, any developmental delay or any particular support that might benefit the child (DfE 2017)
Inter-professional	Practitioners from different professional backgrounds work together to respond to the needs of children and their families who encounter complex challenges (Payler et al. 2016)
Multi-agency	Practitioners from different professional groups could be working together in the same location, though their work might not be collaborative (Leadbetter at al. 2007)
Multi-disciplinary	Practitioners from two or more different disciplines work alongside though independently from each other (Malin and Morrow 2007)
Trans-disciplinary	Practitioners across different professional backgrounds have space to explore and develop new perspectives to manage the complexities of practice (Cartmel et al. 2013)

approach to provide support to children and their families is a familiar concept, terminology concerning this area of professional work can be problematic. There is a tendency to use different terms inconsistently to denote collaborative working and terms may be applied interchangeably (Wong and Sumsion 2013). Examples of terms that could be used to denote how professionals work together are detailed in Table 7.1.

Co-production is a further term that might be applied to service provision in the early years sector. Co-produced services are distinguished by an equal and reciprocal relationship between the user and provider in order to achieve an identified outcome (Whalley 2013). When professionals are involved in co-produced service delivery, they take on the role of catalysts and facilitators; this involves building social networks that can help to address underlying issues and extend the capacity of service provision (New Economics Foundation 2008). Examples of co-production in early years provision can include parents coordinating activities and groups or parents taking responsibility for designing and implementing services (Whalley 2013).

Bronfenbrenner's ecological model of human development

Collaborative practice in ECEC draws on Bronfenbrenner's (1979) ecological perspective on the influence of key determinants on the child's development. Bronfenbrenner's ecological model proposes that there are family, school, wider community and global influences on the child's development. Bronfenbrenner positioned the child at the centre of layers of nested social contexts and suggested that the child's development is shaped by shared relationships and reciprocal interactions across these contexts so that the child is influenced by and also influences their surrounding environment. The nested contexts are represented as interdependent systems, which are detailed in Table 7.2.

Bronfenbrenner (1986) later identified the *chronosystem* as a further layer to his model. This context relates to how the timing of the child's interaction with

Table 7.2 Bronfenbrenner's (1979) ecological system

Microsystem	The system that is nearest to the child, which includes their immediate family and friends
Mesosystem	The immediate system to the child, which incorporates their early years setting, school, peers and wider family
Exosystem	Covers different contexts that exert influence on the child, though they may not directly participate with these contexts. These include social services, health care, neighbours and parent workplaces
Macrosystem	The wider legal, socio-economic, political and cultural context affecting the child's development

social contexts during their childhood affects their development, such as their transition from nursery to school.

Reflective task 7.1

Interaction

Reflect on interaction that takes place between the early years setting and the home.

Think!

- How might the use of technology, such as smartphones, support interaction between the setting and the home?

You may find it helpful to refer to the discussion on interaction with parents in Chapter 3.

Children's holistic development

Collaborative practice between early childhood professionals, parents and colleagues has been suggested in a number of key reports that emphasise the importance of professionals working with parents and each other to support young children's holistic development (DES 1990; Laming 2003; Marmot 2010; Allen 2011; Tickell 2011; Nutbrown 2012; Ofsted 2016). This process is in accordance with articles of the 1989 United Nations Convention on the Rights of the Child (UNCRC), which cover child protection and provision of children's services.

Support for integrated service provision is provided by findings from the research study, *Effective Provision of Pre-School Education* (EPPE) (Sylva et al. 2004), which indicated that early years provision that integrated education, childcare and family services was beneficial for children's development. EPPE also found that the most effective settings supported parental involvement and shared information about children's learning and development between parents and staff (Sylva et al. 2004). This view is aligned with socio-cultural theory, which acknowledges the holistic nature of children's learning and development and recognises the significance of early intervention in a child's life to promote their current and future outcomes (Wong and Sumsion 2013). Early intervention involves identifying as soon as possible any issues that are adversely affecting a child's health or development and then seeking the necessary support (Wolfe 2013). The significance of early intervention is supported by a growing recognition that the early stages of life are a crucial time for determining cognitive development, social and emotional well-being and the roots of physical health (Marmot 2010; Tickell 2011; Wolfe 2013).

Reflective task 7.2

Identifying language skills

Reflect on the following statement concerning the importance of early identification of children's language skills:

'*Law et al. (2017a) report that evidence demonstrates the likelihood of children's early language difficulties adversely affecting their progression in school and future employment opportunities. They advise early identification of children's language difficulties and support with language skill development in order to promote positive outcomes for children's cognitive and socio-emotional development.*'

Think!

- How would you involve the child's family in the process of early identification of language delay?
- What information or specialist support could help to inform an assessment of a child's language delay?
- What support could be found to help identify the cause(s) of a child's language delay, if this has been identified?

Practice initiatives to support children's holistic development

Holistic and informed assessment of a child, which is supported by professionals working together to collectively review the child's progress and provide support, is seen to be critical for realising positive outcomes for children and their families (Easton and Gee 2012). Early years settings and schools have a crucial role in early identification, early intervention and provision of support for young children who have additional needs or are at risk of significant harm (Laming 2009). This view is supported by Ofsted, who advise that effective support for children and their families is reliant on the processes of 'early assessment, early identification and early intervention that are shared across a children's services department' (2016: 21). A collaborative assessment process helps with the early identification of a child's additional needs; this process can be supplemented by contributions from the child's parents, their key person (KP) and other practitioners who work in the setting, and by other professionals, such as educational psychologists, health visitors and social workers (Howard et al. 2016).

As discussed in Chapter 3, being attuned to children's needs is crucial. Engagement in sensitive observation and respectful listening to children facilitates the early childhood professional's role in contributing to the process of identifying children's interests, capabilities and any additional support they might need. By forming

Table 7.3   Maslow's (1943) hierarchy of needs

Lower-level needs	• Physiological needs (e.g. drinking, eating and sleeping) • Safety needs (e.g. physical and mental health)
Higher-level needs	• Social needs (e.g. sense of belonging and friendship) • Esteem needs (e.g. self-respect and confidence) • Self-actualisation (realising potential, although Maslow felt only a small percentage of people would attain this level)

trusting and constructive relationships with the children in their care, the early childhood professional can help to ensure that the child's voice is being represented authentically in documentation that is shared with others. This, in turn, supports the task of identifying relevant strategies or interventions that support their needs and holistic development (Hiscott 2013).

Although not intended specifically for ECEC, Maslow's (1943) theory of a hierarchy of human needs, shown in Table 7.3, supports this view of children's holistic development. Maslow's hierarchy indicates that progression to higher-level needs is not attainable until lower-level needs have been realised.

The importance of safety needs being met was highlighted by Munro's (2011) report on child protection. Munro stated that support for children's access to quality education is only made possible when they are subject to beneficial care and feel they are safe. By providing a physically and emotionally secure environment, being attuned to individual children and contributing to the collaborative process of support for holistic development, the early childhood professional helps children to realise the needs identified by Maslow. Examples of this might be supporting a child's transition to the setting to help them develop a sense of belonging or by providing healthful, balanced and nutritious drinks, snacks and meals, as specified by the EYFS framework's *Safeguarding and Welfare Requirements* (DfE 2017: Section 3).

The importance of attending to children's holistic development has long been recognised by pioneers of early years provision in their theoretical perspectives on education and care, including by the following innovators of practice.

- **Friedrich Fröbel** initiated kindergarten provision in Germany in 1840 as an educational system that promoted the importance of play and creativity in young children's learning and development. He encouraged children's active exploration of the indoor and outdoor environments to support their holistic development. Areas of the garden were allocated to children so they could grow plants and develop an understanding of the natural environment. Fröbel recognised the importance of relationships between children and adults and believed parents should actively support their child's education.

- **Maria Montessori** qualified as a doctor before establishing her Casa dei Bambini (Children's House) for three- to six-year-olds in 1907 in Rome, following requests for childcare for migrant workers who worked in the city's factories. Montessori recognised the importance of the early years in children's overall development. Provision for children was based on adult observations of the children's individual needs and interests to promote their holistic development and inner motivation. She thought children should have opportunities for active learning and sensory experiences within a clean, orderly environment. Montessori promoted the use of structured resources that provided a range of sensory experiences. Furniture and resources were scaled to children's size and were readily accessible to facilitate their use and promote children's independence. Montessori believed children should be encouraged to take responsibility for caring for themselves and their environment and encouraged parental involvement in children's education and care.

- **Margaret and Rachel McMillan (the 'McMillan sisters')** began the first 'open-air' nursery for socio-economically disadvantaged children in 1914 in Deptford, London. Recognising that children's learning and development could be affected by family poverty and poor living conditions, which affected children's health and well-being, the McMillan sisters included an outdoor garden area in the nursery that was stocked with natural resources, tools and movable equipment. Children were encouraged to access the garden, which was seen as a site of compensatory education that could improve the quality of life for children who experienced poor health conditions.

- **Rudolf Steiner** opened a school in 1919 in Germany at the invitation of the director of the Waldorf–Astoria–Zigarettenfabrik (Cigarette Factory). Steiner supported a holistic view of children's development and believed strong and respectful relationships should be forged between children, parents and practitioners. His approach to education aimed to support children's emotional and spiritual development through the provision of a range of sensory activities within indoor and outdoor environments. Resources and furniture that were made from natural materials helped to promote children's connection with the natural world. His work led to the development of Steiner Waldorf kindergartens and schools across the world.

- **Loris Malaguzzi** was the founding director of municipal early childhood centres that opened their first pre-school in 1963 in the Reggio Emilia area of Northern Italy. A significant aspect of Malaguzzi's educational philosophy was his view of the strong and competent child who was a communicator from birth. As discussed in Chapters 1 and 2, Malaguzzi (2011: 2) emphasised the importance of listening to children; he proposed they could express themselves through a 'hundred languages', which was a term used to convey how children could communicate through various modes of expression, such as music, art, play and technology. Malaguzzi's view of the child's right to participation is acknowledged in the UNCRC (UNICEF 1989). Parental involvement was also valued by Malaguzzi; he believed that respectful, cooperative relationships between adults and children were essential to support their learning and development. His emphasis on communication is demonstrated by provision of spaces in the early childhood centres to foster children's relationships with others and encourage communication and collaboration. (More information on these theorists can be found in the further reading at the end of the chapter.)

Positive practice impact

Holistic development

The following extracts illustrate how early childhood professionals can enhance provision to support children's holistic development.

Erin, room leader for babies (urban nursery setting)

'*After reviewing provision in the nursery, we decided to rearrange the floor space in the baby room to improve the environment and support children's independence. We created soft, comfortable areas with cushions and carpets and introduced puppets into the book area to encourage communication and language development. The books were arranged so children could access them easily and share them with other children. We also removed doors from the cupboards in the room so the children could access their play resources more easily.*'

Bobbie, home-based childminder

'*I ensure my planning provides opportunities for both indoor and outdoor play, regardless of the weather at the time. I have a fully equipped play room, for the children to independently access toys and resources, and play equipment in the garden. I support the children to climb, explore and take risks and have resources to develop creative, imaginative play.*'

Ayesha, manager of an urban pre-school

'*I encourage children to support one another at all times. Older children take turns laying the table and reading to the younger children. I provide opportunities for children to make plans for the day, be responsible for the resources, and decide what new resources we may need and why. I am always consistent in my expectations of the children to ensure that they feel valued and secure.*'

> **Reflective task 7.3**
>
> **Making the most of your environment**
>
> Reflecting on the resources and activities in the indoor and outdoor environment in your setting or placement, consider how children's holistic development is supported through opportunities in the provision for:
>
> - sensory experiences;
> - gaining independence;
> - developing their understanding of the environment; and
> - communicating and collaborating with others.
>
> Consider support that might be available in your setting, placement or in the wider community to assist you in making provision for children's holistic development.

Policy initiatives

Pascal and Bertram (2013) identify maternal and child health, parenting and ECEC as key areas for action by early years services to combat issues of child poverty, inequality and social immobility. Policy initiatives aimed at supporting children in these focus areas had previously been incorporated within the Sure Start local programmes (SSLPs) in the late 1990s, which offered a range of targeted integrated services in areas of disadvantage to support young children's social, emotional, cognitive and healthy development (see Chapter 1 for more on SSLPs). The development of SSLPs into Sure Start children's centres (SSCCs) at the beginning of the twenty-first century aimed to offer universal provision of services for children and their families, at the early stages of a child's life. However, SSCCs have since been subject to financial constraints and there has been a return to a more targeted approach to service provision in early years policy (Fitzgerald and Kay 2016). Targeted support includes encouragement of evidence-based parenting programmes, an increased number of health visitors, an extension of the Family Nurse Partnership programme that supports parents under the age of 20 during the first two years of their child's life and, from 2014, the introduction of funded provision for two-year-old disadvantaged children, which is discussed in Chapter 2.

An emphasis on collaborative working practices in the early years sector has been influenced by increased concerns about safeguarding of children. The Green Paper, *Every Child Matters* (ECM) (DfES 2003), and the ensuing Children Act (2004) advocated the need for improved collaborative practice by all professionals who were involved in delivering children's services, with the aim of improving the children's well-being and holistic development. The ECM outcomes were five policy objectives for children and young people that were incorporated into the 2008 EYFS framework (DfES). These five outcomes were:

1. stay safe;
2. be healthy;
3. enjoy and achieve;
4. make a positive contribution; and
5. achieve economic well-being. (DfES 2003)

Although ECM policy was later discarded under the Coalition Government (2010–2015), it was a significant initiative at the time of its inception and ECM policy objectives still have relevance for young children's provision, despite the loss of the policy in which they were framed (Fitzgerald and Kay 2016).

The impetus for enhanced collaborative working practices and the five ECM outcomes was driven by the conclusions of Lord Laming's (2003) inquiry into the tragic death of eight-year-old Victoria Climbié in 2000. Lord Laming detailed numerous failings in collaborative working across the key agencies that had responsibility for Victoria and found that the principal failure to protect her from fatal abuse by her carers was the 'result of widespread organisational malaise' (2003: 4). In calling for clear lines of accountability, Lord Laming's report sought to ensure that departments worked more collaboratively together and recommended that each local authority should establish a 'Directorate of Children's Services' to oversee the process of more effective integrated working. Lord Laming's report also suggested that agencies should share information more effectively, and the subsequent Children Act 2004 set out clear expectations for improving information sharing. The current process of information sharing explains that professionals should share appropriate information in a timely manner and should discuss any concerns about a child with colleagues and relevant staff in the local authority (DfE 2018a).

However, safeguarding is a wide-ranging and complex issue (Nikiforidou and Anderson 2016). Despite the policy agenda that was implemented following the death of Victoria Climbié, further tragic child abuse cases have occurred that have highlighted failures in effective collaborative working by the services involved in children's lives. Following the death of baby Peter Connelly ('Baby P') in 2007, Lord Laming was asked to report on the progress being made towards effective safeguarding arrangements for children. Lord Laming (2009) noted that the recommendations in his previous report (2003) had not been fully implemented and challenges still remained in providing efficient safeguarding and child protection processes.

The 2009 Laming report led to a subsequent review of child protection led by Munro (2011: 6), who reported that attention was being paid to 'process over the quality and effectiveness of help given' by children's services. Rather than focusing on 'doing things right', in terms of following procedures, Munro (2011: 6) advised that the system should focus on 'doing the right thing' by checking that children received help. Munro's (2011) report detailed ways in which child protection could be improved, recommending that unhelpful or unnecessary government direction should be removed to leave a focus on essential regulation for effective integrated working and underpinning principles of good practice.

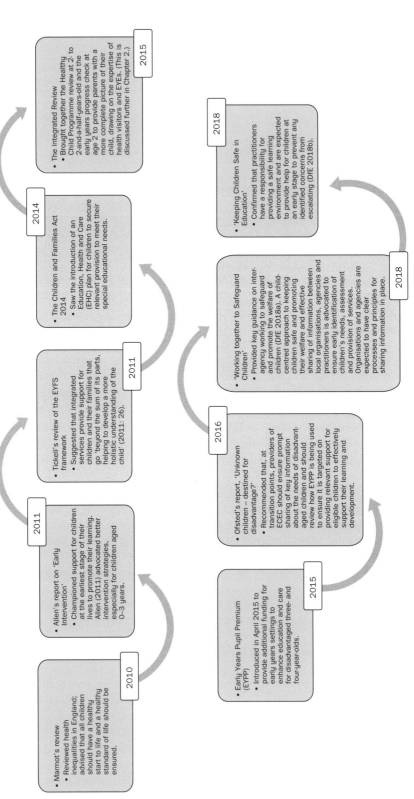

Figure 7.1 Key reports and policy initiatives in collaborative working

- Marmot's review
  - Reviewed health inequalities in England; advised that all children should have a healthy start to life and a healthy standard of life should be ensured.

2010

- Allen's report on 'Early Intervention'
  - Championed support for children at the earliest stage of their lives to promote their learning. Allen (2011) advocated better intervention strategies, especially for children aged 0–3 years.

2011

- Tickell's review of the EYFS framework
  - Suggested that integrated services provide support for children and their families that go 'beyond the sum of its parts, helping to develop a more holistic understanding of the child' (2011: 26).

2011

- The Children and Families Act 2014
  - Saw the introduction of an Education, Health and Care (EHC) plan for children to secure relevant provision to meet their special educational needs.

2014

- The Integrated Review
  - Brought together the Healthy Child Programme review at 2- to 2-and-a-half-years-old and the early years progress check at age 2 to provide parents with a more complete picture of their child, drawing on the expertise of health visitors and EYEs. (This is discussed further in Chapter 2.)

2015

- Early Years Pupil Premium (EYPP)
  - Introduced in April 2015 to provide additional funding for early years settings to enhance education and care for disadvantaged three- and four-year-olds.

2015

- Ofsted's report, 'Unknown children – destined for disadvantage?'
  - Recommended that, at transition points, providers of ECEC should ensure prompt sharing of key information about the needs of disadvantaged children and should review how EYPP is being used to ensure it is targeted on providing relevant support for eligible children to effectively support their learning and development.

2016

- 'Working together to Safeguard Children'
  - Provided key guidance on inter-agency working to safeguard and promote the welfare of children (DfE 2018a). A child-centred approach to keeping children safe and promoting their welfare and effective sharing of information between local organisations, agencies and practitioners is advocated to ensure early identification of children's needs, assessment and provision of services. Organisations and agencies are expected to have clear processes and principles for sharing information in place.

2018

- 'Keeping Children Safe in Education'
  - Confirmed that practitioners have a responsibility for providing a safe learning environment and are expected to provide help for children at an early stage to prevent any identified concerns from escalating (DfE 2018b).

2018

This view is supported by Skattebol et al. (2016), who note that a culture of regulation within ECEC can act as a constraint on discussion and recognition of professional practice undertaken by early childhood professionals in their everyday work. Skattebol et al. (2016) cite the work of Fenech et al. (2006), who suggest that regulation is a double-edged sword, as it confers legitimacy but can also confine the early childhood professional's ability to apply their wisdom and knowledge to the situation at hand.

Further policy initiatives relating to collaborative working within integrated services include the following key reports and policy initiatives, detailed in Figure 7.1.

Reflective task 7.4

The Early Years Toolkit

Reflect on different approaches to support children who are eligible for EYPP supplementary funding that are suggested in the 'Early Years Toolkit' (EEF 2018), discussed in Chapter 1.

Think!

- Consider if any of these approaches might be appropriate for the setting where you work or are on placement. If a similar strategy has already been implemented, explore its use and likely impact.

Collaborative practice: Working in teams

The Rumbold Report (DES 1990) identified that teamwork is at the root of good practice in the early years sector. Members of a team can operate with a coordinated approach to advance a shared aim and can provide a wider reach than an individual working alone (Jelphs and Dickinson 2008). A useful model of team working is offered by Tuckman and Jensen (1977), which has been adapted in Table 7.4. Their five-stage model of team development helps to identify processes that might occur. However, team formation in practice may not follow the sequence of these stages and teams may spend more time in one stage than another or even omit one. The right-most column includes some suggested actions that might be taken by an early childhood professional during the different stages of team formation.

A further model of team working that is useful to consider in the early years context is offered by Edgington (2004). This shown in Table 7.5 model consists of three types of teams: the cosy team, the turbulent team and the rigorous and challenging team.

Table 7.4   Stages of team development

Stage	Features of stage	Suggested actions by early childhood professional
1. *Forming*	• members start working together • some members may feel unsure about their role or team goals	• welcome new members to the team • explore group tasks • establish group systems • hear any concerns
2. *Storming*	• possible disagreement between team members • dominant team member may emerge	• listen respectfully to different views expressed • help to resolve any discord within the group
3. *Norming*	• disagreements within group are reconciled • team members begin to cooperate	• acknowledge development of the team • focus on team's planned tasks
4. *Performing*	• emergent sense of cooperation as team members start to perform as a group	• keep team focused on group goals • encourage team members to act more autonomously
5. *Adjourning*	• team disbands as goals are achieved • members may exhibit mixed feelings	• review completion of team goals • celebrate team members' achievements

Source: Adapted from Tuckman and Jensen (1977).

Reflective task 7.5

Working in a team

• Can you recognise any stages of Tuckman and Jensen's (1977) model of team formation?
• Can you identify any challenges about working in the team structures identified by Edgington (2004)?
• Can you see any similarities between these models and other team models that you know?
• What improvements could you make to your setting's team working?

Table 7.5 Model of team working

The cosy team	• team may be well established • members believe their systems are effective • new members are unwelcome, especially if they have suggestions for change
The turbulent team	• team appears to be outwardly receptive to change but may act subversively • turmoil in the team may prevent members from managing change effectively
The rigorous and challenging team	• team members are receptive to change • team engages in critical discussion and seeks to analyse problems • team may feel dissatisfied with their actions

Source: Adapted from Edgington (2004).

Enhancing collaborative practice

Collaborative practice in ECEC takes place in a fluid landscape of young children's services. The role of the early childhood professional has broadened in scope and complexity and is subject to a shifting policy and practice environment in which the professional role is performed (Edwards and Daniels 2012). Skattebol et al. (2016) suggest that the dynamic nature of early childhood service provision requires practitioners to have a depth of knowledge and commitment to support children and their families to confidently access the services they might require at the earliest stage of the child's life. Early childhood professionals interact with a range of children in diverse contexts of practice. It is therefore important for you to regularly review your professional knowledge and skills and seek opportunities for professional development so you can effectively engage in collaborative practice. (This subject is considered further in Chapter 9.)

As discussed in Chapter 6, Dalli (2011: 40) reported three main thematic elements of professionalism that emerged from her survey of New Zealand early years teachers' perspectives on professionalism and ethics in their practice. These three elements are:

1. Professional knowledge and practice
2. Pedagogical strategies and style
3. Collaborative relationships

Features of 'collaborative relationships' that were noted by Dalli included supportive engagement and respectful communication with others. By engaging in collaborative relationships, professionals can be guided beyond their own specialist knowledge of early years practice by the knowledge and expertise of others (Douglass and Gittell 2012).

Reflective task 7.6

Collaborative relationships

- Reflect on examples of collaborative relationships with others from your own or others' practice.
- Consider how these might facilitate a planned goal and any associated challenges.

Example of 'collaborative relationships' from your own or others' practice	Did the collaborative relationships facilitate a planned goal?	Were there any associated challenges?

Earlier in the chapter, we considered the findings of Laming (2003, 2009), which indicated failings of service providers to communicate in a timely and effective manner to share information about the life circumstances of Victoria Climbié and Peter Connelly. Collaborative practice relies on effective communication strategies and sharing of information. According to Melasalmi and Husu (2016), early childhood professionals construct their professional knowledge and understanding through the process of reciprocal interaction, so professional communication that is focused on practice is crucial to effective participation with children, families and other professionals.

Hierarchy is another key factor that can influence the process and outcome of collaborative practice. Power issues can have a negative impact on relationships between members of the group, affecting the thinking and efficacy of the group's work (Edwards and Daniels 2012). Therefore, it is also important to build strong, positive relationships to support the efficient process of collaborative practice and to enable you to draw on the resources of others' expertise to effectively support a child's development trajectory. The final task of this chapter includes examples of strategies that will support you to enhance your collaborative practice.

Reflective task 7.7

Collaborative practice

Reflect on the following points drawn from a case study of early years practice that demonstrate effective collaborative practice. The context of the setting is a social enterprise managed by parents and staff that offers provision for children under three years of age (Ofsted 2015b). Consider how the examples of collaborative practice detailed in this case study might support provision for children and their families who attend the setting.

- Sharing of information and good practice, which helps practitioners to be aware of professional development opportunities and keep their professional knowledge current.
- Visiting other settings to see a range of different practice and consider if their own practice would benefit from change.
- Welcoming practitioners into the setting to support colleagues and receive informal feedback from a fresh perspective.
- Working collaboratively with a neighbouring outstanding provider; staff from both settings meet regularly to share good practice and access a range of training.
- Making strong links with leading early years experts and taking part in early years research, testing new ways of working and sharing their findings by contributing to publications.
- Making good use of professional support available through the local authority and specialist services. This helped the team learn about and implement strategies to support children with special educational needs and disabilities (SEND), such as learning from the speech and language service.
- Leading on carrying out local and national projects and strategies designed to support children's communication, language and literacy development.

(Adapted from Ofsted 2015b: 3)

Summary and moving on

This chapter has focused on the early childhood professional's role of engagement in collaborative practice. Melasalmi and Husu (2016) emphasise the importance of practitioners developing pedagogical, reflective practices and skills to enhance their practice in this field. In the next chapter, we focus on the subject of reflective practice and consider how this process can support you to be responsive and proactive when supporting children's learning and development.

Further reading

Duhn, I., Fleer, M. and Harrison, L. (2016) Supporting multidisciplinary networks through relationality and a critical sense of belonging: Three 'gardening tools' and the Relational Agency Framework, *International Journal of Early Years Education*, 24 (3): 378–391.

Education Endowment Foundation (2018) *Preparing for Literacy: Improving Communication, Language and Literacy in the Early Years.* Available at: https://educationendowmentfoundation.org.uk/tools/guidance-reports/preparing-for-literacy (accessed 19 January 2019).

Gray, C. and MacBlain, S. (2015) The founding fathers and philosophies of learning, in *Learning Theories in Childhood*, 2nd edn. London: Sage.

Moss, P. (2016) Loris Malaguzzi and the schools of Reggio Emilia: Provocation and hope for a renewed public education, *Improving Schools*, 19 (2): 167–176.

8 Reflective practice in the early years

> This chapter explores how the act of reflection enhances practice and discusses how reflection becomes a powerful resource to support creative, 'outside the box' thinking. Reflective theory and practice are defined to explore the processes and skills involved during reflection and self-evaluation. Individual experiences, values and perspectives influence professional judgements. The personal and professional judgements we make impact on practice and the changes we make. This chapter argues that reflecting on the 'right thing at the right time' and applying reflective practice is a pivotal skill to generate positive changes.

Introduction

Reflective practice within the early years is a relatively new concept for many early childhood professionals and represents a shift within their practice. The skills associated with the concept of reflection have been applied within professional qualifications across a number of disciplines with the expectation that the act of reflection will become a dominant and normalised process to improve outcomes and provision and effect change. However, if the concept, intent and act of reflection are not fully understood or engaged with, then reflection can be a superficial act preventing 'real thinking' or 'real change'.

Reflection offers options, choice and opportunities so that individual actions are undertaken with foresight to fully understand the impact they will have on others. Cable and Miller (2011), Melhuish and Gardiner (2017) and Osgood et al. (2016) recognise that for reflection to be more effective within practice, professionals are required to engage with each other via reflective dialogue and self-assessment. This chapter builds upon Chapters 6 and 7 to explore how early childhood professionals can 'get to know better' their own reflective styles in order to enhance daily interactions, dialogue, experience and expression to bring about change. This theme is continued in Chapter 9, which explores how the challenges of change can most effectively be managed.

Change

Change happens throughout life and can be intentional or unintentional, positive or negative, either initiated by self or others or due to external situations that are out of our control (Fullan 2016). Research suggests that staff who regularly self-evaluate, reflect and engage in dialogic discussion to critique practice and outcomes are more likely to sustain and maintain high-quality communication and engagement with two- to four-year-olds (Melhuish and Gardiner 2017). If reflection is a tool that can bring about change, it is vital that changes planned or made enhance the quality of working with children and families.

One definition of change limits it to the act of making something different. Fullan (2016), however, encourages practitioners also to consider the *process* and *levels* of change. Planning and implementing change demands reflection; it is for this reason that any practice committed to bringing about positive change must invest intellectual energies in decoding what reflection is and what reflective practice entails. Schön (1987) suggested that reflective practice is more than a technical skill to be applied. Rather, reflection in the early years is a multi-faceted cognitive and creative dance, where personal, professional and academic identities engage with unique thinking processes that underpin early years pedagogy. Reflection can be a resource for change only if we 'tap into' our thinking to know when we are reflecting, what we are reflecting about and why. Without reflection, there is a risk of repeating cycles that may prevent practice moving forward or innovation being implemented.

For early childhood professionals, change is a daily experience; this is deemed essential for high-quality provision and undertaken in response to often complex and rapidly shifting demands and responsibilities (Cable and Miller 2011; Fullan 2016; Osgood et al. 2016; Melhuish and Gardiner 2017). Schön's constructionist reflective theory (1987) asserts that professionals can shape and interact with challenges according to their unique understanding, experiences and expectations through experimental practices or by generating innovation.

Early childhood provision and practice has undergone – and continues to undergo – a raft of policy changes and paradigm shifts. In line with the government-led agenda, early childhood provision is viewed as critical to narrowing gaps in educational achievement, improving school readiness, developing lifelong skills and inspiring individual aspirations (DfE 2016). Such an agenda impacts on professional identity and the expected leadership skills required to deliver high-quality provision. 'Leadership' here does not refer to the role of a manager, leader or director of a setting; rather, it is about leading and managing 'self', being accountable for our own practice, interactions with others and the resources we use every day to support learning and development. It is about knowing why changes are made and taking responsibility for choices and reasons why change is needed (Melhuish and Gardiner 2017).

Two types of change that occur during early years practice are intentional and unintentional change. An *intentional* change is when the act and art of reflection are knowingly engaged with and when a solution is sought to solve an identified problem or issue. An *unintentional* change occurs during everyday practice, may not be identified or focused on and is a consequence of an action that has not been consciously considered or planned. Unintentional change can develop into intentional change by becoming more aware of the issue during reflective practice.

RARA Key model

The RARA Key model (Scollan 2009) demonstrates how professionals can modify or focus their thinking during reflective practice to make changes. The model developed from research with early childhood professionals, systematising data collected through interviews and reviews of professionals' reflective journals. The RARA Key model describes four stages of reflection for early childhood professionals, as shown in Figure 8.1:

> Recognise
> Adjust
> Review
> Act

The RARA Key model is applied in Table 8.1.

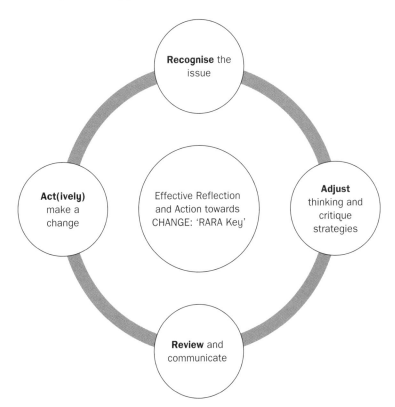

Figure 8.1   Reflective RARA Key

Table 8.1 RARA Key model

Recognise	What has been recognised as an area to change?	**Example:** Literacy outcomes and engagment with children because ...
Adjust	What area(s) needed to be adjusted and why?	**Example:** Change of environment and literacy resources because ...
Review	Change needs to happen. How? Evidence to be used will be?	**Example:** Children were not engaging with indoor mark-making or literacy because ...
Action	Will change occur straight away or after discussion with peers to share ideas via a two-way dialogic discussion? Why?	**Example:** Peers shared observation and outcomes to seek a different approach because ...

Referring to the following case study, identify where the practitioner:

- recognises issues that require change;
- adjusts, to plan and make changes;
- reviews changes; and
- acts to make changes.

Case study 8.1

Anita, nursery teacher in her second year of teaching working in a primary school

'*During a recent inspection, I was very nervous when Ofsted came to our setting and, whilst being observed, I was questioned as to why we had moved the writing area and resources outside. At first, I wasn't confident justifying this; I doubted myself and the changes made. However, we recently undertook some peer observations and, during a weekly staff meeting, justified the literacy changes made in the nursery regarding the writing focus and outdoor environmental shift. Other staff critiqued these changes and the focus, which I appreciated, whilst I was a bit shocked at the reaction of some staff. I responded by sharing why changes were made and provoked those critiquing to justify why they have not made changes in view of recent literacy results. I stood my ground, sharing our nursery team reflections and pedagogy using solid outcomes from our observations, progression outcomes and tracking data. The data had been used to capture the movements and next steps of our current cohort and we needed to do something different to meet the children's needs. The children's interests and focus related more to being outside for many social, emotional, physical and economic reasons. Therefore, this developed our nursery pedagogy and underpinned reasons towards change. Using a wider range of resources whilst outside, we can develop hand–eye coordination and relive the 'Bear Hunt' story using props, dressing up resources, video recorders and cameras so that our bear hunt play and talk can be captured first-hand and reflected upon later with the children, team and parents.*

'During the discussion with the inspector, I felt I was being judged, and I lacked confidence when leading the change. Reflecting on this event, I wondered why I was so nervous and unconfident about leading the change. I took responsibility to bring about change – now I was being accountable for the change. I knew my theory, my children and the reasons why changes were made. Why did I feel so ill at ease, so tested, so unsure?'

Think!

- Who did Anita work with to bring about the change?
- What evidence was used to determine if the change was needed or not?
- Was this a big or small change? Why?
- Was the change well received? Why?
- Is Anita a leader of change? Why? How?

Self-assessment and accountability

Children need inclusive access to high-quality experiences, provision and interactions in a complex and challenging environment. At the same time, early childhood professionals are responsible for the quality of their practice. The combination of these two contextual factors highlights the importance of self-assessment and reflection on individual practice and accountability, particularly when the reality of practice imposes the need for change (NCTL 2013; Mathers et al. 2016; Osgood et al. 2016; Callanan et al. 2017; Melhuish and Gardiner 2017).

Leadership cannot be separated from accountability. It is vital that early childhood professionals who engage with children at any level of practice can justify what they do. Reflective practice is crucial for the development of accountable leadership, coupling action and decision-making with self-awareness and flexibility, leading to positive change.

The act of reflection

Many theorists, including Dewey (1966), Kolb (1981, 1984), Schön (1987), Moon (1999) and Bolton (2010), recognise the challenges associated with agreeing on a definition of reflection. Through an educational lens, reflection is captured by Dewey as a dialectic approach to thinking, where our thoughts and experiences clash and oppose in an internal dialogue to formulate new meaning. In Dewey's enquiry model, a *reflective act* on its own is not enough, as reflection can become too technical or mechanical, which prevents opportunities for the development of our unique, creative and individual *out of the box thinking*. For instance, during a swimming session, a five-year-old girl became distressed when she realised her swimming costume was not the right one and could not be worn because it had a dog's head with long floppy puppy ears hanging off the costume. The child was embarrassed and refused to change into it. The following options explain a mechanical reflective response and a creative reflective response.

> **Response 1:** The early childhood professional reflected that next week, bags should be checked before children leave and the child will have to sit out and watch if she does not put her costume on.

> **Response 2:** The reflection was thought about, and then other possible options and outcomes were engaged with. The early childhood professional used previous experiences and picked up the costume, turned it inside out and indicated the costume was now plain with no evidence of the floppy ears.

Reflection can be applied to both thought processes and practical aspects of practice. The success of strategies and levels of reflective practice are dependent on the extent of thoughtful engagement whilst thinking about our own thinking. Flavell (1979) termed this *metacognition*: our thinking about thinking, fuelled by the intention to self-assess, which contributes towards self-regulation. Knowing when and how thinking occurs can support individuals to understand the unique thought patterns developed during lifelong experiences and learning journeys (Schön 1987; Solomon 1987; Moon 1999; Bolton 2010). This, in turn, enables management of behaviour, choices and responses. These experiences are connected and link to a wealth of transferable skills and knowledge that, once realised, are empowering for individuals to create and recreate new meaning or possibilities. When early childhood professionals are conscious of their unique thought processes and style, or the cognitive lens used to make sense of their world, the technical act of reflection is set in motion.

Creativity and criticality are the ingredients that enrich the act of reflection towards the *art of reflection* that makes *reflective acts* imaginative, conscious thought. Reflection is empowered by creativity and criticality because these make thinking more purposeful and focused. During the process of reflection, we think about something and then focus on areas requiring attention. Both the act (technique) and art (conscious creativity) are needed during reflection to bring about appropriate changes for self and others. Of course, space and time are needed for reflection so that reflectors have time to consider if they are making changes for the right reason or outcome.

Technical and creative reflection is recognised as a powerful tool towards problem-solving and decoding daily situations that are, at times, fast and furious. For early childhood professionals, trying to find the space to think about outcomes, interactions and issues involving parents, children or colleagues can be challenging. Responding quickly to situations becomes a complex balancing act. For example, ensuring there is enough time to revisit interactions with parents or reflect on the effectiveness of the next steps for key children to support their progression, whilst at the same time recording evidence to share with parents, colleagues or visitors. The space and time for reflection within daily interactions and routines can be rare commodities.

What might the act of reflection look like in practice and how does this bring about change? The STARR model, illustrated in Figure 8.2, captures processes and characteristics of reflection that consider how to use reflective space creatively to maximise opportunities for change. In the process represented by the STARR model, the concept of *reflexivity* begins to evolve, enabling individuals to distance themselves from the main issue to become more objective about change and the characteristics of reflective thinking.

Reflective task 8.1

Reflecting on challenges and risks

Consider the main challenges or risks in your setting or placement to how you:

- review how much reflective dialogue is undertaken with colleagues during an average week and identify the space available to reflect upon events;
- consider how team members react if reflective dialogue presents challenges; and
- reflect on the potential impact on quality outcomes of not applying reflection in practice with peers, children or self.

How much time or space is there during the working day to reflect?

Space to be reflective

Schön's reflective theory (1987) provokes early childhood professionals to enquire, challenge and consider the act of reflection as being more than just one movement of thought. Schön separates the act of reflection into two concepts: reflecting 'in' action, which means reflecting on what is happening or what we are doing as it happens, and reflecting 'on' action, which occurs after the event. Early childhood professionals will directly or indirectly consider positive or negative outcomes of

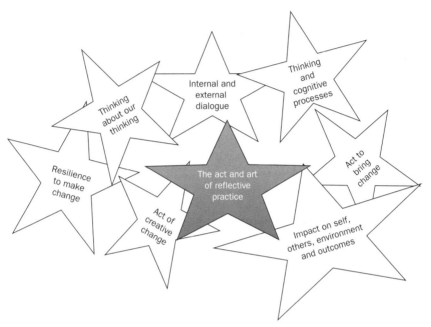

Figure 8.2   STARR model

their practice both when reflecting *in* their practice and *on* their own practice. For example, when reading a story to children, an early childhood professional might need to adjust their voice, pitch or pace if it is observed in action that a group of children are not fully engaged. Reflecting in action enables changes to be made during the event. If reflective thinking occurs after the story has finished, then the event cannot be altered, although changes can be made for future story time sessions. Raelin (2001) and Ron et al. (2006) build on Schön's concept of reflecting in and on action, defining the act of reflection as periodically returning to a place or space to immerse back into a situation, feeling or event and to look at it from all angles.

Reflective theory into practice

The Teachers' Standards (DfE 2011b), Nutbrown Review (2012), Teachers' Standards (Early Years) (DfE 2013b) and the EYFS framework (DfE 2017) all advocate that early childhood professionals need to be self-critical within their role in the best interests of children and their families. There are many generic traits that are identifiable during the act of reflection to systematically measure practice. Reflective traits and characteristics are identified as: reviewing; doing; action; engaging in; examining; deciding; exploring; analysing; assessing; feeling; critically evaluating; sharing; communicating; critiquing; clarifying; listening; thinking; experiencing; and decoding (Dewey 1966; Schön 1987; Moon 1999; Bolton 2010).

Early childhood professionals need to be mindful of the impact that their language, identity and pedagogical beliefs have on everyday practice and outcomes. This is very clear for Schön (1987) and Callanan et al. (2017) when they identify the benefit from reflection and its impact on professional progression and well-being. Schön uses the term generative metaphor, which combines creative reflection and cognitive skills to enable individuals to see things from a new perspective when conceptual and perceptual changes occur. Seeing things in a new way also requires internal and external discussion so that ideas and thoughts can be expressed, critiqued and transformed. (This is also discussed in Chapter 4 as a feature of an enabling environment and in Chapter 9 as an area for professional development.)

Schön suggested that the most important area for reflective practice is probably language. Language is highly influential for identity formation. According to Erikson (1950) and Marcia (1966; Marcia et al. 1993), identity develops across the lifespan, starting from the early ideas we maintained from a young age that contribute to the belief system that we hold regarding who we are in adulthood. Therefore, the identity seeds that adults sow during everyday interactions and communications with children require thoughtful consideration and conscious reflection. Early childhood professionals need to be mindful during their interactions with children so that reflection is an active process that offers opportunity to reshape and challenge thinking and practice for positive outcomes (Eraut 1994; Alversson and Svenigsson 2008; Colwell 2015).

The use of professional language to describe children during observation and assessment of their progress will influence how others view a child and their abilities. For instance, describing a child's behaviour during these assessments as positive, challenging or disruptive results in labels, responses and expectations that connect to pre-existing perspectives. Language and labels transmit messages or ideas about a child's identity, achievements, ability, behaviour and characteristics. Such terms can impact on children's well-being. Consequently, the early childhood workforce requires skilful and reflective professionals who are advocates for the rights of children, identifying and challenging 'out-of-date' perspectives, labels and the 'use' of tokenistic or damaging language. There is strong evidence that it is vital to maintain respectful and cohesive teams, working collaboratively towards change in order to ensure overprotective gatekeepers do not inhibit new ideas (Pollard 1987; Sedgwick 1988; Colwell 2015). This can include early childhood professionals being mindful of their own bias and challenging aspects of practice, attitudes, language and interactions that are not appropriate to maximising children's well-being. However, challenging colleagues or managers who are less reflective or less aware of their impact on others requires tact, courage and training to support understanding and empathy (this will be a focus of the final chapter).

Reflective task 8.2

Assessment comments

Read the following two examples of assessment comments on the same child and consider what is being focused on and why. Consider how the comments about the child, who is transitioning from one class to another, might impact on how their new teacher perceives the child's character, ability and behaviour.

'Eva is hyperactive and will not listen to a word you tell her. It is best to keep Eva in a separate group during story or group time, rather than try to deal with her behaviour. I've actually asked her mum to come in and take her home 15 minutes before the end of the session, so we can enjoy the story and get through it all.'

*****

'Eva seems to find sitting down in large groups a challenge at the moment, so her mum and I are working together to strengthen this with the use of two-way turn-taking via speaking and listening. Currently, we are trialling one-to-one support during large group work and sometimes Eva is leaving earlier at the end of the day, so she only has two minutes of group time to deal with. We will monitor and amend this strategy depending on how Eva gets on.'

Think!

- How is language used to describe the child's behaviour?
- How does the adult form an assessment?
- Which words or phrases have informed your view of the assessments?
- How might the statements present bias or inform professional practice and future training?
- Reflect on whether the seeds sown regarding the child's identity and behaviour are factual, fair or positive. How might Eva's parents read the assessment? Thinking back to Chapter 4, where is Eva's own voice?

Shared reflection: The act of reflection to bring about change via self and others

When professionals strive to offer high-quality early years provision, interpersonal and reflective skills impact greatly on the levels of reflection reached, either individually or within a group. The impact of internal thought processes and reflection within early years provision will depend upon 'willing' colleagues who are reflective and open to dialogue. If an early childhood professional is unable to engage others in a reflective discussion, then developing reflective practice for oneself or implementing high-quality provision for children may be more challenging.

Reflection is an ongoing process that can be an internal or external dialogue. In fact, until we become aware or conscious that we are reflecting it can be habitual, meaning we are not aware it is happening. There are many theories, reflective models and cycles that capture processes of reflective thinking and it is important to realise that internal dialogic discussion is continuous – expecting to measure it fully is like using a butterfly net to catch an aeroplane. However, similar features found in reflective theory and cycles across disciplines recognise dialogue, cognitive awareness and critical evaluation of everyday actions, interactions and outcomes. Therefore, early childhood professionals should aim to think, discuss and reflect not only individually, but also through dialogue with others. Bohm (1996) celebrates the use of dialogue because it has no fixed agenda and, when individuals explore issues together, this can bring about collective change. Cable and Miller (2011), Nutbrown (2012), Osgood et al. (2016) and Melhuish and Gardiner (2017) all recognise that for reflection to be more effective within practice, professionals are required to engage with each other via reflective dialogue and self-assessment.

The RARA Key model (Figure 8.1) can be used in shared reflection whilst assessing interactions, outcomes and challenges in the daily professional journey. For example, information sharing can be distorted and misunderstood. Professional language and attitudes during everyday communication influence positive relationships, how partnership roles and expectations unfold and how mutual two-way communication is shared.

Reflective task 8.3

Self-assessment

The four themes of the RARA Key model (Figure 8.1) can be used to self-assess and reflect on practice to think about how communication and interactions affect others. For example, consider how a recent interaction with a parent or colleague might provoke feelings, reactions or possible miscommunication. Ask yourself:

- How can a message that needs to be shared and received be open to miscommunication?
- How can I seek to ensure that a message is perceived as clear, accurate, articulate and relevant by the recipient of the message?

Positive practice impact

Peter, nursery teacher

Peter illustrates a practising nursery teacher engaging in RARA reflection.

'When I speak to parents during pick-up or drop-off time, I recognise I have mainly been approaching parents only if I have something to inform them about. I rarely initiate interaction with parents, unless I want something or have something to say. So, I began to wonder if that was positive from a parental perspective and wondered what it must feel like to be a parent when only approached for technical issues or information-receiving. I reflected further about my role and this aspect of my practice and I planned to make a change. I adjusted my routine during pick-up and drop-off time and started to talk to parents about their children to find out what they wanted to talk about. I asked parents questions rather than sending out requests or informing them of my agenda.

'My change was interesting to observe, because I began to review the reaction from parents and children. At first, I observed parents who were observing me, to work out what had changed. I could tell they were waiting to be approached by me, to hear information from me. When I didn't do what I normally did, there were sometimes quiet spaces, with no one talking or approaching. We were unsure of what to talk about; we had learnt our drop-off and pick-up roles and rituals and now we were unlearning them, changing them. This was when I realised how much power my role takes for granted and expects. This needed to change.'

The role of communication

Communication with peers on a regular basis is a powerful resource for reflection that enables articulation of our thinking to share ideas, whilst involving others in experiential learning opportunities (Kolb 1984). Talking things through, or sharing our thinking and ideas during dialogic discussion, offers opportunities to negotiate and learn from each other. Talking with others offers opportunities to gain an insight into why changes are being suggested or made. This creates a *shared space* to challenge existing practice and co-construct new strategies, frameworks and shared ideas. Co-construction of strategies and frameworks promotes shared meaning, participation and agency within the early years setting so that practice, pedagogical styles and aims or targets are understood and owned by all those involved (Bohm 1996). Professional dialogue and two-way discussion enhance the act and process of reflection and take professionals on a shared intellectual journey. However, it should always be remembered that making a change or challenging existing practice can be viewed by some as a confrontational or negative act, something that will be explored further in Chapter 9.

Reflective task 8.4

Communication skills

Use the reflective questions in the following table to focus on your communication skills.

Recognise	What has been recognised as an area to change during a recent communication or interaction?	**Example:** Did you talk too much, too little or was there a good balance of communication during a recent interaction with a parent/peer?
		• How do you know? • What was the agenda of the message? • Do you think there was equal two-way communication? Why (or why not)?
Adjust	What needs to be adjusted and why?	**Example:** Prioritise the above reflective points and plan to adjust future communication or practice. (Plan adjustments via small steps.)
Review	Self-assess your choice to change: aim to identify why you have noticed something that needed to change or be challenged. Is it something new or has it always been happening? If it has always happened, why are you noticing it now? What else is impacting on the issue and on your own thinking? Have you as a professional changed your practice, view, expectations or approach (how/why)? Considering these changes will make you notice and see things differently. Refer to Figure 4.2: this offers opportunity to think about layers within the environment that you might now be engaging with.	**Example:** Review changes and adjustments to consider impact (i.e. who/what has been impacted?). • Is the change the best option? Who for? Why? • Who and what are the main benefits of the planned adjustments or changes? Do others agree? Do they need to agree? • Have children been consulted about planned adjustments or changes? Why (or why not)?

Action	Will change occur straight away or after discussion with peers to share ideas via a two-way dialogic discussion?	**Example:** Is the planned adjustment working? Should it change? What has been learnt during the review? Continue to apply the RARA Key model via a cycle of continuous change.

The act and art of reflective practice allow for the creative problematising of issues. Outcomes from practice are revisited and reconsidered to acknowledge others' perspectives and unravel miscommunication, intentions and interpretations. This can include a critique of our responses and taking ownership of weaker aspects of practice. Responsibility and ownership of outcomes does not show weakness; rather, it shows insight and strength towards change. Relational thinking and depth of reflective practice are vital for personal and professional changes to take place. Effective change requires reflectors who are creative and resourceful during challenging situations and who can assess impact, responsibility and accountability for themselves and others. Reflective characteristics, which were discussed at the beginning of this chapter, interrelate during multi-dimensional and layered thinking, which enables creativity to flow and escape – this is the act and art of reflection.

Our thinking and beliefs continue to evolve during personal, professional and academic journeys, although it is difficult to pinpoint exactly when a shift or change has occurred. According to Piagetian theory (1954), this is because we continuously accommodate and assimilate new knowledge that expands and pushes what we thought or knew. Challenges from others relating to individual beliefs or concrete knowledge of what works well in our practice, combined with successful strategies developed during years of practice, can be disarming, shocking and emotional to experience (Goleman 1996). However, early childhood professionals are expected to undertake a continuous spiral of cognitive and professional growth to keep abreast of rapid educational reform whilst managing their complex roles in practice. Therefore, the skills and strategies required to consciously develop reflective thinking are powerful multi-dimensional *tools of trade*, required at micro and macro levels, to make changes *for* early years practice *from* reflective early childhood professionals (Schön 1987; Skemp 1989; Pound 1999; Barnes et al. 2014, 2015; Callanan et al. 2017).

Many personal and professional investments are made by those aiming to make changes. Change occurs by taking risks, dealing with trial and error, learning from past experiences, and picking oneself up when the challenges encountered have not been successful or well received. When aiming to adapt practice to make things better, early childhood professionals need to consider who else should be involved and what or who will be affected during the act of reflection (refer to table 8.2). Here, it is vital to comprehend that 'what we think' or 'a truth arrived at during the act of reflection' will be the truth of that time-frame, context and environment only. Reflective examples in this chapter have aimed to demonstrate the notion that reflective practice offers the opportunity to be aware of the 'here and now' to bring about change. Changes made are not always transferable to a different context, time or environment, and a successful strategy used once to make a change might not work at another time. This can be viewed positively: freedom and liberation for creative thinking bring about change to make way for new ideas to evolve (Kuhn 1970; Schön 1987).

If changes made are unsuccessful or not well received by colleagues, it is pertinent to carefully review the impact that the change had on:

- self;
- children;
- colleagues;
- practice; and
- the setting environment.

Knowing what to focus on or to prioritise when making a change is challenging and the effectiveness of a change will vary depending on roles, experiences and the contexts in which we find ourselves. Dewey (1966) and Schön (1987) believe that our focus, thinking styles and paradigms (the framework within which we view the world) are based on concepts formulated through social interaction, function and behaviour, which influence our definition and interpretation of a situation.

Table 8.2 Professional self-audit

Critique your practice and style of interaction with children, peers and parents to identify what is positive about your pedagogy and impact	
Positive things about my practice or communication are:	Less positive aspects about my practice and communication are:
Strategies to improve my practice and make change possible are:	I need to be mindful of the following things that may prevent professional growth, the development of leadership skills or opportunity to make effective change:

Action plan: <Date to review impact>

Reflective task 8.5

The depth of change

Fullan (2016) encourages us to consider whether changes made are at a deep or surface level. Think back to an experience in practice or on placement when a change made did not work as expected and consider why this was not successful. Use the reflective audit plan to facilitate your personal reflection and then complete the following audit plan.

What change was made and why?	What was the outcome of the change?
What were the strengths and weaknesses of the change?	How did others respond to the changes you led?
What would you do differently next time, and why?	How could you involve others in the revised change?

To fully engage in the reflective processes, techniques and strategies requires space, dialogic discussion, mentoring and understanding. Schön (1987) uses a murky water metaphor to capture the many layers or levels that occur during the act of reflection. This metaphor encourages early childhood professionals to self-assess: is this reflection on safe, still water or going deeper to explore murkier issues that are harder to deal with, challenge, articulate or understand? At times, it is easier to explore shallower waters, reflecting on issues that are less threatening or less time-consuming and that will not present conflict, cause offence or upset those with whom we work. However, staying safe can also prevent much-needed changes. Early childhood professionals are employed for their training, experience, knowledge of childcare and pedagogical expertise to ensure children have the best opportunities available to them. The ethical and professional response should always be intended to privilege the needs of the children and resilience is needed to deal with reflective dilemmas.

Reflective task 8.6

The process of thinking

• Evaluate your reflective process and style to explore what and how you think when reflecting.
• Aim to write down the processes of your thinking and how the act and art of reflection work for you.
• What are the main challenges within your setting or placement to:

- bring about change via reflective dialogue with colleagues?
- respond to others who are not enthusiastic to bring about change?
- find space for reflective dialogue to critique practice?

Summary and moving on

The act and art of reflection have been explored and reflective tasks offered for early childhood professionals to 'think about thinking' in and on their practice. Reflection requires strength to constitute a change of perspective or strategy and therefore will, at some level, involve a shift that will impact on the environment and those within it. Identifying potential challenges within the workplace can be stressful but at the same time it is developmental, exciting and stimulating. In the next chapter, ongoing professional development is posited as part of the reflective cycle and an essential element for all early childhood professionals in effecting changes to and developments in practice.

Further reading

Miller, L. and Cable, C. (eds.) (2011) *Professionalization, Leadership and Management in the Early Years*. London: Sage.

Moon, J. (1999) *Reflection in Learning and Professional Development*. London: Kogan Page.

Schön, D. (1983) *The Reflective Practitioner: How professionals think in action*. New York: Basic Books.

٩   Owning professional development and managing change

> We will inaugurate this final chapter with a clear and important statement:
>
> *Professional development must be owned.*
>
> *It demands the professional to act, where action refers to learning by doing; learning from others; and being resourceful, creative and mindfully daring in managing change. This chapter explores the question of the early childhood professional's ownership and responsibility for their professional development throughout all stages of the process. We discuss the theoretical position underpinning professional development, arguing that for professional development to be owned by the individual, it must be continuously renewed and challenged via reflective processes that are at once individual and social, nurtured by dialogue between professionals.*

Introduction

There is an acknowledged duty for all professionals to undertake a learning journey.

Nutbrown (2012) alludes to this with the term *pedagogical processes*. Pedagogical processes include training, mentoring and continuing professional development (CPD) within the workplace. (This builds on Chapter 8, which discussed the characteristics of the pedagogical process and its reflective nature, aimed at continuously improving routines, thinking and practices.)

Mentoring, Level Three training programmes, Postgraduate Early Years Initial Teacher Training (EYITT) and Qualified Teacher Status (QTS) professional standards all converge in requiring 'reflection' to be developed effectively as part of professional development. The notion of lifelong elsewhere learning applies to everyone working within early childhood services, where the individual is committed to personal development and innovative practice. Within the revised Early Years Foundation Stage (EYFS) framework (DfE 2017), practitioners are required to use reflection to observe, evaluate and plan appropriate provision for children to meet their unique needs. Reflection is explicitly instrumental to high-quality provision and it is at once a condition and an outcome of professional development (Dahlberg et al. 2006). Although quality is an essential pillar of practice and the ultimate rationale for professional development, as per our earlier discussion in Chapter 5, establishing a secure definition of what quality means is complex. It should not be assumed that because a qualification has been achieved or a professional development programme has been completed, an individual will understand how to interact appropriately with children and adults, how to bring about change, or how to challenge practice (Pascal and Bertram 2014). The concept of quality requires clarity and needs to be contextualised via dialogue with all stakeholders so that its essence is unpicked, co-constructed, mutually engaged with and fully understood by all concerned (Moss 2016). This has implications for the nature, aims and scope of professional development, challenging individualistic and strictly outcome-driven interpretations.

Reflective task 9.1

The origin of thinking

Reflect on how your own education, personal, professional and/or academic experiences have influenced your thinking and current knowledge. How might your knowledge and experiences collectively impact on future or past decisions or changes made?

It is agreed within key findings from the *Effective Provision of Pre-school Education* (EPPE) report (1997–2003) that access to high-quality provision has a very positive impact on the child (Sylva et al. 2004: 6). In Chapter 4, we discussed how young children who have access to enabling environments and enabling adults benefit from the care and education experiences with which they interact. Attending high-quality early years provision can improve the child's holistic life skills by, firstly, building on what children already know and, secondly, communicating with children respectfully. A key characteristic of high-quality provision is interacting with the child first and then the child as a learner (Penn 2006; Alderson 2012). Sylva et al. (2004) recognise that it is vital to engage respectfully and meaningfully with children to discuss, clarify and construct a shared understanding. Only then is it possible to tap into the rich tapestry of the child's reality, to enable the child 'in the moment'. All of these points intertwine in that moment and, hence, the challenge is to unpick the skills, knowledge and know-how to provide high-quality provision.

A 2018 report from the Early Intervention Foundation (EIF) defined quality as early childhood provision and experiences that effect positive outcomes for children. The report, *Teaching, Pedagogy and Practice in Early Years Childcare: An evidence review* (EIF 2018), measured outcomes of 108 studies relating to children's language and literacy; numeracy and mathematics; and cognitive, socio-emotional and physical outcomes. Two main themes within high-quality provision are recognised: *structural* quality and *process* quality. Structural quality pertains to measurable criteria such as daily management roles and safeguarding responsibilities, staff qualifications, training and retention, whilst process quality refers to how daily experiences, communication, interactions and partnerships evolve. Both themes within high-quality provision bring about change, emphasising the importance of professional development.

Reflective task 9.2

Quality provision

Explore your understanding and experience of quality provision by undertaking the following tasks:

- Identify key characteristics that contribute towards high-quality experiences for children.
- Discuss with colleagues or other students how to define high-quality provision (for instance, ask a peer or colleague to define quality; share examples and compare). Were there any differences in your definitions? What might be the reasons for this?

Creating change and managing resistance

Professional development is a powerful force that can bring about change within the professional setting. It is at once both a genuinely individual and genuinely social process (Moyles 2006; Cable and Miller 2011; Nutbrown 2012; Siraj and Hallet 2014; DfE 2017). It demands flexibility and the ability to challenge established assumptions while interacting with others, which Schön (1987) elegantly defines as *professional artistry* at the intersection of an internal and external driven dilemma (Kolb 1981; McKenzie 1990). As an example of external forces that can limit the impact of professional development within settings, resistance may be shown by those being affected following CPD, reflection and the introduction of change, which Fisher (2012) identifies as a *transitional curve* cycle of cause and effect. Reactions from colleagues or others affected by a reflective outcome will influence the possibilities for learning through professional development (Bolton 2010; Colwell 2015; Lindon and Trodd 2016).

Reflective task 9.3

Thinking and change

How have recent changes impacted on your thinking and practice? Refer to changes that:

- you made;
- you have been part of;
- have been 'done' to you;
- involved micro or macro change levels.

Are the changes you have identified or experienced at practice, management or policy level? Why? How?

- Identify how, personally and professionally, you have reacted to and dealt with change.
- How do colleagues react to change, responding to professional development via: training; CPD; peer critique; peer review; reflective dialogue; and appraisals?
- How do the children you work with or have encountered on placement react to changes to the routine, outside access, planned activities, new staff, new rules, new children joining the class?
- Identify how reactions to change impact on: emotions, self-esteem, confidence, friendships, morale, enthusiasm, motivation, leadership, outcomes, impact, ownership and responsibility levels.
- Identify the stakeholders involved in a recent change. Why was the change made? How did you envisage it would enhance the quality of the children's experience? Who was involved in making changes? Identify whether the roles within making changes were clear, understood and negotiated. How do you know?

Collaboration

Fisher's 'transitional curve' cycle was developed from Kelly's (1955/1991) psychology of personal constructs theory, aimed at capturing how learners may experience or encounter *challenging* reactions from others. A factor here may be the range of professionals and disciplines involved in the lives of children. Professionals working on behalf of and for children share the same goal: to keep children safe. However, each professional will prioritise the needs of children differently and apply contrasting strategies. Professional boundaries become blurred. Therefore, it is vital to acknowledge that professional core skills, training and ethical codes that underpin practice are different across professional disciplines. For instance, Banks (2004) uses the term *multi-professional* where each profession and professional working within their field has a traditional identity, way of working and knowledge bank. However, because the early years and education sector has a range of professionals working within it, expectations and perspectives vary and sometimes collide. Subsequently, reflective discussions or reactions to change, or to bring about change, can be an emotional labour (Hochschild 1983). A broad definition of emotional labour is when it becomes an effort to manage emotions. Emotional labour requires individuals to make a conscious effort to manage and regulate personal feelings and emotions when they respond professionally to others. We all have our own original life journey, family and childhood experiences and belief systems that, when merged together, create unique individuals who feel, think and perceive experiences differently (Goleman 1996; Rodd 2013). Therefore, when a case study, work scenario or professional challenge arises, a plethora of perspectives and ideas are put forward.

Fisher's 'transitional curve' and Hochschild's definition of emotional labour recognise that any suggestions or changes made at work may result in resistance, which can cause pressure. Change and reactions require conscious interaction to prompt individuals to evaluate how their own behaviour, attitudes and involvement can improve or hinder performance or outcomes (Kotter 1996; Fisher 2012). However, as discussed in the previous chapter, the level of ownership and depth of reflection – Schön's (1987) *murky or shallow waters* metaphor – will create either accurate or inaccurate connections and realities. This position reinforces the need for a continuing and intense discussion with colleagues to explore why and how outcomes occurred, including a form of internal dialogue for self-reflection and CPD, which might include coaching, mentoring or professional guidance (Siraj and Hallet 2014).

Dimensions of change and development

The concepts of personal and professional change on the one hand and professional development on the other do not involve the same processes or outcomes. Nevertheless, change and development interlink and co-exist on both personal and professional levels. Personal changes and development impact on professional identity and vice versa (Chalke 2015; Osgood et al. 2016).

Early childhood professionals should be aware that individual development or change in practices can impact on the cultural structures, shared beliefs or team ideology of a setting. Therefore, reactions from others may alter when innovations or adjustments to routine or practice are introduced. Making changes can be challenging on many levels and this is a responsibility that the developing practitioner must accept (Reed and Canning 2012; Siraj and Hallet 2014; Chalke 2015). Changes introduced following professional development may impact on well-being, knowledge and resilience levels within a setting (Goleman 1996; Corrie 2003; Moyles 2006; Nutbrown 2012). A safe learning environment and community of trust are essential to support new initiatives and to test new strategies. The social dimension and perspective must be part of the reflective process in professional development, complemented by knowledge and 'know-how' gained via experience. Only such awareness can ensure that developing professionals can progress on their own 'intellectual journey' that is at the same time shared and co-constructed with others. Developing professionals continue to learn and evolve, forming their professional identity whilst impacting on others. Change is stronger when support is both given and received. Early childhood professionals are responsible for their own learning journey and for seeking appropriate support, resources and information. Chalke's (2015) work on three expressions of identity and professionalism was outlined in Chapter 6 and you might like to look back at that now. These three expressions also have relevance when considering the importance of professional development:

- **the head** – reflections on knowledge, reason and thinking;
- **the heart** – passion, feelings, values and beliefs; and
- **the hands** – professionalism as worked out in practice in the workplace.

Each expression provides a way of ethically exploring practice so that professional integrity and individual professional stories are owned and developed by the early childhood professional within practice and via professional development. Combining these aspects of self enables our creativity and challenges thinking to construct a 'reflective key' to problem-solving.

Responsibility for change model

Reflective task 9.4

Murky or shallow waters

Refer to Schön's murky or shallow waters metaphor to reflect on the following:

- When you decide to make a change or ask a peer for guidance or help, who do you ask and why do you ask them in particular? What is it about certain individuals that draws you to them?
- Self-assess what motivates you to seek out support from others and what it is that might be achieved:

    - Who is the change for and who will benefit?
    - Is the help being sought challenging Schön's (1987) shallow or murky waters metaphor?
    - Is the change something quick and superficial or a huge shift?
    - Will the level of change influence who it is you will seek support from? Why?
    - From where do you receive support?

- Why do you ask for support and how do you decide where the best or most appropriate support can be found?
- Identify the core characteristics that underpin the 'effective and enabling' support you have received or offered.

The implication of a socially conscious approach to professional development is that each professional is intrinsically responsible for the impact of their own professional development and should accept ownership of the change generated and the related consequences for *self* and *other* (Schön 1987).

Reflective task 9.5

SWOT analyses

A SWOT analysis (an analysis of strengths, weaknesses, opportunities and threats, seen in the following table) provides a useful tool for exploring your practice and drawing up a personal development plan. A SWOT analysis enables reflection and self-audits to identify, categorise and acknowledge personal, professional or academic skills, challenges and areas requiring development.

Focus on either your personal, professional or academic 'self'. Identify the things that are going well (strengths), the things that are not going so well (weaknesses), the things that may develop or get better with some support (opportunities) and the issues that continue to threaten your professional or academic development (threats).

SWOT analysis

My strengths are (things I do well or achieve in):	The areas or skills I feel I am weaker in are (I need to develop further or seek support because …):
Opportunities I can use to support progression (e.g. accessing CPD, training, mentoring, material to read or reflective discussion with colleagues):	Current threats to my own development or opportunities (e.g. limited support or understanding from myself, colleagues or home or funding issues):

Reflective task 9.6

Creating a development plan

Once the SWOT analysis is complete, it is time to construct a development plan that relates to your personal, professional or academic development. Utilise the SWOT analysis to make a plan to challenge and build upon recognised weaknesses and/or threats. Your recognised strengths and opportunities will support your journey. Reflect 'how' your individual strengths and unique skills support you.

Name:

Professional/Personal/Academic Development Focus (choose one area per plan):

Area/skill to develop (be clear as to why development is needed and for whom – identify the purpose):	Main challenges (identify potential barriers that make change or professional development difficult to achieve or move forward; for instance, time, resources, attitude, self-belief, complexity of role or demanding work–life balance):
Plan of action (how to achieve set goals):	Support/resources required (what will make the plan work?):
Small steps in place (how will each step support you?):	How progression will be measured (how do you know if progress is being made?):
How change will be managed (think about other plans, strategies or support):	Review date: (it is vital to reach a date to assess impact of the plan and small step achievements):
Next steps and plan:	

The impact of professional development: Reaction to change

It is vital to offer guidance, space and strategies to those at the forefront of change by reflecting on what is required to meet their needs within a complex and demanding professional role. It is an ethical responsibility (at all levels) to consider the needs and position of all involved in professional development. Making changes to develop practice and 'self' impacts on the lives and experiences of others. Professionals need to nurture positive emotions and resilience to support all involved in possible change, development and progression (Roberts 2010; Cable and Miller 2011; Lindon 2012; Rodd 2013).

Reflecting on the consequences of change through professional development is intrinsically an act of responsibility for all involved in early childhood provision – responsibility to take ownership of change and its implications. It is particularly an act of responsibility for managers and leaders to equip and support staff to make changes. This may be through training activity that embeds the strategies and skills to mentor colleagues and stakeholders towards developing resilience when facing changes (Solomon 1987; Murray 2017).

Dialogue to challenge practice and quality

The role of the early childhood professional is complex, diverse, fluid and challenging and is rather like unravelling a ball of knotted and tangled string (Friedland 2007). Research undertaken by Melhuish and Gardiner (2017) found that personal and professional support is needed for all staff within the current climate. They found CPD opportunities to be key for the well-being of early childhood professionals and, ultimately, for the sector. This is even more relevant in a context where qualifications, technical knowledge and core skills are used as a measure of quality to ensure professionals working with children are fit for purpose to meet the needs of their role (Anning and Edwards 2006; Cable and Miller 2011; Moss 2016; DfE 2017; NatCen Social Research 2017). Such qualifications and core skills can be perceived as 'must-have' requirements to maintain quality levels and ensure due adherence to policy drives.

At the same time, Melhuish and Gardiner's report found that practice and provision in England is diverse and staffing structures are not fixed. Therefore, providing professional progression and development opportunities via a one-stop professional development or CPD package is not possible. It must be owned by the individuals involved, directly or indirectly, via reflective dialogue and open discussion around the concept of quality, as this will mean something different to each stakeholder. Based on the idea of a dynamic and changing concept of quality, Moss (2016) makes the case that the design and objective of professional development should be mutually agreed, owned by all subjects involved and challenged to prevent misunderstanding and complacency.

Professional development is also a pillar of quality provision because professional frameworks and routines are an example of how complacency can creep into practice (Dahlberg et al. 2006; Callanan et al. 2017). Routines within early childhood education and care (ECEC) settings need reflection, updating or, at times, restructuring rather than adhered to because they have always worked well (Rodd 2013). Professional development should provide professionals with the skills and resources to lead on revision and to challenge routines that can limit children's access to resources or provision that are inherited from a pedagogical style no longer relevant to current structures or transitional requirements within the setting. As discussed in Chapter 4, if a routine in a setting has been in place and unchallenged for a long time, then adult- and child-led pedagogies or structures within the routine may clash or not be in harmony with newer pedagogies (Brooker 2008). Professional development is understood as a core asset to equip professionals to innovate, whilst keeping a sensitive eye on the limits of the pace and scope of change that the professional environment can tolerate without excessive stress.

Reflective task 9.7

Reacting and responding to change

Read the following reactions to change from two early childhood professional colleagues who have completed CPD together.

'*I've recently completed CPD to develop outside access for children. I really don't think children learn anything more when outside than they do when they are inside and I'm not really liking going outside for too long – it's too cold.*'

'*I really enjoy being outside with children, I see them so differently and learn much more about them and from them when we are outside exploring. Recent training has enabled me to make connections about how children interact with the environment.*'

Think!

- Why might the reactions about being outside with children be so different?
- Identify how personal and professional values and beliefs impact on attitudes about 'being outside'.
- Who is responsible for developing practice and outdoor access?
- How might future CPD support or challenge each example?

Trust is essential to change professional practice and professional self

Professionals need a safe learning environment and community of trust to interact, communicate and 'test out' possible meanings of quality and, subsequently, reflective strategies or outcomes to bring about change and professional development. However, it is vital to define the concept of trust to consider how it embeds pedagogy, professional practice and relationships at micro and macro levels within ECEC. Professional expertise and interpersonal closeness, together with personal identity, interweave to build trust in relationships. However, for trust to flourish when taking the risk to trust others, the realisation of *distrust* also exists. Baraldi and Farini (2013: 132) define trust as a sociological perspective: they argue that trust is observed as a function in society, providing a way of dealing with the disappointment of expectations.

Sustainable change-making

The acts of reflection and development that fuel change can be separated into a cognitive process, moving from intrapersonal self-evaluation towards interpersonal reflections and dialogue with peers, to co-construct meaning (Schön 1987). Distinguishing between *reflection towards change* and *domesticated reflection* can help clarify the characteristics of effective training towards professional development (Pascal and Bertram 2013, 2014). Domesticated reflection, and the connected domesticated professional development, occur when professionals react to issues habitually, dealing with problems at the surface level and seeking a quick-fix solution. However, Dewey (1966) explained that learning does not only stem from experience – much more is learnt when thinking about an experience. Reflection facilitates changes (or challenges) to dominant thinking patterns, assumptions and taken-for-granted routines. For this reason, the act of reflection must be a springboard for effective professional development. The final outcome of reflective, socially aware professional development and training is to extend possibilities, to make change happen through a spiral process of observation, evaluation, planning and doing. Reflective dialogue with and openness to others requires a level of trust so that ideas or feedback do not evoke a negative reaction but are rather seen as developmental towards changing practice.

Professional development can create the conditions for genuine learning, where 'genuine' indicates the capability to challenge pre-existing knowledge (Dewey 1933, 1966). Reflection links with and empowers professional development and reinforces the key message of this chapter: that professional development must be owned by the individual in a continuing, constructive dialogue with the environment. Trust in self and others is needed to do this effectively.

CPD and the nature of change in practice: Primary and secondary change

It is important to distinguish between *primary* change and *secondary* change. Primary change is when a professional makes a conscious effort to interpret the environment and to consider what personal impact this can have, has had or will have (Giddens 1995). Secondary change, which does not deny but complements primary change, occurs via external support, guidance and interactions from and with others (Katz 1985; Kotter 1996; Rodd 2013; NDNA 2015). Secondary change cannot happen without primary change. Therefore, CPD, training and purposeful intent to develop or produce stimulating and enabling environments are only effective when engaged with and owned by the one making the change – that is, *the developing professional*. This highlights the professional's unavoidable responsibility towards ownership of professional development that generates change, assuming an active role in working with others.

In the previous chapter, the level of ownership and depth of reflection was discussed. This is critical in creating either accurate or inaccurate connections and realities, with a clear impact on the potential for change to be anchored in practice. Two factors are particularly important in anchoring new approaches in a setting's culture. The first is a conscious attempt to show people how specific behaviours and attitudes have helped improve performance. The second is the need for open dialogue with colleagues to explore why and how outcomes occurred. This is particularly important when change concerns established patterns and professional routines. The following case study captures how Fisher's 'transitional curve' cycle (2012) can be applied to observe the impact and process of change.

Case study 9.1

Janet, teacher in a maintained nursery

Janet works in a maintained nursery within a primary school. She has followed broadly the same daily routine for 20 years. The routine is structured around register time and circle time to introduce the focus of the day and introduce children to adult- or child-led activities. The routine continues with staff taking turns to work inside or outside for 30-minute slots, followed by fruit time and book bag exchange before the end of session story is shared, prior to pick up.

The existing team is well established and have followed Janet's lead for many years. Jo is a newly qualified teacher and the newest member of the nursery team. Janet is friendly and welcoming whilst assertive and adamant that the routine is followed by the new teacher because it is an effective routine that works well. Jo has reflected upon the established routine and suggests that children 'do not really have to sit down at fruit time, registration or book bag times as doing so prevents free-flow and child-initiated play'. The different pedagogical approaches and values begin to impact on team morale and leadership with a clash of proposed pedagogical changes and teaching styles.

Think!

- Identify and discuss the main issue in the case study to consider how training, roles, power and leadership impact on how change is:

  - received;
  - reacted to; and
  - brought about.

- Should Jo introduce new ideas that upset the team and established routine?
- If yes, how could Jo successfully introduce changes? What could Janet and Jo do to compromise and develop ideas?
- If Jo does not achieve a change in routines, consider the potential impact on:

  - team morale;
  - children's learning opportunities;
  - role modelling good practice; and
  - opportunities for reflective dialogue and openness.

Reflecting on daily routines offers opportunity of insight into practice as to why specific routines or rituals exist and to explore who they benefit. It is pertinent here to consider:

- why a routine is in place and who it benefits;
- how a routine is used to maximise learning opportunities; and
- the extent to which a routine enables or limits the way individual needs can be met via flexible provision.

Bolton (2010) and Rodd (2013) recognise that, whilst change can be inherited from the past, it also exists and manifests itself in the present. Therefore, new behaviours and shared values or beliefs brought about by personal development within practice require ownership and active engagement by all (Dewey 1966; Kotter 1996; Siraj and Hallet 2014; Lindon and Trodd 2016). The socialisation of change requires individuals to be flexible thinkers who can de-centre and view limitations or inherited gatekeeping routines, roles and behaviour. This requires deep reflection (Dewey 1933; Peeters and Vandenbroeck 2011). Solomon (1987) describes these levels and layers of reflection connected with professional development and change as a form of social practice requiring colleagues to articulate their ideas, share thoughts and open opportunities for critical discussion so that mutual understanding and frameworks can be constructed to bring about effective and owned change.

Positive practice impact

Change in a setting

These extracts illustrate how reflection, characteristics of quality, taking risks and/or professional interaction interweave and influence change.

'Nothing stays the same: we are always changing'

'*During recent CPD, I have been really positive and excited about developing reflective skills for my own personal growth, but I also aim to develop assertiveness within my professional role. To enable me to be more assertive, I did a SWOT analysis, to consider professional areas of strength and areas needing development, and devised several action plans. I was not ready for the fact that if a strategy to bring about change was once successful, it might not be successful the next time. This was a shock! When the changes I made stopped working, I thought my reflection was not working anymore. I felt very demotivated. This was a very upsetting and a scary outcome of trying to develop my reflective skills.*

'*For example, to begin with, I could deal with staff who were resisting change, but two weeks later the resistance from some of the staff resulted in conflicts. I didn't have a reserve of strategies to deal with this. I became really upset, unconfident and resentful of the concept of reflection (because I thought it wasn't working). After a discussion with my mentor, I realised that this was all part of the reflective cycle. I was planning, doing and reviewing, but it became evident that this was a never-ending cycle. For instance, I reflected on an aspect of practice that needed to be changed; I put a plan into action; I expected everyone to be delighted with the new changes and ideas and felt secure about my impact. However, I hadn't considered further reactions. I hadn't considered what to do about cycles of change and possible resistance or conflict from peers who didn't want or like the change. At this point, again, I really hated the idea of making changes, challenging outcomes and using reflection to develop – it was stressful and tiring. Reflecting further on this example, I realised that when I bring about change, then so will others. Everyone you interact with will communicate, challenge, respond, interact and reflect because one person will impact on everyone else and vice versa.*'

Creating space

'*My manager is a delegator and constantly likes to pass exciting roles and responsibilities my way. What I need to do is to learn how to say "no". I did not realise this was my issue and kept blaming her for her delegation style. Learning to reflect supports me to devise strategies to deal with this style. Now, when I inherit new tasks, I use the following strategy: "If I take on this extra role you are asking me to do, then what would you like to delegate from my current workload to someone else?" When I first used this strategy, I was both scared and excited at the same time. When I used my new strategy, my manager paused for a moment. I felt really empowered. However, I had to change my strategy because the next time we met, my manager used other techniques to delegate her agenda to me. I then used the phrase, "Can I get back to you?", which gave me time to think about issues before responding. These strategies and changes were both positive and empowering because I was becoming more effective in my role and less stressed. I felt in control and able to communicate if workloads were getting too much. Previously, I would get annoyed and despondent. Reflection provides me with the space to think and grow within my role and I can self-assess how I impact on outcomes, aims and the environment rather than be unhappy in my job.'*

Change via reflection

'My time management, whether at home, work or university, was not good. But I was so busy blaming my job, family and degree commitments for a lack of time that nothing changed. I was always late, never meeting deadlines and constantly feeling stressed. I felt like a failure. Reflection enabled me to find space and reasons to look at myself. The only reason I was not coping was because I was not changing or doing anything differently. I was always doing what I always did. I needed to dig deeper to consider what I was or was not doing that could change so as to manage my commitments rather than my commitments managing me. I sharpened my focus and stopped looking at others first and began looking at myself. This was very hard, emotional and challenging because it's easier to reflect on others, isn't it?'

Communities of practice

Communities of practice are shared social learning spaces that evolve during collaboration, reflective dialogue and shared problem-solving discussions and interactions (Lave and Wenger 1991; Wenger 1998). Individuals share good practice and knowledge with each other, promoting social capital and exploring ways to do things better. When change occurs from these exchanges, CPD can enable individuals to see things from a new perspective (Schön 1987). Reflective CPD supports creative interconnections between experiences, knowledge and observations to challenge what has been focussed on and changed. Schön recognised that training needs to be complemented with knowledge and know-how so that training, learning and understanding take reflectors on an intellectual journey (Rodd 2013). Skemp (1989) promoted the importance of the relational thinking patterns and consciousness applied during cognitive growth and professional development. Building on Schön's work, Canning

(2010) argued that depth to relational thinking and reflection is vital because effective reflection occurs through cognitive, psychological and emotional connections. Kline (1999, 2009) asserted that everything we do is connected to others; this is firstly derived from our own thinking and how we treat others.

Reflective task 9.8

Kline's 10 components

Kline developed 10 components within a community of practice that enhance shared and individual learning: being and practice; attention; equality; ease; appreciation; encouragement; feelings; information; diversity; incisive questions; and place.

- Refer to the Positive Practice Impact above. In what ways are Kline's 10 components relevant? How? Why?

Collective dialogical reflection

Sternberg (2003) and Rodd (2013) recognise how early childhood professionals require the freedom to be creative within their reflective practice and self-evaluative processes so they can engage in meaningful change, development and understanding with peers (Anning and Edwards 2006; McFarland et al. 2009; Whalley 2011; Reed and Canning 2012). Reflection and evaluation are two separate processes that early childhood professionals can use to critically analyse their practice with children and families and the implications, potentialities and challenges of utilising CPD to nurture changes in practice. These processes allow early childhood professionals to develop as practitioners and contribute to changing ECEC provision and practice through a greater depth and understanding (McFarland et al. 2009: 505)

Pollard (2002, cited in Paige-Smith and Craft 2008) has identified seven reflective traits required to reflect professionally and self-regulate during professional development:

- active focus;
- continuous cycle of monitoring and evaluation;
- judgements using evidence;
- open-mindedness and perspectives;
- capacity to reframe;
- reflective discussion; and
- adapting external frameworks.

Pollard's list captures the impact that *self-evaluation* and *self-reflection* have on an individual's internal strength and resilience to deal creatively with the outcomes or challenges of – or for – change. Not all reflections need to bring about change. The skill is to know when, if and what to change. Creative imagination and evaluation involve risk-taking: individuals have a strong sense of what is right or wrong. Realities, however, will differ depending on context and interpretation and therefore will need careful consideration when applying the art of reflection. Predictable outcomes can be unpredictably reflected on and understood (Faulkner 1965, cited in Penn 2005). Reflective interpretation and dialogue with peers can offer the opportunity to make sense of personal development, to construct meaningful understanding and have confidence in doing so.

Resilience and change

It is important to recognise that change within practice often presents challenges and it is therefore vital to foster the resilience needed to empower change. Resilience means to recoil and return to a natural state of equilibrium or safety (Goleman 1996). It presents itself in many forms, including: humour, empathy, emotional literacy, determination and inner strength. Emotional resilience applies internal self-assessment and regulation to adapt to new situations when reflection and self-evaluation take place (Goleman 1996). Dunn (1988) identifies how individuals aim to keep a secure equilibrium between thoughts and feelings when applying reflection: through action, interaction and communication with others.

Reflective change combines both the technical expertise of the *professional* and the emotional qualities of the *individual* (Williams 2002). This definition emphasises the importance of resilience, emotional intelligence, active learning, cognitive development and creativity, all of which affect how professionals interact during their developmental learning journey. With any decisive action, thought or reflection, improved outcomes are identified, challenged and developed using combined skills, a reflective mechanism and a cycle that naturally formulates thinking and refines it towards a deeper level of exploration and firmer cognitive understanding (Schön 1987; Roberts 2010).

Dunn (1988) and Goleman (1996) argue that cultural and ecological perspectives and interactions affect our well-being and unique levels of resilience. Rutter (1987) and Roberts (2010) agree, identifying that physical and psychological resilience is internally driven whilst being externally developed during exposure to difficult and sometimes challenging circumstances. Reactions experienced during a reflective critical incident, for example connected to resistance to change, can prevent further challenges being made or can cause immense stress (Dunn 1988; Goleman 1996). Rutter (1987) argues that any challenge needs to be manageable and, if it becomes too difficult, emotional, physical or psychological damage may leave a permanent mark. Multiple mothering is a term used by Rutter, indicating the need for the development of resilience within a caring relationship or team. This facilitates the development of resilience, enabling the individual to embrace change, survive, explore and continue. Such a dyad of reflective dialogue and practice enables all team members and groups to be active participants within reflection and change (Moyles 2006; Penn 2006).

Goleman (1996) and Corrie (2003) suggest that emotional and internal dispositions influence the level of resilience that individuals have during change. The reasons why some people can get over something much quicker than others are difficult to quantify, with factors linked to individual dispositions and internal experiences. Roberts (2010) identifies the four main factors that impact on how resilience is maintained and supported: an individual's standard of living; their temperament; the level of care; and their network of support and friends. The factors that support resilience link closely to the EYFS framework's (DfE 2017) principles and commitments and to a number of other landmark reports and research (DfES 2004; Melhuish et al. 2017). Ongoing professional challenges may represent long-term developmental opportunities when emotional, physical and cognitive needs are fully supported (Goleman 1996; Moyles 2006; Rodd 2013). The support received during periods of change, either from within oneself or from others, leads to the development of resilience to nurture and protect self-esteem, image and confidence (Kline 1999, 2009; Roberts 2010).

Summary

In this chapter, we have explored how reflection and professional development are intertwined and interlinked. Both are pivotal in introducing change into the early years landscape. High-quality provision can only be reached through change and continuous evolvement. Managing change can be a complex journey requiring skills, knowledge and resilience but is critical in impacting on the quality of the enabling environment. Individual resilience is strengthened because the resilient individual does not travel alone. To be resilient is to know when to ask for help from those we care about, trust and know or to know when to offer support to enable and be enabled. Such support can often be a necessary training or change programme or involve a mentor, coach or professional guide. Professional development offers opportunities for early childhood professionals to access essential time and space for personal and professional growth. It enables them to sail on the ocean and look at the island, landscape and horizon from a range of positions.

Further reading

Gabriel, N. (2017) *The Sociology of Early Childhood: Critical perspectives*. London: Sage (Chapters 1, 2 and 4).

Goleman, D. (1996) *Emotional Intelligence*. London: Bloomsbury.

Nutbrown, C. (2006) *Key Concepts in Early Childhood Education and Care*. London: Sage.

Bibliography

Ainsworth, M.D.S. (1968) Object relations, dependency and attachment: A theoretical review of the infant mother relationship, *Child Development*, 40: 969–1025.

Alderson, P. (2000) School students' views on school councils and daily life at school, *Children & Society*, 14:121–134.

Alderson, P. (2004) Ethics, in S. Fraser, V. Lewis, S. Ding, M. Kellett and C. Robinson (eds.) *Doing Research with Children and Young People*. London: Sage.

Alderson, P. (2008) *Young Children's Rights: Exploring beliefs, principles and practice*, 2nd edn. London: Jessica Kingsley.

Alderson, P. (2010) Younger children's individual participation in all matters affecting the child, in B. Percy-Smith and N. Thomas (eds.) *A Handbook of Children and Young People's Participation: Perspectives from theory and practice*. London: Routledge.

Alderson, P. (2012) Rights respecting research: A commentary on the 'right to be properly researched: research with children in a messy, real world', *Children's Geographies*, 10 (2): 233–239.

Alderson, P. and Morrow, V. (2011) *The Ethics of Research with Children and Young People: A practical handbook*. London: Sage.

Alderson, P., Hawthorne, J. and Killen, M. (2005) The participation rights of premature babies, in H. Van Beers, A. Invernizzi and B. Milne (eds.) *Beyond Article 12: Essential readings on children's participation*. Bangkok: Black & White Publications.

Alexander, E. (2010) A successful child: early years practitioners' understandings of quality, *Early Years*, 30 (2): 107–118.

Allen, G. (2011) *Early Intervention: The Next Steps. An independent report to Her Majesty's Government*. London: Cabinet Office. Available at: https://assets. publishing.service.gov.uk/government/uploads/system/uploads/attachment_data/file/284086/early-intervention-next-steps2.pdf (accessed 14 October 2015).

Allen, S. and Gordon, P. (2011) *How Children Learn 4: Thinking on special educational needs and inclusion*. London: MA Education.

Allen, S. and Whalley, M. (2010) *Supporting Pedagogy and Practice in Early Years Settings*. Exeter: Learning Matters.

Allen, T. (2013) *Drivers and Barriers to Raising Achievement: A focus on school and classroom level influences*. London: Institute of Education, University of London. Available at: https://core.ac.uk/download/pdf/18491486.pdf (accessed 16 April 2016).

Almond, D. and Currie, J. (2011) *Human Capital Development Before Age Five*. National Bureau of Economic Research (NBER) Working Paper. Cambridge, MA: NBER.

Alvesson, M. and Sveningsson, M. (2008) *Changing Organizational Culture: Cultural change work in progress.* Abingdon: Routledge.

Andrews, K. (2015) Why Britain's schools are failing to tackle racism, *The Guardian*, 12 August. Available at: www.theguardian.com/commentisfree/2015/aug/12/racism-schools-government-reforms-targets (accessed 13 October 2016).

Anning, A. and Edwards, A. (2006) *Promoting Children's Learning from Birth to Five: Developing the new early years professional.* Maidenhead: Open University Press.

Anning, A. and Edwards, A. (2010) Creating contexts for professional development, in L. Miller, C. Cable and G. Goodliff (eds.) *Supporting Children's Learning in the Early Years*, 2nd edn. London: Routledge.

Appleby, K. and Andrews, M. (2011) Reflective practice is the key to quality improvement, in M. Reed and N. Canning (eds.) *Quality Improvement and Change in the Early Years.* London: Sage.

Archard, D. (1993) *Children: Rights and childhood.* London: Taylor & Francis.

Arnett, J. (1989) Caregivers in day-care centres: Does training matter?, *Journal of Applied Developmental Psychology*, 10 (4): 541–552.

Arnold, C. (2003) *Observing Harry: Child development and learning 0–5.* Maidenhead: Open University Press.

Arnold, C. and the Pen Green Team (2010) *Understanding Schemas and Emotion in Early Childhood.* London: Sage.

Atherton, F. and Nutbrown, C. (2013) *Understanding Schemas and Young Children from Birth to Three.* London: Sage.

Athey, C. (2007) *Extending Thought in Young Children.* London: Sage.

Aubrey, K. and Riley, A. (2016) *Understanding and Using Educational Theories.* London: Sage.

Bain, A. and Barnett, L. (1986) *The Design of a Day Care System in a Nursery Setting for Children Under Five.* Document #2T347. London: Tavistock Institute of Human Relations.

Bandura, A. (1977) *Social Learning Theory.* Englewood Cliffs, NJ: Prentice-Hall.

Banks, S. (2004) *Ethics, Accountability and the Social Professions.* Basingstoke: Palgrave Macmillan.

Baraldi, C. (2014a) Children's participation in communication systems: A theoretical perspective to shape research, in M.N. Warehime (ed.) *Soul of Society: A focus on the lives of children and youth.* Bingley: Emerald Group Publishing.

Baraldi, C. (2014b) Formulations in dialogic facilitation of classroom interactions, *Language and Dialogue*, 4 (2): 234–260.

Baraldi, C. (2015) Promotion of migrant children's epistemic status and authority in early school life, *International Journal of Early Childhood*, 47 (1): 5–25.

Baraldi, C. and Farini, F. (2013) Trust and facilitation in educational interactions, in H. Warming (ed.) *Participation, Citizenship and Trust in Children's Lives.* London: Palgrave Macmillan.

Barnardos (2016) *The Key Person Approach: Positive relationships with children in the early years.* Dublin: Barnardos. Available at: http://www.donegalchildcare.com/wp-content/uploads/2015/08/Barnardos_KeyPersonBooklet_final-draft.pdf (accessed 20 November 2018).

Barnes, C., Archer, D.T., Hogg, B., Bush, M. and Bradley, P.S. (2014) The evolution of physical and technical performance parameters in the English Premier League, *International Journal of Sports Medicine*, 35: 1095–1100.

Barnes, C., Boutron, I., Gireaudeau, B., Porcher, R., Altmann, D.G. and Ravaud, P. (2015) Impact on an online writing aid tool for writing a randomized trial report: The COBWEB (Consort-based Web tool) randomized controlled trial, *BMC Medicine*, 13 (1): 221. Available at: https://doi.org/10.1186/s12916-015-0460-y.

Barnes, J. (2015) *Cross-Curricular Learning 3–14*, 3rd edn. London: Sage.

Bath, C. (2011) Participatory concepts of multidisciplinary/professional working on an Early Childhood Studies degree course in the UK, *Early Years*, 31 (2): 181–192.

Ben-Ari, E. (1996) From mothering to othering: organization, culture, and nap time in a Japanese day-care center, *Ethos*, 24 (1): 136–164.

Bilton, H. (2010) *Playing Outside*. Abingdon: Routledge.

Bilton, H., Bento, G. and Dias, G. (2016) *Taking the First Steps Outside: Under threes learning and developing in the natural environment*. Abingdon: Routledge.

Blackwell, S. and Pound, L. (2011) Forest Schools in the early years, in L. Miller and L. Pound (eds.) *Theories and Approaches to Learning in the Early Years*. London: Sage.

Blades, R., Greene, V., Wallace, E., Loveless, L. and Mason, P. (2014) *Implementation Study: Integrated review at 2–2½ years – Integrating the Early Years Foundation Stage Progress Check and the Healthy Child Programme Health and Development Review*. Research Report DFE-RR350. London: Department for Education. Available at: www.gov.uk/government/publications/integrated-review-at-age-2-implementation-study (accessed 20 February 2016).

Blanden, J., Del Bono, E., Hansen, K., McNally, S. and Rabe, B. (2014) *Evaluating a Demand-Side Approach to Expanding Free Pre-School Education*. Colchester: Institute for Social and Economic Research.

Bohm, D. (1996) *On Dialogue*. Abingdon: Routledge.

Bolton, G. (2010) *Reflective Practice: Writing and professional development*. London: Sage.

Borgia, E.T. and Schuler, D. (1996) *Action Research in Early Childhood Education*. Available at: www.ericdigests.org/1997-2/action.htm (accessed 28 July 2016).

Borkett, P. (2019) Inclusion and participation, in D. Fitzgerald and H. Maconochie (eds.) *Early Childhood Studies: A student's guide*. London: Sage.

Bottle, G. (2007) Research in the early years, in A. Nurse (ed.) *The New Early Years Professional: Dilemmas and debates*. London: David Fulton.

Bowlby, J. (1953) *Child Care and the Growth of Love*. London: Pelican/Penguin.

Bradford, H. (2012) *The Wellbeing of Children Under Three*. Abingdon: Routledge.

Brodie, K. (2018) *The Holistic Care and Development of Children from Birth to Three: An essential guide for students and practitioners*. Abingdon: Routledge.

Brock, A. (2011) Perspectives on professionalism, in A. Brock and C. Rankin (eds.) *Professionalism in the Early Years Interdisciplinary Team: Supporting young children and their families*. London: Continuum.

Brock, A. (2012) Building a model of professionalism from practitioners' perspectives, *Journal of Early Childhood Research*, 11 (1): 27–45.

Brock, A. (2015) What does professionalism mean for me?, in A. Brock (ed.) *The Early Years Reflective Practice Handbook*. Abingdon: Routledge.

Brock, A. and Thornton, T. (2015) Capable, confident children: A reception class teacher's pedagogical reflections, in A. Brock (ed.) *The Early Years Reflective Practice Handbook*. Abingdon: Routledge.

Bronfenbrenner, U. (1979) *The Ecology of Human Development*. Cambridge, MA: Harvard University Press.

Bronfenbrenner, U. (1986) Ecology of the family as a context for human development, *American Psychologist*, 32: 513–531.

Brooker, L. (2008) *Supporting Transitions in the Early Years*. Maidenhead: Open University Press.

Brooker, L. (2010) Constructing the triangle of care: Power and professionalisation in practitioner/parent relationships, *British Journal of Educational Studies*, 58 (2): 181–196.

Bruce, T. (2006) *Early Childhood*. London: Sage.

Bruce, T. (2012) *Early Childhood Practice*. London: Sage.

Brymer, E., Davids, K. and Mallabon, L. (2014) Understanding the psychological health and well-being benefits of physical activity in nature: an ecological dynamics analysis, *Ecopsychology*, 6 (3): 189–197.

Burdette, H.L. and Whitaker, R.C. (2005) Looking beyond fitness and fatness to attention, affiliation, and affect, *Archives of Pediatrics and Adolescent Medicine*, 159 (1): 46–50.

Cable, C. and Miller, L. (2011) A new professionalism, in L. Miller and C. Cable (eds.) *Professionalization, Leadership and Management in the Early Years*. London: Sage.

Callanan, M., Anderson, M., Haywood, S., Hudson, R. and Speight, S. (2017) *Study of Early Education and Development: Good practice in early education*. Research Report. London: Department for Education. Available at: www.foundation-years.org.uk/files/2017/01/SEED-Good-Practice-in-Early-Education.pdf (accessed 14 March 2017).

Campbell-Barr, V. and Leeson, C. (2016) *Quality and Leadership in the Early Years: Research, theory and practice*. London: Sage.

Canning, N. (2010) *Reflective Practice in the Early Years*. London: Sage.

Canning, N. (2014) *Play and Practice in the Early Years Foundation Stage*. Maidenhead: Open University Press.

Carpenter, J. and Dickinson, H. (2008) *Interprofessional Education and Training*. Bristol: Policy Press.

Carr, M. and Lee, W. (2012) *Learning Stories: Constructing learner identities in early education*. London: Sage.

Cartmel, J., Macfarlane, K. and Nolan, A. (2013) Looking to the future: Producing transdisciplinary professionals for leadership in early childhood settings, *Early Years*, 33 (4): 398–412.

Centre for Excellence and Outcomes (C4EO) (2010) *Grasping the Nettle: Early intervention for children, families and communities*. London: C4EO.

Chalke, J. (2015) *Negotiating and developing professionalism: Early years practitioners' stories of professionalism*. Doctoral thesis, University of Sheffield.

Cherrington, S. (2018) Early childhood teachers' thinking and reflection: A model of current practice in New Zealand, *Early Years*, 38 (3): 316–332.

Children's Workforce Development Council (CWDC) (2006) *Early Years Professional Prospectus*. Leeds: CWDC.

Clark, A. and Moss, P. (2011) *Listening to Young Children: The Mosaic approach*, 2nd edn. London: National Children's Bureau for the Joseph Rowntree Foundation.

Clark, A., McQuail, S. and Moss, P. (2003) *Exploring the Field of Listening to and Consulting with Young Children*. Nottingham: DfES Publications.

Clark, A., Moss, P. and Kjörholt, A.T. (2005) *Beyond Listening: Children's perspectives on early childhood services*. Bristol: Policy Press.

Clark, M. and Waller, T. (2007) *Early Childhood Education and Care: Policy and practice*. London: Sage.

Colwell, J. (2015) *Reflective Teaching in Early Education*. London: Bloomsbury.

Conkbayir, M. and Pascal, C. (2014) *Early Childhood Theories and Contemporary Issues*. London: Bloomsbury.

Constable, K. (2014) *Bringing the Forest School Approach to Your Early Years Practice*. London: Taylor & Francis.

Corrie, C. (2003) *Becoming Emotionally Intelligent*. Stafford: Network Educational Press.

Council for Disabled Children (2015) *SEN and Disability in the Early Years: A toolkit*. Available at: https://councilfordisabledchildren.org.uk/sites/default/files/field/attachemnt/early-years-toolkit-merged.pdf.

Craft, A. (2011) Creativity and early years settings, in A. Paige-Smith and A. Craft (eds.) *Developing Reflective Practice in the Early Years*, 2nd edn. Buckingham: Open University Press.

Crown, H. (2016) Providers cut EYT courses due to low demand, *Nursery World*, 2 May. Available at: www.nurseryworld.co.uk/nursery-world/news/1157040/providers-cut-eyt-courses-due-to-low-demand (accessed 13 August 2016).

Dahlberg, G. and Moss, P. (2005) *Ethics and Politics in Early Childhood Education*. London: Routledge.

Dahlberg, G., Moss, P. and Pence, A. (1999) *Beyond Quality in Early Childhood Education and Care*. London: Falmer Press.

Dahlberg, G., Moss, P. and Pence, A. (2006) *Beyond Quality in Early Childhood Education and Care*, 2nd edn. London: Falmer Press.

Dahlberg, G., Moss, P. and Pence, A. (2013) *Beyond Quality in Early Childhood Education and Care*, 3rd edn. London: Routledge.

Dalli, C. (2008) Pedagogy, knowledge and collaboration: Towards a ground-up perspective on professionalism, *European Early Childhood Education Research Journal*, 16 (2): 171–185.

Dalli, C. (2011) Pedagogy, knowledge and collaboration: Towards a ground-up perspective on professionalism, in C. Dalli and M. Urban (eds.) *Professionalism in Early Childhood Education and Care: International perspectives*. London: Routledge.

Dalli, C. (2014) *Quality for Babies and Toddlers in Early Years Settings*. TACTYC Occasional Paper #4. Available at: tactyc.org.uk/occasional–papers (accessed 20 December 2014).

Dalli, C. (2016) *Love, care and professionalism: Reflections on why we must engage emotionally in infant and toddler pedagogy*. Keynote speech given at the 7th Annual Baby Room Conference, Canterbury Christ Church University, 15 April.

Dalli, C. and Urban, M. (2011) Introduction, in C. Dalli and M. Urban (eds.) *Professionalism in Early Childhood Education and Care: International perspectives*. London: Routledge.

Degotardi, S. and Pearson, E. (2014) *The Relationship Worlds of Infants and Toddlers*. Maidenhead: Open University Press.

Department for Children, Schools and Families (DCSF) (2007) *Children's Plan – Building Brighter Futures*. Norwich: HMSO.

Department for Children, Schools and Families (DCSF) (2008a) *Mark Making Matters: Young children making meaning in all areas of learning and development*. Nottingham: DCSF.

Department for Children, Schools and Families (DCSF) (2008b) *Statutory Framework for the Early Years Foundation Stage*. Nottingham: DCSF.

Department for Education (DfE) (2010) *Review of Early Years Foundation Stage*. London: DfE.

Department for Education (DfE) (2011a) *The Early Years: Foundations for life, health and learning – An independent report on the Early Years Foundation Stage to Her Majesty's Government*. London: Department for Education. Available at: https://www.gov.uk/government/publications/the-early-years-foundations-for-life-health-and-learning-an-independent-report-on-the-early-years-foundation-stage-to-her-majestys-government (accessed 18 June 2019).

Department for Education (DfE) (2011b) *Teachers' Standards*. London: DfE.

Department for Education (DfE) (2013a) *More Great Childcare: Raising quality and giving parents more choice*. London: DfE. Available at: www.gov.uk/government/uploads/system/uploads/attachment_data/file/219660/More_20Great_20 Childcare_20v2.pdf (accessed 20 February 2016).

Department for Education (DfE) (2013b) *Teachers' Standards (Early Years)*. London: DfE. Available at: https://www.gov.uk/government/publications/early-years-teachers-standards (accessed 18 June 2019).

Department for Education (DfE) (2014) *Early Years: Guide to the 0 to 25 SEND Code of Practice*. London: DfE. Available at: https://assets.publishing.service.gov.uk/government/uploads/system/uploads/attachment_data/file/350685/Early_Years_Guide_to_SEND_Code_of_Practice_-_02Sept14.pdf (accessed 13 November 2017).

Department for Education (DfE) (2016) *Initial Teacher Training Criteria and Supporting Advice*. London: DfE.

Department for Education (DfE) (2017) *Statutory Framework for the Early Years Foundation Stage: Setting the standards for learning, development and care for children from birth to five*. London: DfE. Available at: www.foundation-years.org.uk/files/2017/03/EYFS_STATUTORY_FRAMEWORK_2017.pdf (accessed 15 March 2017).

Department for Education (DfE) (2018a) *Working Together to Safeguard Children: A guide to inter-agency working to safeguard and promote the welfare of children*. London: DfE. Available at: https://assets.publishing.service.gov.uk/government/uploads/system/uploads/attachment_data/file/729914/Working_Together_to_Safeguard_Children-2018.pdf (accessed 24 August 2018).

Department for Education (DfE) (2018b) *Keeping Children Safe in Education: Statutory guidance for schools and colleges*. London: DfE. Available at: https://assets.publishing.service.gov.uk/government/uploads/system/uploads/attachment_data/file/741314/Keeping_Children_Safe_in_Education__3_September_2018_14.09.18.pdf (accessed 30 September 2018).

Department for Education (DfE) (2019) *Assessment Framework: Reception baseline assessment*. London: DfE. Available at: https://www.gov.uk/government/publications/reception-baseline-assessment-framework (accessed 16 March 2019).

Department for Education/ National College for Teaching and Leadership (DfE/NCTL) (2018) *Guidance – Early Years Initial Teacher Training: Accredited providers*. London: DfE. Available at: https://www.gov.uk/government/publications/early-years-initial-teacher-training-itt-providers-and-school-direct-early-years-lead-organisations/early-years-initial-teacher-training-itt-providers-and-school-direct-lead-organisations (accessed 29 January 2019).

Department for Education and Skills (DfES) (2001) *Early Years Sector Endorsed Foundation Degree: Statement of requirement*. London: HMSO.

Department for Education and Skills (DfES) (2003) *Every Child Matters: Green Paper*. Norwich: TSO.

Department for Education and Skills (DfES) (2004) *Every Child Matters: Change for children*. Nottingham: DfES Publications.

Department for Education and Skills (DfES) (2006a) *Children's Workforce Strategy: A strategy to build a world-class workforce for children, young people and families. The government's response to the consultation*. Nottingham: DfES Publications.

Department for Education and Skills (DfES) (2006b) *Childcare Act 2006*. London: HMSO.

Department for Education and Skills (DfES) (2006c) *Learning Outside the Classroom: Manifesto*. London: DfES. Available at: http://www.lotc.org.uk/wp-content/uploads/2011/03/G1.-LOtC-Manifesto.pdf (accessed 18 June 2019).

Department for Education and Science (DES) (1990) *The Rumbold Report: Starting with quality*. London: DES.

Department of Education Northern Ireland (2013) *Learning to Learn. A framework for early years education and learning.* Available at: www.education-ni.gov.uk/sites/default/files/publications/de/a-framework-for-ey-education-and-learning-2013.pdf (accessed 21 August 2018).

Department of Health and Social Care (DHSC) (2009) *Healthy Child Programme: Pregnancy and the first 5 years of life.* London: DHSC. Available at: https://www.gov.uk/government/publications/healthy-child-programme-pregnancy-and-the-first-5-years-of-life (accessed 18 June 2019).

Desforges, C. with Abouchaar, A. (2003) *The Impact of Parental Involvement, Parental Support and Family Education on Pupil Achievements and Adjustment: A literature review.* London: Department for Education.

Devarakonda, C. (2013) *Diversity and Inclusion in Early Childhood.* London: Sage.

Dewey, J. (1933) *How We Think: A restatement of the relation of reflective thinking to the educative process.* New York: D.C. Heath.

Dewey, J. (1966) *Democracy and Education.* New York: Free Press.

Dickins, M. (2002) All about … anti-discriminatory practice, *Nursery World*, 3 January: 15–22.

Douglass, A. and Gittell, J. (2012) Transforming professionalism: relational bureaucracy and parent–teacher partnerships in child care settings, *Journal of Early Childhood Research*, 10 (3): 267–281.

Dowling, M. (2005) *Young Children's Personal, Social and Emotional Development*, 2nd edn. London: Paul Chapman.

Duhn, I., Fleer, M. and Harrison, L. (2016) Supporting multidisciplinary networks through relationality and a critical sense of belonging: Three 'gardening tools' and the Relational Agency Framework, *International Journal of Early Years Education*, 24 (3): 378–391.

Dunn, J. (1988) *The Beginnings of Social Understanding.* Oxford: Basil Blackwell.

Dunn, J. (1993) *Young Children's Close Relationships.* London: Sage.

Early Education (2011) *Code of Ethics.* London: British Association for Early Childhood Education. Available at: https://www.early-education.org.uk/sites/default/files/Code%20of%20Ethics.pdf (accessed 31 May 2017).

Early Education (2012) *Development Matters in the Early Years Foundation Stage (EYFS).* London: British Association for Early Childhood Education. Available at: www.foundationyears.org.uk/files/2012/03/Development-Matters-FINAL-PRINT-AMENDED.pdf (accessed 12 February 2016).

Early Education (2016) *Learning Together About Learning.* Project Report. Available at: https://www.early-education.org.uk/sites/default/files/EYPP%20final%20report%20May%202016.pdf (accessed 3 May 2017).

Early Intervention Foundation (EIF) (2018) *Teaching, Pedagogy and Practice in Early Years Childcare: An evidence review.* London: EIF. Available at: https://www.eif.org.uk/files/pdf/teaching-pedagogy-and-practice-in-early-years-childcare.pdf (accessed 29 September 2018).

Easton, C. and Gee, G. (2012) *Early Intervention: Informing local practice.* LGA Research Report. Slough: NFER.

Edgington, M. (2004) *The Foundation Stage Teacher in Action: Teaching 3, 4 and 5 year olds*, 4th edn. London: Sage.

Education Endowment Foundation (EEF) (2018) *EEF Early Years Toolkit*. Available at: https://educationendowmentfoundation.org.uk/evidence-summaries/early-years-toolkit/ (accessed 26 November 2018).

Education and Skills Funding Agency (ESFA) (2018) *Early Years National Funding Formula: Operational guide*. Available at: https://www.gov.uk/government/publications/early-years-national-funding-formula-allocations-and-guidance (accessed 30 August 2018).

Edwards, A. (2010) *Being an Expert Professional Practitioner: The relational turn in expertise*. London: Springer.

Edwards, A. and Daniels, H. (2012) The knowledge that matters in professional practices, *Journal of Education and Work*, 25 (1): 39–58.

Edwards, C., Gandini, L. and Forman, G.E. (eds.) (2011) *The Hundred Languages of Children: The Reggio Emilia Experience in Transformation*. Santa Barbara, CA: Greenwood Press.

Edwards, M. (2019) Childhood in a global context, in D. Fitzgerald and H. Maconochie (eds.) *Early Childhood Studies: A student's guide*. London: Sage.

Edwards, S., Skouteris, H., Cutter-Mackenzie, A., Rutherford, L., O'Conner, M., Mantilla, A. et al. (2016) Young children learning about well-being and environmental education in the early years: A funds of knowledge approach, *Early Years*, 36 (1): 33–50.

Einarsdóttir, J. (2014) Children's perspectives on play, in L. Brooker, M. Blaise and S. Edwards (eds.) *The SAGE Handbook of Play and Learning in Early Childhood*. London: Sage.

Eisenstadt, N. (2002) Sure Start: Key principles and ethos, *Child: Care, Health and Development*, 28 (1): 2–3.

Elfer, P. and Dearnley, K. (2007) Nurseries and emotional well-being: Evaluating an emotionally containing model of professional development, *Early Years*, 27 (3): 267–279.

Elfer, P., Goldschmied, E. and Selleck, D.Y. (2012) *Key Persons in the Early Years: Building relationships for quality provision in early years settings and primary schools*, 2nd edn. Abingdon: Routledge.

Engdahl, I. (2015) Early childhood education for sustainability: The OMEP World Project, *International Journal of Early Childhood*, 47 (3): 347–366.

Epstein, A., Johnson, S. and Lafferty, P. (2011) The High Scope Approach, in L. Miller and L. Pound (eds.) *Theories and Approaches to Learning in the Early Years*. London: Sage.

Eraut, M. (1994) *Developing Professional Knowledge and Competence*. London: Routledge.

Eraut, M. (2008) Knowledge creation and knowledge use in professional context, *Studies in Higher Education*, 10 (2): 117–133.

Erikson, E.H. (1950) *Childhood and Society*. London: Imago.

European Commission (2011) *Early Childhood Education and Care: Providing all our children with the best start for the world of tomorrow*. Available at: eur-lex.

europa.eu/LexUriServ/LexUriServ.do?uri=COM:2011:0066:FIN:EN:PDF (accessed 13 July 2016).

Evans, K. (2016) Beyond a logic of quality: Opening space for material-discursive practices of 'readiness' in early years education, *Contemporary Issues in Early Childhood*, 17 (1): 65–77.

Farson, R.E. (1974) *Birthrights: A Bill of Rights for children*. New York: Macmillan.

Faulkner, W. (1965) *Uncle Willy and Other Stories*. London: Penguin.

Felstead, A., Fuller, A., Jewson, N. and Unwin, L. (2009) *Improving Working as Learning*. London: Routledge.

Fenech, M. (2011) An analysis of the conceptualisation of 'quality' in early childhood education and care empirical research: 'blind spots' as foci for future research, *Contemporary Issues in Early Childhood*, 12 (2): 102–117.

Fenech, M., Sumison, J. and Goodfellow, J. (2006) The regulatory environment in long day care: A 'double-edged sword' for early childhood professional practice, *Australian Journal of Early Childhood*, 31 (3): 49–58.

Field, F. (2010) *The Foundation Years: Preventing poor children becoming poor adults. The report of the Independent Review on Poverty and Life Chances*. London: Cabinet Office. Available at: http://www.bristol.ac.uk/poverty/downloads/keyofficialdocuments/Field%20Review%20poverty-report.pdf (accessed 15 March 2016).

Fisher, J. (2012) John Fisher Personal Transition Curve concept and content 2000–13; Fisher & Savage Personal Construct Psychology article 1999; edit and contextual material Alan Chapman 2000–2013. Available at: https://www.businessballs.com/change-management/personal-change-stages-john-fisher/.

Fitzgerald, D. and Kay, J. (2016) *Understanding Early Years Policy*, 4th edn. London: Sage.

Flavell, J.H. (1970) Developmental studies of mediated memory, in H.W. Reese and L.P. Lipsitt (eds.) *Advances in Child Development*, Vol. 5. New York: Academic Press.

Flavell, J.H. (1979) Metacognition and cognitive monitoring, *American Psychologist*, 34 (10): 906–911.

Forest School Association (2018) Available at: https://www.forestschoolassociation.org/what-is-forest-school/ (accessed 9 April 2018).

Fortin, J. (2003) *Children's Rights and the Developing Law*. Cambridge: Cambridge University Press.

Fox, N.A. and Rutter, M. (2010) Introduction to the special section on the effects of early experience on development, *Child Development*, 81 (1): 23–27.

Freeman, M. (1983) *The Rights and Wrongs of Children*. London: Francis Pinter.

Freeman, M. (1998) The sociology of childhood and children's rights, *International Journal of Children's Rights*, 6 (4): 433–444.

Freeman, M. (2007) Why it remains important to take children's rights seriously, *International Journal of Children's Rights*, 15 (1): 5–23.

Freeman, M. (2011) *Human Rights: An interdisciplinary approach*. Cambridge: Polity Press.

Freire, P. (1985) *The Politics of Education: Culture, power and liberation*. South Hadley, MA: Bergin & Garvey.

Freire, P. (1998) *Pedagogy of Freedom: Ethics, democracy, and civic courage.* New York: Rowman & Littlefield.

Freire, P. (2004) *Pedagogy and Hope: Reliving pedagogy of the oppressed.* London: Continuum.

Friedland, H. (2007) Navigating through narratives of despair: Making space for the Cree reasonable person in the Canadian justice system, *University of New Brunswick Law Journal*, 67 (1): 269–312.

Friedson, E. (2001) *Professionalism: The third logic.* Cambridge: Polity Press.

Fullan, M. (2016) *Indelible Leadership: Always leave them learning.* Thousand Oaks, CA: Corwin Press.

Gabriel, N. (2017) *The Sociology of Early Childhood: Critical perspectives.* London: Sage.

Gambaro, L., Stewart, K. and Waldfogel, J. (2015) A question of quality: Do children from disadvantaged backgrounds receive lower quality early childhood education and care?, *British Educational Research Journal*, 41 (4): 553–574.

Gardner, H. (1983) *Changing Minds: The art and science of changing our own and other people's minds.* Boston, MA: Harvard Business School Press.

Gardner, H. (1993) *Multiple Intelligences.* New York: Basic Books.

Garner, M., Wagner, C. and Kawulick, B. (2009) *Teaching Research Methods in the Social Sciences.* Abingdon: Routledge.

Gaunt, C. (2018) Government scraps early years workforce strategy's graduate plans, *Nursery World*, 19 July. Available at: https://www.nurseryworld.co.uk/nursery-world/news/1165036/government-scraps-early-years-workforce-strategys-graduate-plans (accessed 25 January 2019).

Georgeson, J., Campbell-Barr, V., Mathers, S., Boag-Munroe, G., Parker-Rees, R. and Caruso, F. (2014) *Two-Year-Olds in England: An exploratory study.* Available at: tactyc.org.uk/wp-content/uploads/2014/11/TACTYC_2_year_olds_Report_2014.pdf (accessed 29 December 2016).

Gibb, J., Jelicic, H., La Valle, I., Gowland, S., Kinsella, R., Jessiman, P. et al. (2011) *Rolling Out Free Education for Disadvantaged Two Year Olds: An implementation study for local authorities and providers.* Research Report DFE-RR131. London: Department for Education. Available at: www.natcen.ac.uk/media/26401/rolling-out-free-early-education.pdf (accessed 30 March 2016).

Giddens, A. (1990) *The Consequences of Modernity.* Stanford, CA: Stanford University Press.

Giddens, A. (1995) *Surveillance and the Capitalist State: A contemporary critique of historical materialism*, 2nd edn. Basingstoke: Macmillan.

Goldschmied, E. and Jackson, S. (1994) *People Under Three: Young children in day care.* Abingdon: Routledge.

Goldschmied, E. and Jackson, S. (2004) *People Under Three: Young children in day care*, 2nd edn. Abingdon: Routledge.

Goleman, D. (1996) *Emotional Intelligence.* London: Bloomsbury.

Goodfellow, J. (2003) Practical wisdom in professional practice: The person in the process, *Contemporary Issues in Early Childhood*, 4 (1): 48–63.

Goouch, K. and Powell, S. (2013) *The Baby Room*. Maidenhead: Open University Press.

Goulden, C. (2010) *Cycles of Poverty, Unemployment and Low Pay*. York: Joseph Rowntree Foundation. Available at: www.jrf.org.uk/publications/cycles-unemployment-low-pay (accessed 30 March 2016).

Gov.UK (2013) *Equality Act 2010: Guidance*. Available at: www.gov.uk/equality-act-2010-guidance (accessed 13 November 2016).

Gov.UK (2014) *Landmark Children and Families Act 2014*. Available at: https://www.gov.uk/government/news/landmark-children-and-families-act-2014-gains-royal-assent (accessed 13 March 2016).

Gov.UK (2015) *Parents to Get Complete Picture of Child Development*. Available at: https://www.gov.uk/government/news/parents-to-get-complete-picture-of-child-development (accessed 30 August 2018).

Gov.UK (2018) *Free Education and Care for 2-Year-Olds*. Available at: https://www.gov.uk/help-with-childcare-costs/free-childcare-2-year-olds (accessed 13 April 2018).

Gregoriadis, A., Papandreou, M. and Birbili, M. (2018) Continuing professional development in the Greek early childhood education system, *Early Years*, 38 (3): 271–285.

Grenier, J. (2011) *Child Care and Early Years Education: The ideas of Susan Isaacs, Melanie Klein and Anna Freud*. Available at: http://juliangrenier.blogspot.com/2011/03/child-care-and-early-years-education.html (accessed 31 March 2016).

Grenier, J. (2013) *When Is a Teacher Not a Teacher*. Available at: http://juliangrenier.blogspot.com/2013/03/when-is-teacher-not-teacher.html (accessed 14 January 2017).

Hadfield, M., Jopling, M., Needham, M., Waller, T., Coleyshaw, L., Emira, M. et al. (2012) *Longitudinal Study of Early Years Professional Status: An exploration of progress, leadership and impact*. Final Report RR DFE-RR239c. London: Department for Education. Available at: www.gov.uk/government/uploads/system/uploads/attachment_data/file/183418/DfE-RR239c_report.pdf (accessed 3 November 2016).

Hakim, L. and Dalli, C. (2018) 'To be professional is a never-ending journey': Indonesian early childhood practitioners' views about the attitudes and behaviours of a professional teacher, *Early Years*, 38 (3): 244–257.

Hallet, E. (2016) *Early Years Practice for Educators and Teachers*. London: Sage.

Handley, G. (2005) Children's rights to participation, in T. Waller (ed.) *Early Childhood: A multi-disciplinary approach*. London: Paul Chapman.

Harms, T., Jacobs, E. and White, D. (1996) *School Age Care Environment Rating Scale*. New York: Teachers College Press.

Harms, T., Cryer, D. and Clifford, R.M. (2003) *Infant/Toddler Environment Rating Scale – Revised edition (ITERS-R)*. New York: Teachers College Press.

Harms, T., Clifford, R.M. and Cryer, D. (2005) *Early Childhood Environment Rating Scale – Revised edition*. New York: Teachers College Press.

Harms, T., Cryer, D. and Clifford, R.M. (2007) *Family Child Care Rating Scale: Revised edition*. New York: Teachers College Press.

Hayes, N. and Filipović, K. (2017) Nurturing 'buds of development': From outcomes to opportunities in early childhood practice, *International Journal of Early Years Education*, 26 (3): 220–232.

Heckman, J.J. (2011) The economics of inequality: The value of early childhood education, *American Educator*, 35 (1): 34–47.

Hedges, H. (2012) Teachers' funds of knowledge: A challenge to evidence based practice, *Teachers and Teaching: Theory and Practice*, 18 (1): 7–24.

Helsby, G. (1996) Professionalism in English secondary schools, *Journal of Education for Teaching*, 22 (2): 135–148.

HM Treasury and Department for Education and Skills (2007) *Aiming High for Children: Supporting families*. London: TSO.

Hevey, D. (2013) *Different but Equal*. Available at: https://www.newvisionsforeducation.org.uk/about-the-group/home/2013/03/28/different-but-equal/ (accessed 14 November 2016).

Hillman, J. and Williams, T. (2015) *Early Years Education and Care: Lessons from evidence and future priorities*. London: The Nuffield Foundation.

Hinde, R.A. (1979) *Towards Understanding Relationships*. London: Academic Press.

Hiscott, D. (2013) Accessing support through outreach, in L. Trodd (ed.) *Transitions in the Early Years: Working with children and families*. London: Sage.

Hochschild, A.R. (1983) *The Managed Heart: The commercialization of feeling*. Berkeley, CA: University of California Press.

Hodgman, L. (2015) *Enabling Environments in the Early Years: Making provision for high quality and challenging learning experiences in early years settings*. Salisbury: Practical Pre-School Books.

Holt, J. (1974) *Escape from Childhood*. New York: Holt Associates.

Hopkins, D. (2000a) Powerful learning, powerful teaching and powerful schools, *Journal of Educational Change*, 1 (2): 135–154.

Hopkins, D. (2001) *School Improvement for Real*. London: Routledge-Falmer.

Houston, G. (2015) Dealing with racist incidents, in A. Brock (ed.) *The Early Years Reflective Practice Handbook*. Abingdon: Routledge.

Howard, S., Nicholson, N. and Williamson, C. (2016) Assessment, in I. Palaiologou (ed.) *The Early Years Foundation Stage: Theory and practice*. London: Sage.

Hoyle, E. and John, P.D. (1995) *Professional Knowledge and Professional Practice*. London: Cassell.

Hutchin, V. (2013) Meeting individual needs, in T. Bruce (ed.) *Early Childhood: A guide for students*. London: Sage.

Jackson, S. and Forbes, R. (2014) *People Under Three: Play, work and learning in a childcare setting*. Abingdon: Routledge.

James, A. (2007) Giving voice to children's voices: Practices and problems, pitfalls and potentials, *American Anthropologist*, 109 (2): 261–272.

James, A. (2009) Agency, in J. Qvortrup, G. Valentine, W. Corsaro and M.S. Honig (eds.) *The Palgrave Handbook of Childhood Studies*. Basingstoke: Palgrave Macmillan.

James, A. and James, A.L. (2004) *Constructing Childhood. Theory, policy and social practice.* Basingstoke: Palgrave Macmillan.

James, A. and James, A.L. (2008) *Key Concepts in Childhood Studies.* London: Sage.

James, A. and Prout, A. (eds.) (1990) *Constructing and Reconstructing Childhood.* London: Falmer Press.

James, A., Jenks, C. and Prout, A. (1998) *Theorizing Childhood.* Cambridge: Polity Press.

Jelphs, K. and Dickinson, H. (2008) *Working in Teams.* Bristol: Policy Press.

Jones, P. (2011) Participation and provision across disciplines: Child rights for, and by, children, in P. Jones and G. Walker (eds.) *Children's Rights in Practice.* London: Sage.

Jones, P. and Walker, G. (eds.) (2011) *Children's Rights in Practice.* London: Sage.

Jones, P. and Welch, S. (2010) *Rethinking Children's Rights: Attitudes in contemporary society.* London: Continuum.

Jones, P. and Welch, S. (2013) *Rethinking Children's Rights.* London: Bloomsbury Academic.

Johnson, J. (2010) *Positive and Trusting Relationships with Children in Early Years Settings.* Exeter: Learning Matters.

Joyce, R. (2012) *Outdoor Learning: Past and present.* Maidenhead: Open University Press.

Katz, L.G. (1985) Dispositions in early childhood education, *ERIC/EECE Bulletin,* 18 (2): 1–3.

Katz, L.G. (1993) Multiple perspectives on the quality of early childhood programmes, *European Early Childhood Education Research Journal,* 1 (2): 5–9.

Kearney, N. (1987) The historical background, in *Social Work and Social Work Training in Ireland: Yesterday and Tomorrow,* Occasional Paper Series #1. Dublin: Department of Social Studies, Trinity College.

Kelly, G.A. (1955/1991) *The Psychology of Personal Constructs.* London: Routledge.

Kline, N. (1999) *Time to Think: Listening to ignite the human mind.* London: Ward Lock.

Kline, N. (2009) *More Time to Think: A way of being in the world.* London: Ward Lock.

Knight, S. (2009) *Forest School and Outdoor Learning in the Early Years.* London: Sage.

Knight, S. (ed.) (2012) *Forest School for All.* London: Sage.

Knight, S. (2013) *Forest School and Outdoor Learning in the Early Years,* 2nd edn. London: Sage.

Knight, T., Tennant, R., Dillon, L. and Weddell, E. (2006) *Evaluating the Early Years Sector Endorsed Foundation Degree: A qualitative study of students' views and experiences.* Research Report RR751. London: Department for Education and Skills. Available at: https://webarchive.nationalarchives.gov.uk/20130323021502/https://www.education.gov.uk/publications/eOrderingDownload/RR751.pdf (accessed 23 April 2017).

Kolb, D.A. (1981) Learning styles and disciplinary differences, in A. Chickering (ed.) *The Modern American College.* San Francisco, CA: Jossey-Bass.

Kolb, D.A. (1984) *Experiential Learning: Experience as the source of learning and development.* Englewood Cliffs, NJ: Prentice-Hall.

Kolb, D., Rubin, I.M. and McIntyre, J. (eds.) (1984) *Organizational Psychology: Readings on human behaviour in organizations*, 4th edn. Englewood Cliffs, NJ: Prentice-Hall.

Kolb, D.A. (2014) *Experiential Learning: Experience as the source of learning and development*, 2nd edn. Upper Saddle River, NJ: Pearson FT Press.

Kotter, J.P. (1990) What leaders really do, *Harvard Business Review*, 68 (3): 101–111.

Kotter, J.P. (1995) Leading change: Why transformation efforts fail, *Harvard Business Review*, 73 (2): 59–67.

Kotter, J.P. (1996) *Leading Change.* Cambridge, MA: Harvard Business School Press.

Kuhn, T.S. (1970) *The Structure of Scientific Revolution*, 2nd edn. Chicago, IL: University of Chicago Press.

Laming, Lord H. (2003) *The Victoria Climbié Enquiry: Report of an inquiry by Lord Laming*, Cm 5730. London: HMSO. Available at: https://assets.publishing. service.gov.uk/government/uploads/system/uploads/attachment_data/ file/273183/5730.pdf (accessed 18 June 2019).

Laming, Lord H. (2009) *The Protection of Children in England: A progress report.* London: TSO. Available at: https://www.gov.uk/government/publications/the-protection-of-children-in-england-a-progress-report (accessed 18 June 2019).

Lane, J. (2008) *Young Children and Racial Justice: Taking action for racial equality in the early years – understanding the past, thinking about the present, planning for the future.* London: National Children's Bureau.

Lang, S.N., Tolbert, A.R., Schoppe-Sullivan, S.J. and Bonomi, A.E. (2016) A cocaring framework for infants and toddlers: Applying a model of coparenting to parent–teacher relationships, *Early Childhood Research Quarterly*, 34: 40–52.

Lansdown, G. (2001) Children's welfare and children's rights, in P. Foley, J. Roche and S. Tucker (eds.) *Children in Society: Policy and practice.* Basingstoke: Palgrave Macmillan.

Lansdown, G. (2005) *The Evolving Capacities of Children: Implications for the exercise of rights.* Florence: UNICEF Innocenti Research Centre.

Lansdown, G. (2010) The realisation of children's participation rights: Critical reflections, in B. Perry-Smith and N. Thomas (eds.) *A Handbook of Children and Young People's Participation.* Abingdon: Routledge.

Lave, J. and Wenger, E. (1991) *Situated Learning: Legitimate peripheral participation.* Cambridge: Cambridge University Press.

Law, J., Charlton, J., Dockrell, J., Gascoigne, M., McKean, C. and Theakston, A. (2017a) *Early Language Development: Needs, provision, and intervention for preschool children from socio-economically disadvantage backgrounds. A report for the Education Endowment Foundation.* London: EEF and Public Health England. Available at: https://educationendowmentfoundation.org.uk/ public/files/Law_et_al_Early_Language_Development_final.pdf (accessed 30 September 2018).

Law, J., Charlton, J. and Asmussen, K. (2017b) *Language as a Child Well–being Indicator.* London: Early Intervention Foundation. Available at: https://www.eif.

org.uk/report/language-as-a-child-wellbeing-indicator/ (accessed 30 September 2018).

Leadbetter, J., Daniels, H., Edwards, A., Martin, D., Middleton, D., Popova, A. et al. (2007) Professional learning within multi-agency children's services: Researching into practice, *Educational Research*, 49 (1): 83–98.

Learning and Teaching Scotland (LTS) (2006) *The Reggio Emilia Approach to Early Years Education*. Glasgow: LTS. Available at: education.gov.scot/improvement/Documents/ELC/ELC35_ReggioEmilia/ELC35_ReggioAug06.pdf (accessed 2 February 2017).

Leather, M. (2012) *Seeing the Wood from the Trees: Constructionism and constructivism for outdoor and experiential education*. Edinburgh: University of Edinburgh.

Lee, W., Carr, M., Soutar, B. and Mitchell, L. (2013) *Understanding the Te Whāriki Approach*. London: Routledge.

Lindon, J. (2011) *Too Safe For Their Own Good?*, 2nd edn. London: National Children's Bureau.

Lindon, J. (2012) *Equality in Early Childhood: Linking theory and practice*, 2nd edn. London: Hodder Arnold.

Lindon, J. and Trodd, L. (2016) *Reflective Practice and Early Years Professionalism: Linking theory and practice*, 3rd edn. London: Hodder Education.

Lloyd, E. and Hallet, E. (2010) Professionalising the Early Childhood Workforce in England: Work in progress or missed opportunity?, *Contemporary Issues in Early Childhood*, 11 (1): 75–88.

Lumsden, E. (2016) The time is right for a Royal College for Early Childhood, *Nursery World*, 3 May. Available at: https://www.nurseryworld.co.uk/nursery-world/opinion/1157092/the-time-is-right-for-a-royal-college-for-early-childhood (accessed 24 May 2016).

Lundy, L. (2007) 'Voice is not enough': Conceptualising Article 12 of the United Nations Convention on the Rights of the Child, *British Education Research Journal*, 33 (6): 927–942.

Macintosh, P. (1988) *White Privilege and Male Privilege: A personal account of coming to see correspondence through work in women's studies*. Working Paper #189. Wellesley, MA: Wellesley Centers for Women. Available at: https://www.wcwonline.org/Publications-by-title/white-privilege-and-male-privilege-a-personal-account-of-coming-to-see-correspondences-through-work-in-women-s-studies-2 (accessed 30 September 2018).

Macleod, S., Sharp, C., Bernardinelli, D., Skipp, A. and Higgins, S. (2015) *Supporting the Attainment of Disadvantaged Pupils: Articulating success and good practice*. London: Department for Education. Available at: https://assets.publishing.service.gov.uk/government/uploads/system/uploads/attachment_data/file/473974/DFE-RR411_Supporting_the_attainment_of_disadvantaged_pupils.pdf (accessed 16 April 2017).

MacNaughton, G. (2003) *Shaping Early Childhood*. Maidenhead: Open University Press.

Malaguzzi, L. (1995) *A Journey into the Rights of Children*. Reggio Emilia, Italy: Reggio Children.

Malaguzzi, L. (1997) No way. The hundred is there, in T. Fillipini and V. Vecchi (eds.) *The Hundred Languages of Children: Narratives of the possible.* Reggio Emilia, Italy: Reggio Children.

Malaguzzi, L. (2011) The hundred is there, in C. Edwards, L. Gandini and G. Forman (eds.) *The Hundred Languages of Children: The Reggio Emilia experience in transformation.* Westport, CT: Praeger.

Malin, N. and Morrow, G. (2007) Models of interprofessional working within a Sure Start 'Trailblazer' programme, *Journal of Interprofessional Care,* 21 (4): 445–457.

Marcia, J.E. (1966) Development and validation of ego-identity status, *Journal of Personality and Social Psychology,* 3 (5): 551–558.

Marcia, J.E., Waterman, A.S., Matteson, D.R., Archer, S.L. and Orlofsky, J.L. (1993) *Ego Identity.* New York: Springer.

Marmot, M. (2010) *Fair Society, Healthy Lives: The Marmot Review.* London: Department of Health. Available at: https://www.parliament.uk/documents/fair-society-healthy-lives-full-report.pdf.

Marsh, J. and Hallet, E. (2008) *Desirable Literacies: Approaches to language and literacy in the early years,* 2nd edn. London: Sage.

Maslow, A.H. (1943) A theory of human motivation, *Psychological Review,* 50 (4): 370–396.

Maslow, A.H. (1970) *Motivation and Personality.* New York: Harper & Row.

Mathers, S., Singler, R. and Karemaker, A. (2012) *Improving Quality in the Early Years: A comparison of perspectives and measures.* London: Nuffield Foundation.

Mathers, S., Eisenstadt, N., Sylva, K., Soukakou, E. and Ereky-Stevens, K. (2014) *Sound Foundations: A review of the research evidence on quality of early childhood education and care for children under three.* London: The Sutton Trust. Available at: https://www.suttontrust.com/wp-content/uploads/2014/01/1sound-foundations-jan2014-3.pdf (accessed 26 May 2016).

Mathers, S., Hardy, G., Clancy, C., Dixon, J. and Harding, C. (2016) *Starting Out Right: Early education and looked after children.* London: University of Oxford/Family and Childcare Trust. Available at: https://www.nuffieldfoundation.org/sites/default/files/files/Starting%20out%20right_%20early%20education%20and%20looked%20after%20children.pdf (accessed 18 June 2019).

Mayall, B. (2002) *Towards a Sociology for Childhood.* Buckingham: Open University Press.

Maykut, P. and Morehouse, R. (1994) *Beginning Qualitative Research.* London: Falmer Press.

Maynard, T. and Waters, J. (2007) Learning in the outdoor environment: A missed opportunity?, *Early Years,* 27 (3): 255–265.

McDermott, D. (2008) *Caring Relationships Among Parents, Children, Schools and Communities.* London: Sage.

McDowall Clark, R. (2016) *Exploring the Contexts for Early Learning: Challenging the school readiness agenda.* London: Routledge.

McFarland, E., Saunders, R. and Allen, S. (2009) Reflective practice and self-evaluation in learning positive guidance: Experiences of early childhood practicum students, *Early Childhood Education Journal,* 36 (6): 505–511.

McGillivray, G. (2011) Nannies, nursery nurses and early years professionals, in C. Dalli and M. Urban (eds.) *Professionalism in Early Childhood Education and Care: International perspectives.* London: Routledge.

McInnes, K., Howard, J., Crowley, K. and Miles, G. (2013) The nature of adult–child interaction in the early years classroom: Implications for children's perceptions of play and subsequent learning behaviour, *European Early Childhood Education Research Journal,* 21 (2): 268–282.

McKenzie, R.H. (1990) *Prior Learning and Reflection: Analytic thinking from experience.* Dubuque, IA: Kendall Hunt.

Melasalmi, A. and Husu, J. (2016) The content and implementation of shared professional knowledge in early childhood education, *Early Years,* 36 (4): 426–439.

Melhuish, E. and Gardiner, J. (2017) *Study of Early Education and Development (SEED): Study of quality of early years provision in England.* Research Report. London: Department for Education. Available at: https://assets.publishing.service.gov.uk/government/uploads/system/uploads/attachment_data/file/723736/Study_of_quality_of_early_years_provision_in_England.pdf (accessed 18 June 2019).

Melhuish, E., Gardiner, J. and Morris, S. (2017) *Study of Early Education and Development (SEED): Impact study on early education use and child outcomes up to age three.* Research Report. London: Department for Education. Available at: https://assets.publishing.service.gov.uk/government/uploads/system/uploads/attachment_data/file/627098/SEED_ECEC_impact_at_age_3.pdf (accessed 13 July 2017).

Meltzoff, A.N., Kuhl, P.K., Movellan, J. and Sejnowski, T.J. (2009) Foundations for a new science of learning, *Science,* 325 (5938): 284–288.

Melyn, B. (2009) Boundaries – not barriers, *Community Care,* November. Available at: https://www.communitycare.co.uk/2009/11/13/professional-boundaries-in-childrens-homes/# (accessed 2 June 2016).

Miller, L. (2008) Developing professionalism within a regulatory framework in England: Challenges and possibilities, *European Early Childhood Education Research Journal,* 16 (2): 255–268.

Miller, L. (2011) Developing professionalism within a regulatory framework in England: Challenges and possibilities, in C. Dalli and M. Urban (eds.) *Professionalism in Early Childhood Education and Care: International perspectives.* London: Routledge.

Miller, L. and Cable, C. (2011) The changing face of professionalism in the early years, in C. Cable and L. Miller (eds.) *Professionalization, Leadership and Management in the Early Years.* London: Sage.

Monk, D. (2004) Problematising home education: Challenging 'parental rights' and 'socialisation', *Legal Studies,* 24 (4): 568–598.

Montessori, M. (1912/2012) *The Montessori Method: Scientific pedagogy as applied to child education in 'the children's houses' with additions and revisions by the author.* New York: Frederick A. Stokes.

Moon, J. (1999) *Reflection in Learning and Professional Development.* London: Kogan Page.

Mooney, A. (2007) *The Effectiveness of Quality Improvement Programmes for Early Childhood Education and Care*. London: Thomas Coram Research Unit and Institute of Education, University of London.

Morrow, V. (2011) *Understanding Children and Childhood*. Background Briefing Series #1. Lismore, NSW: Centre for Children and Young People, Southern Cross University.

Moss, P. (2006) Structures, understanding and discourses: Possibilities for re-envisioning the early childhood worker, *Contemporary Issues in Early Childhood*, 7 (1): 30–41.

Moss, P. (2007) *Bringing Politics into the Nursery: Early childhood education as a democratic practice*. The Hague: Bernard van Leer Foundation.

Moss, P. (2009) *There are Alternatives! Markets and democratic experimentalism in early childhood education and care*. The Hague: Bernard Van Leer Foundation.

Moss, P. (2014) *Transformative Change and Real Utopias in Early Childhood Education: A story of democracy, experimentation and potentiality*. London: Routledge.

Moss, P. (2016) Why can't we get beyond quality?, *Contemporary Issues in Early Childhood*, 17 (1): 8–15.

Moss, P. and Dahlberg, G. (2008) Beyond quality in early childhood education and care – languages of evaluation, *New Zealand Journal of Teachers' Work*, 5 (1): 3–12.

Moyles, J. (1989) *Just Playing?* Milton Keynes: Open University Press.

Moyles, J. (2001) Passion, paradox and professionalism in early years education, *Early Years*, 21 (2): 81–95.

Moyles, J. (2006) *Effective Leadership and Management in The Early Years*. Maidenhead: McGraw-Hill.

Moyles, J. (2010) *The Excellence of Play*, 3rd edn. Maidenhead: Open University Press.

Moyles, J. (2015) *The Excellence of Play*, 4th edn. Maidenhead: Open University Press.

Moyles, J., Adams, S. and Musgrove, A. (2002) *SPEEL: Study of Pedagogical Effectiveness in Early Learning*. Research Report RR363. London: Department for Education and Skills. Available at: https://dera.ioe.ac.uk/4591/1/RR363.pdf (accessed 12 April 2016).

Muijs, D. (2004) How do they manage? A review of the research on leadership in early childhood, *Journal of Early Childhood Research*, 2 (2): 157–169.

Munro, E. (2011) *The Munro Review of Child Protection, Final Report: The child's journey*. London: Department for Education.

Munton, A.G., Mooney, A. and Rowland, L. (1995) Deconstructing quality: A conceptual framework for the new paradigm in day care provision for the under eights, *Early Childhood Development and Care*, 114: 11–23.

Murray, C. and Hallet, C. (2000) Young people's participation in decisions affecting their welfare, *Childhood*, 7 (1): 11–25.

Murray, J. (2017) *Building Knowledge in Early Childhood Education: Young children are researchers*. London: Routledge.

NatCen Social Research, University of Oxford, Department of Education (2017) *Study of Early Education and Development: Wave 2, 2014–2015* [data collection]. UK Data Service. SN: 8278. Available at: http://doi.org/10.5255/UKDA-SN-8278-1.

National Audit Office (2004) *Early Years: Progress in developing high quality childcare and early education accessible to all.* London: TSO.

National Autistic Society (2016) *Autism: What is autism?* Available at: https://www.autism.org.uk/about/what-is/asd.aspx (accessed 13 May 2016).

National Children's Bureau (NCB) (2012) *A Know How Guide: The EYFS progress check at age two.* Available at: https://www.foundationyears.org.uk/files/2012/03/A-Know-How-Guide.pdf (accessed 11 January 2016).

National College for Teaching and Leadership (NCTL) (2013) *Teachers' Standards (Early Years): From September 2013.* London: Department for Education. Available at: www.gov.uk/government/publications/early-years-teachers-standards (accessed 12 July 2018)

National Day Nurseries Association (NDNA) (2015) *NDNA Workforce Survey 2015.* Huddersfield: NDNA. Available at: https://www.ndna.org.uk/NDNA/News/Reports_and_surveys/Workforce_survey_results_2015.aspx (accessed 28 March 2018).

National Scientific Council on the Developing Child (NSCDC) (2004) *Young Children Develop in an Environment of Relationships.* Working Paper #1. Cambridge, MA: NSCDC. Available at: http://developingchild.harvard.edu/wp-content/uploads/2004/04/Young-Children-Develop-in-an-Environment-of-Relationships.pdf (accessed 23 February 2016).

National Scientific Council on the Developing Child (NSCDC) (2007) *The Science of Early Childhood Development: Closing the gap between what we know and what we do.* Cambridge, MA: NSCDC. Available at: https://developingchild.harvard.edu/resources/the-science-of-early-childhood-development-closing-the-gap-between-what-we-know-and-what-we-do/ (accessed 20 November 2016).

New Economics Foundation (NEF) (2008) *Co-production: A manifesto for growing the core economy.* London: NEF.

Nikiforidou, Z. and Anderson, B. (2016) Working together to safeguard children, in I. Palaiologou (ed.) *The Early Years Foundation Stage: Theory and practice.* London: Sage.

Nursery World (2015) *Guide to Early Years Teacher Status.* London: Nursery World/Department for Education. Available at: https://www.nurseryworld.co.uk/digital_assets/877/Guide-to-Early-year-teacher-Singles.pdf (accessed 12 January 2016).

Nutbrown, C. (2006) *Key Concepts in Early Childhood Education and Care.* London: Sage.

Nutbrown. C. (2012) *Foundations for Quality: The independent review of early education and childcare qualifications. Final Report.* London: Department for Education. Available at: https://assets.publishing.service.gov.uk/government/uploads/system/uploads/attachment_data/file/175463/Nutbrown-Review.pdf (accessed 12 September 2016).

Nutbrown, C. (2013) *Shaking the Foundations of Quality? Why 'childcare' policy must not lead to poor-quality early education and care.* Available at: https://

www.newvisionsforeducation.org.uk/about-the-group/home/2013/03/27/shaking-the-foundations-of-quality-why-childcare-policy-must-not-lead-to-poor-quality-early-education-and-care/ (accessed 23 February 2016).

Oberhuemer, P. and Scheryer, I. (2008) What professional? *Children in Europe. Aiming High: A Professional Workforce for the Early Years*, 15: 9–12.

O'Brien, E.A. and Murray, R. (2007) 'Forest School' in England: An evaluation of three case study settings, *Environmental Education*, 84: 8–9.

O'Brien, L. and Murray, R. (2006) *A Marvellous Opportunity for Children to Learn: A participatory evaluation of Forest School in England and Wales.* Norwich: HMSO. Available at: https://www.forestschooltraining.co.uk/_webedit/uploaded-files/All%20Files/Research%20papers/Marvellous%20opportunity.pdf (accessed 14 October 2018).

Office for Standards in Education, Children's Services and Skills (Ofsted) (2014) *Are You Ready? Good practice in school readiness.* London: Ofsted. Available at: https://assets.publishing.service.gov.uk/government/uploads/system/uploads/attachment_data/file/418819/Are_you_ready_Good_practice_in_school_readiness.pdf (accessed 26 April 2016).

Office for Standards in Education, Children's Services and Skills (Ofsted) (2015a) *Teaching and Play in the Early Years: A balancing act?* London: Ofsted. Available at: https://www.gov.uk/government/publications/teaching-and-play-in-the-early-years-a-balancing-act (accessed 16 April 2016).

Office for Standards in Education, Children's Services and Skills (Ofsted) (2015b) *Collaborating to Support Early Years Teaching and Learning: Broomhall Nursery School and Children's Centre.* London: Ofsted. Available at: https://dera.ioe.ac.uk/23469/ (accessed 26 April 2016).

Office for Standards in Education, Children's Services and Skills (Ofsted) (2016) *Unknown Children – Destined for disadvantage?* London: Ofsted. Available at: https://www.gov.uk/government/publications/helping-disadvantaged-young-children-ofsted-thematic-report (accessed 1 July 2016).

Office for Standards in Education, Children's Services and Skills (Ofsted) (2017) *Early Years Inspections: Myths.* London: Ofsted. Available at: https://www.gov.uk/government/publications/inspecting-registered-early-years-providers-guidance-for-inspectors (accessed 16 June 2017).

Office for Standards in Education, Children's Services and Skills (Ofsted) (2019) *Early Years Inspection Handbook.* London: Ofsted. Available at: https://assets.publishing.service.gov.uk/government/uploads/system/uploads/attachment_data/file/801429/Education_inspection_framework.pdf (accessed 15 July 2019).

Ólafsdóttir, S. and Einarsdóttir, J. (2017) 'Drawing and playing are not the same': Children's views on their activities in Icelandic preschools, *Early Years*, 39 (1): 51–63.

Organisation for Economic Co-operation and Development (OECD) (2017) *Starting Strong 2017: Key indicators on early childhood education and care.* Paris: OECD Publishing. Available at: https://read.oecd-ilibrary.org/education/starting-strong-2017_9789264276116-en#page1 (accessed 3 July 2017).

Organisation for Economic Co-operation and Development (OECD) (2018) *Equity in Education: Breaking down barriers to social mobility*. Paris: OECD Publishing. Available at: www.oecd.org/education/equity-in-education-9789264073234-en. htm (accessed 30 September 2018).

Organisation Mondiale pour l'Education Prescolaire (OMEP) (2010) *OMEP 2010 World Assembly and Congress*. Available at: www.worldomep.org (accessed 24 January 2017).

Osgood, J. (2009) Childcare workforce reform in England and the 'early years professional': A critical discourse analysis, *Journal of Education Policy*, 24 (6): 733–751.

Osgood, J. (2012) *Narratives from the Nursery: Negotiating professional identities in early childhood*. London: Routledge.

Osgood, J., Elwick, A., Robertson, L., Sakr, M. and Wilson, D. (2016) *Early Years Teacher and Early Years Educator: A scoping study of the impact, experience and associated issues of recent early years qualifications and training in England*. Available at: http://www.mdx.ac.uk/__data/assets/pdf_file/0019/363313/Early-Years-Teacher-and-Early-Years-Educator.pdf?bustCache=84797373 (accessed 17 October 2017).

Osler, A. (2011) Teacher interpretations of citizenship education: National identity, cosmopolitan ideals, and political realities, *Journal of Curriculum Studies*, 43 (1): 1–24.

Osler, A. and Starkey, H. (2010) *Teachers and Human Rights Education*. Stoke-on-Trent: Trentham Books.

Otero, M. and Melhuish, E. (2015) *Study of Early Education and Development (SEED): Study of the quality of childminder provision in England*. Available at: https://www.gov.uk/government/publications/study-of-early-education-and-development-childminder-provision (accessed 3 December 2016).

Oxford Dictionaries (2018) *Definition of 'trust' in English*. Available at: https://en.oxforddictionaries.com/definition/trust (accessed 12 April 2016).

Page, J. (2008) Permission to love them, in C. Nutbrown and J. Page (eds.) *Working with Babies and Children: From birth to three*. London: Sage.

Page, J. (2011) Do mothers want professional carers to love their babies?, *Journal of Early Childhood Research*, 9 (3): 310–323.

Page, J., Lahmar, J., Clare, A., Clough, P., Kitchen, K., Jinks, P. et al. (2015) *Professional Love in Early Years Settings: A report of the summary of findings*. University of Sheffield/Fennies Day Nursery and Preschool. Available at: https://pleysproject.files.wordpress.com/2017/06/pleys-report_singlepages.pdf (accessed 18 June 2019).

Pahl, K. (2007) Creativity in events and practices: A lens for understanding children's multimodal text, *Literacy*, 41 (2): 86–92.

Paige-Smith, A. and Craft, A. (2008) *Developing Reflective Practice in the Early Years*. Maidenhead: Open University Press.

Palaiologou, I. (2012) *Childhood Observation for the Early Years*, 2nd edn. Exeter: Learning Matters.

Palaiologou, I. (ed.) (2016) *The Early Years Foundation Stage*. London: Sage.

Paley, V.G. (1991) *The Boy Who Would Be a Helicopter.* Harvard, MA: Harvard University Press.

Papatheodorou, T. (2009) Exploring relational pedagogy, in T. Papatheodorou and J. Moyles (eds.) *Learning Together in the Early Years: Exploring relational pedagogy.* Abingdon: Routledge.

Parker-Rees, R. (2018) Editorial, *Early Years*, 38 (3): 241–243.

Pascal, C. and Bertram, T. (2013) *The Impact of Early Education as a Strategy in Countering Socio-economic Disadvantage.* Research Paper #130155-RR-005. London: Centre for Research in Childhood. Available at: http://www.crec.co.uk/docs/Access.pdf (accessed 11 January 2016).

Pascal, C. and Bertram, T. (2014) *Early Years Literature Review.* Available at: https://www.early-education.org.uk/early-years-literature-review (accessed 16 July 2016).

Pascal, C., Bertram, A.D., Ramsden, F., Georgeson, J., Saunders, M. and Mould, C. (1996) *Evaluating and Developing Quality in Early Childhood Settings: A professional development programme.* Worcester: Amber Publishing.

Payler, J., Georgeson, J. and Wong, S. (2016) Young children shaping interprofessional practice in early years settings: Towards a conceptual framework for understanding experiences and participation, *Learning, Culture and Social Interaction*, 8: 12–24.

Peeters, J. and Vandenbroeck, M. (2011) Child care practitioners and the process of professionalization, in L. Miller and C. Cable (eds.) *Professionalization and Management in the Early Years.* London: Sage.

Penn, H. (2000) *Early Childhood Services.* Buckingham: Open University Press.

Penn, H. (2005) *Understanding Early Childhood: Issues and controversies.* Maidenhead: Open University Press.

Penn, H. (2006) *Unequal Childhoods: Young children's lives in poor countries.* Abingdon: Routledge.

Penn, H. (2011) *Quality in Early Education and Care: An international perspective.* Maidenhead: Open University Press.

Penn, H. (2012) The rhetoric and realities of early childhood programmes promoted by the World Bank in Mali, in R. Ames and A. Twum Danso Imoh (eds.) *Childhoods at the Intersection of the Local and the Global.* Basingstoke: Palgrave Macmillan.

Penn, H. (2014) *Understanding Early Childhood: Issues and controversies*, 3rd edn. Maidenhead: Open University Press.

Piaget, J. (1954) *The Construction of Reality in the Child* (M. Cook, trans.). New York: Basic Books.

Piaget, J. (1973) *The Child and Reality: Problems of genetic psychology.* London: Frederick Muller.

Podmore, V. (2009) Questioning evaluation in early childhood, in A. Anning, J. Cullen and M. Fleer (eds.) *Early Childhood Education.* London: Sage.

Polat, F. (2011) Inclusion in education: A step towards social justice, *International Journal of Educational Development*, 31 (1): 50–58.

Pollard, A. (1987) Social differentiation in primary schools, *Cambridge Journal of Education*, 17 (3): 158–161.

Pollard, A. (2002) *Reading for Reflective Teaching*. London: Continuum.

Pound, L. (1999) *Supporting Mathematical Development in the Early Years*. Maidenhead: Open University Press.

Powell, S. and Goouch, K. (2014) Whose hand rocks the cradle? Parallel discourses in the baby room, in P. Oberhuemer, L. Brooker and R. Parker-Rees (eds.) *Professional Issues in Work with Babies and Toddlers*. Abingdon: Routledge.

Preschool Learning Alliance (2017) *Growth Through Knowledge*. Available at: https://www.ceeda.co.uk/media/1186/the-facts-on-30-hours_parent-eligbility-and-demand_general-issue_jan-17.pdf (accessed 14 January 2018).

Prout, A. (2000) Children's participation: Control and self-realisation in British late modernity, *Children and Society*, 14 (4): 304–315.

Prout, A. (2003) Participation, policy and the changing conditions of childhood, in C. Hallet and A. Prout (eds.) *Hearing the Voices of Children*. London: Routledge Falmer.

Prout, A. (2008) Participation, policy and changing conditions of childhood, in. B. Lingard, J. Nixon and S. Ranson (eds.) *Transforming Learning in Schools and Communities: The remaking of education for a cosmopolitan society*. New York: Continuum.

Prout, A. and James, A. (1997) A new paradigm for the sociology of childhood?, in A. James and A. Prout (eds.) *Constructing and Reconstructing Childhood: Contemporary issues in the sociological study of childhood*, 2nd edn. London: Falmer Press.

Pugh, G. and Duffy, B. (2006) *Contemporary Issues in The Early Years*, 4th edn. London: Sage.

Purvis, L. and Selleck, D. (1996) *Tuning into Children*. London: BBC Publications.

Raelin, J.A. (2001) Public reflection as the basis of learning, *Management Learning*, 32 (1): 11–30.

Raelin, J.A. (2002) I don't have time to think! Versus the art of reflective practice, *Reflections*, 4 (1): 66–75.

Raelin, J.A. (2005) Don't bother putting leadership into people, *Academy of Management Executive*, 18 (3): 131–135.

Ranns, H., Mathers, S., Moody, A., Karemaker, A., Graham, J., Sylva, K. et al. (2011) *Evaluation of the Graduate Leader Fund: Evaluation overview*. Research Report DFE-RR144d. London: Department for Education. Available at: https://assets.publishing.service.gov.uk/government/uploads/system/uploads/attachment_data/file/181484/DFE-RR144d.pdf (accessed 30 August 2018).

Raven, J. (2011) *Competence, Education, Professional Development, Psychology and Socio-Cybernetics*. Available at: http://www.eyeonsociety.co.uk/resources/CPDAPA_REVISED_FULL_VERSION.pdf (accessed 16 July 2016).

Read, V. (2010) *Developing Attachment in Early Years Settings*. Abingdon: Routledge.

Reed, M. and Canning, N. (eds.) (2012) *Reflective Practice in the Early Years*. Maidenhead: Open University Press.

Reese, H.W. and Lipsitt, L.P. (eds.) (1979) *Advances in Child Development and Behaviour*, Vol. 13. New York: Academic Press.

Ricciardi, A. (2013) Starting at pre-school, in L. Trodd (ed.) *Transitions in the Early Years: Working with children and families*. London: Sage.

Rinaldi, C. (1998) The emergent curriculum and social constructivism: An interview with Lella Gandini, in C. Edwards, L. Gandini and G. Forman (eds.) *The Hundred Languages of Children: The Reggio Emilia approach to early childhood education*, 2nd edn. Norwood, NJ: Ablex.

Rinaldi, C. (2005) *In Dialogue with Reggio Emilia*. London: Routledge.

Rinaldi, C. (2012) The pedagogy of listening: The listening perspective from Reggio Emilia. In C. Edwards, L. Gandini and G.E. Forman (eds.) *The Hundred Languages of Children: The Reggio Emilia experience in transformation* (3rd edn.). Santa Barbara, CA: Praeger.

Ritson, L. (2016) *Adventure Education: Fun games and activities for children and young people*. London: Routledge.

Roberts, H. (2000) Listening to children: And hearing them, in P. Christensen and A. James (eds.) *Research with Children: Perspectives and practice*. London: Falmer Press.

Roberts, R. (2010) *Wellbeing from Birth*. London: Sage.

Robinson, P. and Bartlett, C. (2011) 'Stone crazy': A space where intentional teachers and intentional learners meet, *Early Childhood Folio*, 15 (2): 10–14.

Robson, C. (2002) *Real World Research: A resource for social scientists and practitioner researchers*. London: Blackwell.

Robson, S. (2012) *Developing Thinking and Understanding in Young Children*, 2nd edn. Abingdon: Routledge.

Rockel, J. (2014) Praise for this book, in S. Degotardi and E. Pearson, *The Relationship Worlds of Infants and Toddlers*. Maidenhead: Open University Press.

Rodd, J. (2006) *Leadership in Early Childhood*. Maidenhead: Open University Press.

Rodd, J. (2013) *Leadership in Early Childhood: The pathway to professionalism*, 4th edn. Maidenhead: Open University Press.

Rogoff, B. (1991) *Apprenticeship in Thinking: Cognitive development in social context*. Oxford: Oxford University Press.

Rogoff, B. (2003) *The Cultural Nature of Human Development*. Oxford: Oxford University Press.

Rolfe, S.A. (2004) *Rethinking Attachment for Early Childhood Practice: Promoting security, autonomy and resilience in young children*. Crows Nest, NSW: Allen & Unwin.

Ron, N., Lipshitz, R. and Popper, M. (2006) How organizations learn: Post-flight reviews in an F-16 fighter squadron, *Organization Studies*, 27: 1069–1090.

Rutter, M. (1987) Psychosocial influences: Critiques, findings and research needs, *Development and Psychopathology*, 12 (3): 375–405.

Sammons, P. (2010) Does pre-school make a difference?, in K. Sylva, E. Melhuish, P. Sammons, I. Siraj-Blatchford and B. Taggart (eds.) *Early Childhood Matters: Evidence from the Effective Pre-school and Primary Education project.* London: Routledge.

Sammons, P., Sylva, K., Melhuish, E., Siraj-Blatchford, I., Taggart, B. and Hunt, S. (2008) *Influences on Children's Attainment and Progress in Key Stage 2: Cognitive outcomes in Year 6.* Project Report. Nottingham: DCSF Publications.

Sanghani, R. (2016) The shocking reality of racist bullying in schools, *The Telegraph*, 5 July. Available at: https://www.telegraph.co.uk/family/schooling/the-shocking-reality-of-racist-bullying-in-british-schools/ (accessed 19 July 2016).

Schön, D.A. (1983) *The Reflective Practitioner: How professionals think in action.* New York: Basic Books.

Schön, D.A. (1987) *Educating the Reflective Practitioner: Towards a new design for teaching and learning in the professions.* San Francisco, CA: Jossey-Bass.

Scollan, A. (2009) *Academic and Vocational Progression Routes for Early Years Practitioners Working Towards 'Early Years Professional Status' (EYPS).* Extended Services and Early Years Conference, 23 January, London.

Scollan, A. and McNeill, E. (2019) Ireland: Listening to children's voices in Irish social work through cultural and organisational filters, in F. Farini and A. Scollan (eds.) *Children's Self-Determination in the Context of Early Childhood Education and Services: Discourses, policies and practices.* Dordrecht: Springer.

Sedgwick, F. (1988) Talking about teaching poetry, *Curriculum*, 9 (3): 126–134.

Seligman, M.E.P., Reivich, K., Jaycox, L. and Gillham, J. (1995) *The Optimistic Child.* Boston, MA: Houghton Mifflin.

Sharp, P. (2002) *Nurturing Emotional Literacy.* London: David Fulton.

Sheridan, S. (2007) Dimensions of pedagogical quality in preschool, *International Journal of Early Years Education*, 15 (2): 197–217.

Sieratzki, J. and Woll, B. (2005) Cerebral asymmetry: From survival strategies to social behaviour, *Behavioral and Brain Sciences*, 28 (4): 613–614.

Sim, M., Bélanger, J., Hocking, L., Dimova, S., Iakovidou, E., Janta, B. et al. (2018) *Teaching, Pedagogy and Practice in Early Years Childcare: An evidence review.* Early Intervention Foundation Research Report. Available at: https://www.eif.org.uk/report/teaching-pedagogy-and-practice-in-early-years-childcare-an-evidence-review (accessed 2 February 2019).

Siraj, I. and Hallet, E. (2014) *Effective and Caring Leadership in the Early Years.* London: Sage.

Siraj-Blatchford, I. (2010) A focus on pedagogy: Case studies of effective practice, in K. Sylva, E. Melhuish, P. Sammons, I. Siraj-Blatchford and B. Taggart (eds.) *Early Childhood Matters: Evidence from the Effective Pre-school and Primary Education project.* London: Routledge.

Siraj-Blatchford, I. and Manni, L. (2007) *Effective Leadership in the Early Years Sector: The ELEYS Study.* London: Institute of Education, University of London.

Siraj-Blatchford, I. and Sylva, K. (2004) Researching pedagogy in English pre-schools, *British Educational Research Journal*, 30 (5): 713–730.

Siraj-Blatchford, I. and Wong, Y.-L. (1999) Defining and evaluating 'quality' early childhood education in an international context: Dilemmas and possibilities, *Early Years*, 20 (1): 7–18.

Siraj-Blatchford, I., Sylva, K., Muttock, S., Gilden, R and Bell, D. (2002) *Researching Effective Pedagogy in the Early Years*. DfE Research Report RR356. Available at: https://dera.ioe.ac.uk/4650/1/RR356.pdf (accessed 20 March 2015).

Siraj-Blatchford, I., Kingston, D. and Melhuish, E. (2015) *Assessing Quality in Early Childhood Education and Care: Sustained Shared Thinking and Emotional Well-being (SSTEW) Scale for 2–5-year-olds provision* London: Trentham Books.

Siraj-Blatchford, J., Smith, K.C. and Pramling Samuelsson, I. (2010) *Education for Sustainable Development in the Early Years*. Sweden: Svenska OMEP. Available at: http://www.327matters.org/Docs/ESD%20Book%20Master.pdf (accessed 8 March 2018).

Skattebol, J., Adamson, E. and Woodrow, C. (2016) Revisioning professionalism from the periphery, *Early Years*, 36 (2): 116–131.

Skemp, R. (1989) *Mathematics in the Primary School*. London: Routledge.

Slowie, D. (2014) *Father's Day*. NHS England. Available at: https://www.england.nhs.uk/blog/dominic-slowie/ (accessed 12 March 2016).

Smith, A.B. (2016) *Children's Rights: Towards social justice*. New York: Momentum Press.

Smith, G., Sylva, K., Sammons, P., Smith, T. and Omonigho, A. (2018) *Stop Start: Survival, decline or closure? Children's centres in England 2018*. Available at: https://www.suttontrust.com/wp-content/uploads/2018/04/StopStart-FINAL.pdf (accessed 2 February 2019).

Solly, K. (2015) *Risk, Challenge and Adventure in the Early Years*. Abingdon: Routledge.

Solomon, J. (1987) New thoughts on teacher education, *Oxford Review of Education*, 13 (3): 267–274.

Steiner, R. (1995) *The Kingdom of Childhood: Introductory talks on Waldorf education*. Fair Oaks, CA: Association of Waldorf Schools of North America Publications/Anthroposophic Press.

Steiner, R. (1996) *The Foundation of the Human Experience* (R.F. Lathe and N.P. Whittaker, trans.). Hudson, NY: Anthroposophic Press. Available at: https://www.rsarchive.org/Download/Foundations_of_Human_Experience-Rudolf_Steiner-293.pdf.

Stephen, C. (2010) Pedagogy: The silent partner in early years learning, *Early Years*, 30 (1): 15–28.

Stephens, S. (1995) *Children and the Politics of Culture*. Princeton: NJ: Princeton University Press.

Sternberg, R.J. (2003) Creative thinking in the classroom, *Scandinavian Journal of Educational Research*, 47 (3): 325–338.

Stewart, K. and Waldfogel, J. (2017) *Closing Gaps Early: The role of early years policy in promoting social mobility in England*. London: The Sutton Trust. Available at: https://www.suttontrust.com/research-paper/closing-gaps-early-parenting-policy-childcare/ (accessed 2 February 2019).

Stirrup, J., Evans, J. and Davies, B. (2017) Early years learning, play pedagogy and social class, *British Journal of Sociology of Education*, 38 (6): 872–886.

Sylva, K. (2010) Quality in early childhood settings, in K. Sylva, E. Melhuish, P. Sammons, I. Siraj-Blatchford and B. Taggart (eds.) *Early Childhood Matters: Evidence from the Effective Pre-school and Primary Education project.* London: Routledge.

Sylva, K. and Taylor, H. (2006) Effective settings: Evidence from research, in G. Pugh and B. Duffy (eds.) *Contemporary Issues in the Early Years*, 4th edn. London: Sage.

Sylva, K., Siraj-Blatchford, I. and Taggart, B. (2003) *Assessing Quality in the Early Years: Early Childhood Environment Ratings Scale Extension (ECERS–E): Four curricular sub-scales.* Stoke-on-Trent: Trentham Books.

Sylva, K., Melhuish, E., Sammons, P., Siraj-Blatchford, I. and Taggart, B. (2004) *The Effective Provision of Pre-School Education (EPPE) Project: Final Report.* London: DfES/Institute of Education, University of London. Available at: http://discovery. ucl.ac.uk/10005309/1/sylva2004EPPEfinal.pdf (accessed 18 June 2019).

Sylva, K., Melhuish, E., Sammons, P., Siraj-Blatchford, I. and Taggart, B. (eds.) (2010) *Early Childhood Matters: Evidence from the Effective Pre-school and Primary Education project.* London: Routledge.

Sylva, K., Melhuish, E., Sammons, P., Siraj-Blatchford, I. and Taggart, B. (2012) *Effective Pre-school, Primary and Secondary Education Project (EPPSE 3–14): Final Report from the Key Stage 3 phase: Influences on students' Development from age 11–14.* Research Brief DFE-RB202. London: Department for Education. Available at: https://dera.ioe.ac.uk/14069/7/DFE-RB202.pdf (accessed 18 June 2019).

Sylva, K., Melhuish, E., Sammons, P., Siraj, I., Taggart, B., Smees, R. et al. (2014) *Students' Educational and Developmental Outcomes at Age 16: Effective Pre-school, Primary and Secondary Education (EPPSE 3–16) project.* London: Department for Education. Available at: https://assets.publishing.service.gov. uk/government/uploads/system/uploads/attachment_data/file/351496/ RR354_-_Students__educational_and_developmental_outcomes_at_age_16. pdf (accessed 16 April 2016).

Taggart, B., Sylva, K., Melhuish, E., Sammons, P. and Siraj, I. (2015) *Effective Pre-school, Primary and Secondary Education (EPPSE 3–16+) project: How pre-school influences children and young people's attainment and developmental outcomes over time.* Research Brief DFE-RB455. London: Department for Education. Available at: https://assets.publishing.service.gov.uk/government/uploads/ system/uploads/attachment_data/file/455670/RB455_Effective_pre-school_ primary_and_secondary_education_project.pdf.pdf (accessed 26 May 2016).

Taguma, M., Litjens, I. and Makowiecki, K. (2012) *Quality Matters in Early Childhood Education and Care.* Paris: OECD Publishing.

Tayler, C. (2015) Learning in early childhood: experiences, relationships and 'learning to be', *European Journal of Education*, 50 (2): 160–174.

The Red House Children's Centre (2016) (Re)configuring quality: From a hegemonic framework to story telling, *Contemporary Issues in Early Childhood*, 17 (1): 134–139.

The Scottish Government (2014) *Building the Ambition – National Practice Guidance on Early Learning and Childcare.* Available at: https://www.gov.scot/publications/space-grow-design-guidance-early-learning-childcare-out-school-care/ (accessed 21 August 2018).

Thomas, G. (2007) *Education and Theory: Strangers in paradigms.* Maidenhead: Open University Press.

Tickell, Dame C. (2011) *The Early Years: Foundations for life, health and learning. An independent report on the Early Years Foundation Stage to Her Majesty's Government.* Available at: https://www.gov.uk/government/publications/the-early-years-foundations-for-life-health-and-learning-an-independent-report-on-the-early-years-foundation-stage-to-her-majestys-government (accessed 28 May 2016).

Timpson, E. (2014) Foreword, in *Early Years: Guide to the 0–25 SENS code of practice.* London: department for Education. Available at: https://assets.publishing.service.gov.uk/government/uploads/system/uploads/attachment_data/file/350685/Early_Years_Guide_to_SEND_Code_of_Practice_-_02Sept14.pdf (13 November 2016).

Touhill, L. (2013) Promoting independence and agency, *NQS PLP e-Newsletter,* 64: 1–4.

Tovey, H. (2007) *Playing Outdoors: Spaces and places, risk and challenge.* Maidenhead: Open University Press.

Tovey, H. (2011) *Bringing the Froebel Approach to Your Early Years Practice.* London: David Fulton.

Tovey, H. and Waller, T. (2014) Outdoor play and learning, in T. Waller and G. Davies (eds.) *An Introduction to Early Childhood,* 3rd edn. London: Sage.

Trevarthen, C. (1974) Conversations with a two-month-old, *New Scientist,* 62 (896): 230–235.

Trevarthen, C. (2011) What is it like to be a person who knows nothing? Defining the active intersubjective mind of a newborn human being, *Infant and Child Development,* 20 (1): 119–135.

Trevarthen, C., Barr, I., Dunlop, A.-W., Gjersoe, N., Marwick, H. and Stephen, C. (2003) *Supporting a Young Child's Needs for Care and Affection, Shared Meaning and a Social Place. Review of Childcare and the Development of Children Aged 0–3: Research evidence and implications for out-of-home provision.* Available at: https://www2.gov.scot/resource/doc/933/0007610.pdf (accessed 12 March 2016).

Trodd, L. (2005) Launching into learning: Becoming a reflective practitioner, in L. Dryden, R. Forbes, P. Mukherji and L. Pound (eds.) *Essential Early Years.* London: Hodder Arnold.

Tronick, E. (2005) Why is connection with others so critical?, in J. Nadel and D. Muir (eds.) *Emotional Development.* Oxford: Oxford University Press.

Tuckman, B. and Jensen, M. (1977) Stages of small group development revisited, *Group and Organisational Studies,* 2 (4): 419–427.

Urban, M. (2011) Dealing with uncertainty: challenges and possibilities for the early childhood profession', in C. Dalli and M. Urban (eds.) *Professionalism in Early Childhood Education and Care: International perspectives.* London: Routledge.

UNICEF (1989) *United Nations Convention on the Rights of the Child.* Available at: https://www.unicef.org.uk/what-we-do/un-convention-child-rights/ (accessed 15 March 2015).

United Nations (2013) *General Comment No. 14 (2013) on the Right of the Child to have His or Her Best Interests Taken as a Primary Consideration.* Available at: https://www2.ohchr.org/English/bodies/crc/docs/GC/CRC_C_GC_14_ENG.pdf (accessed 10 October 2016).

Umek, L. (2014) The structural quality of preschools: How it influences process quality and children's achievements, *Journal of Contemporary Educational Studies*, 2: 10–23.

Villumsen, A.M. and Kristensen, O.S. (2016) From management to leadership: A shift towards understanding the organizational complexity of multidisciplinary collaboration, *European Journal of Social Work*, 19 (5): 616–633.

Visković, I. and Jevtić, A.V. (2018) Professional development of the kindergarten teachers in Croatia – a personal choice or an obligation, *Early Years*, 38 (3): 286–297.

Vygotsky, L.S. (1966) Play and its role in the mental development of the child, *Voprosy psihologii*, 12 (6): 62–76.

Vygotsky, L.S. (1978) *Mind in Society: The development of higher psychological processes*. Cambridge, MA: Harvard University Press.

Vygotsky, L.S. (1986) *Thought and Language*. Cambridge, MA: MIT Press.

Waite, S. (2007) 'Memories are made of this': Some reflections on outdoor learning and recall, *Education 3–13*, 35 (4): 333–347.

Wall, S., Litjens, I. and Taguma, M. (2015) *Pedagogy in Early Childhood Education and Care (ECEC): An international comparative study of approaches and policies*. London: Department for Education. Available at: https://assets.publishing.service.gov.uk/government/uploads/system/uploads/attachment_data/file/445817/RB400_-_Early_years_pedagogy_and_policy_an_international_study.pdf (accessed 16 July 2016).

Waller, T. (2007) The trampoline tree and the swamp monster with 18 heads: Outdoor play in the Foundation Stage and Foundation Phase, *Education 3–13*, 35 (4): 393–407.

Waller, T. (2014) Voices in the park: Researching the participation of young children in outdoor play in early years settings, *Management in Education*, 28 (4): 161–166.

Watkins, C., Carnell, E. and Lodge, C. (2007) *Effective Learning in Classrooms*. London: Sage.

Welsh Assembly Government (2008) *Framework for Children's Learning for 3–7 Year Olds in Wales*. Available at: https://learning.gov.wales/docs/learningwales/publications/130424-framework-for-childrens-learning-en.pdf (accessed 17 February 2015).

Wenger, E. (1996) Communities of practice: The social fabric of a learning organization, *Healthcare Forum Journal*, 39 (4): 20–26.

Wenger, E. (1998) *Communities of Practice: Learning, meaning and identity*. Cambridge: Cambridge University Press.

Whalley, M.E. (2011) Leading and managing in the early years, in L. Miller and C. Cable (eds.) *Professionalization, Leadership and Management in the Early Years*. London: Sage.

Whalley, M. (2013) From community development to co-production of services, in M. Whalley, C. Arnold and R. Orr (eds.) *Working with Families in Children's Centres and Early Years Settings*. London: Hodder Education.

Whalley, M.E. (2017) *The role of the graduate pedagogical leader with children from birth to thirty months*. Doctoral thesis, Leeds Beckett University.

Whalley, M.E. and Allen, S. (2011) *Leading Practice in Early Years Settings*, 2nd edn. Exeter: Learning Matters.

Whalley, M. and the Pen Green Team (2007) *Involving Parents in Their Children's Learning*, 2nd edn. London: Sage.

Whalley, M. and the Pen Green Team (2017) *Involving Parents in Their Children's Learning*, 3rd edn. London: Sage.

White, J. (2016) *Introducing Dialogic Pedagogy: Provocations for the early years*. Abingdon: Routledge.

Whitehead, M. (2010) *Language and Literacy in the Early Years*, 4th edn. London: Sage.

Williams, D. (2002) Book review: Reflective Practice: Writing and Professional Development, *Medical Humanities*, 28: 56. Available at: https://mh.bmj.com/content/28/1/56.

Williams, N., King, L., Stephens, M., Edmundson, A. and Smith, L. (2017) *State of Children's Rights in England 2017*. London: CRAE.

Wolfe, I. (2013) Strengthening children's centres through the universalism of healthcare, in National Children's Bureau (NCB) *Partnerships for a Better Start: Perspectives on the role of children's centres*. London: NCB.

Wolfe, S. and Flewitt, R. (2010) New technologies, new multimodal literacy practices and young children's metacognitive development, *Cambridge Journal of Education*, 40 (4): 397–399.

Wong, S. and Sumsion, J. (2013) Integrated early years services: A thematic literature review, *Early Years*, 33 (4): 341–353.

Wood, E.A. (2011) Listening to young children, in A. Paige-Smith and A. Craft (eds.) *Developing Reflective Practice in the Early Years*, 2nd edn. Maidenhead: Open University Press.

Wood, E.A. (2014a) The play–pedagogy interface in contemporary debates, in L. Brooker, M. Blaise and S. Edwards (eds.) *The SAGE Handbook of Play and Learning in Early Childhood*. London: Sage.

Wood, E.A. (2014b) Free choice and free play in early childhood education: Troubling the discourse, *International Journal of Early Years Education*, 22 (1): 4–18.

Wood, E.A. (2015) *De-professionalising or Re-professionalising the Early Childhood Workforce in England*. Available at: https://www.bera.ac.uk/blog/de-professionalising-or-re-professionalising-the-early-childhood-workforce-in-england (accessed 5 July 2016).

Wyness, M.G. (2000) *Contesting Childhood*. London: Falmer Press.

Wyness, M.G. (2012a) Children's participation and intergenerational dialogue: Bringing adults back into the analysis, *Childhood*, 120 (4): 429–442.

Wyness, M.G. (2012b) *Childhood and Society: An introduction to the sociology of childhood*. Basingstoke: Palgrave Macmillan.

Index